The Laws of the Salian Franks

University of Pennsylvania Press
MIDDLE AGES SERIES
Edited by Edward Peters
Henry Charles Lea Professor
of Medieval History
University of Pennsylvania

A complete listing of the books in this series
appears at the back of this volume

The Laws of
the Salian Franks

*Translated and
with an Introduction by
Katherine Fischer Drew*

University of Pennsylvania Press

Philadelphia

Library of Congress Cataloging-in-Publication Data

Lex Salica. English.
    The laws of the Salian Franks / translated and with an
introduction by Katherine Fischer Drew.
        p.   cm.—(Middle Ages series)
    Includes bibliographical references and index.
    ISBN 0-8122-8256-6. — ISBN 0-8122-1322-X (pbk.)
    1. Salic law. 2. Law, Frankish. I. Drew, Katherine Fischer.
II. Title. III. Series.
KJ336.E5   1991
340.5′5—dc20   90-21755
                                               CIP

Second paperback printing 1993

Contents

Foreword

Understanding the transition from the highly civilized urban culture of the Roman world at its height to that of the localized and heavily rural medieval world is a problem that has attracted scholars for many centuries and produced explanations of great variety. In spite of scholarship building upon scholarship and increasingly refined techniques and tools available to a range of interdisciplinary scholars, students of the transition continue to fall into two camps, and this is especially true of those who deal with the transition from Roman Gaul to medieval France. The question is not one of fusion; obviously there was a great deal of fusion involving pre-Roman Celtic elements, Mediterranean immigrants of highly Romanized background, and Germanic invaders belonging to numerous tribal groupings. In spite of much study the problem remains—how great was the Germanic contribution to the new medieval civilization, how much was the Roman? And there is still no general agreement.

Any further attempt to resolve the problem justifies a careful reexamination of all the materials available for this study. The Frankish laws are one of these materials, and a very important one. They have not been utilized as much as one might expect because transmission of the laws has presented some very difficult problems, problems which generations of learned editors have not entirely overcome even today, although a good text (in several versions) has now been produced. The first written Frankish laws date from the late fifth or early sixth centuries—an extremely critical period in the breakup of the western Roman world and the establishment of a number of Germanic kingdoms on former Roman soil. A body of source material dating from this period from the Germanic point of view is obviously of great importance.

By the opening of the sixth century, the western Roman Empire had collapsed, although some independent remnants might still survive in Britain. But on the continent the Franks had established themselves in the northern part of Gaul and would control most of the remainder of Gaul before many years had passed, the Visigoths had Spain, the Ostrogoths had Italy, the Burgundians (soon to be conquered by the Franks) had southeastern Gual, and the Vandals had Africa. The Ostrogothic experiment, although promising much at the time, was destined not to last very long and produced no significant collection of legal materials that has survived; we know very little either about the legal work of the Vandals in Africa. But the Visigoths, the Burgundians, and the Franks all produced legal materials of great importance, materials that undoubtedly were heavily influenced by one another and were produced within a few years of each other—all depending more or less heavily on the availability of specialists in the Roman law who were willing to serve the new Germanic heads of the administrative system in working out a satisfactory legal regime in the new Visigothic, Burgundian, and Frankish kingdoms.

The Visigothic and Burgundian legal materials have been well studied and have helped scholars to understand the more-or-less satisfactory relationship that developed in southwestern and southeastern Gaul and in Spain between the older Gallo-Roman and Ibero-Roman populations, on the one hand, and the more recently arrived Germans, on the other—a relationship that produced a fusion of the two peoples and their cultures by the end of the seventh century and produced a new medieval culture there in which the Roman element was very strong.

But for northern Gaul the picture is different. A fusion between the older Gallo-Roman population and the Germanic newcomers obviously took place, but the end product was very different. The Roman influence here was strong too—the language of north-central Gaul is derived from Latin—but Germanic influence remained strong also: the German tongue survived in the extreme northeastern part of Gaul, the law tended to remain customary rather than Roman derivative, and formal education virtually disappeared.

The Frankish legislation has been recognized for many generations to be the most Germanic of all the barbarian legislation except that of the Anglo-Saxons. A study of it will hopefully provide some clues to the kind of world produced in northern Gaul by the impact of the Gallo-Romans and of Roman law on Frankish legal customs. This book is designed primarily to introduce the significance of legal history to students of medieval history.

It is my pleasure to acknowledge the aid of a number of persons and institutions in the preparation of this translation and introduction. Of greatest help was the work of a research assistant, Dallas Henderson, whose employment at an early stage in this project was made possible by a grant from the Office of Advanced Study and Research at Rice University. Dallas's training in classical Latin came in for some pretty hefty jolts in working with the Latin of several alternate versions of the Salic code, but overall her help was invaluable. I also wish to acknowledge the aid of a fellowship from the National Endowment for the Humanities which, although given for another related project, helped with this one too. And a grant from the American Philosophical Society made possible a summer's work in the musty rooms of the British Library. Finally, sabbatical leave from my own university enabled me to complete the work.

Thanks are due to the American Council of Learned Societies for permission to draw on an article on the early Germanic law written by me for the *Dictionary of the Middle Ages*. Also it should be noted that Theodore John Rivers's *Laws of the Salian and Ripuarian Franks* appeared after my translation of the laws had been completed but not yet submitted for publication. Inevitably my revisions have been influenced by Rivers's work (and I am indebted to him for this), but the two translations remain quite distinct.

Introduction

I. The Roman World and the Germanic Franks

Although the inhabitants of the Mediterranean world knew of the Germanic peoples from the middle of the first millenium B.C., relations with them did not assume major proportions until the third century A.D. when problems within the Roman Empire provided the excuse for withdrawal of the Rhine and Danube troops from their frontier posts, thereby opening the way for a number of Germanic groups to cross over the boundary. These third-century crossings were primarily for plunder not settlement, inasmuch as the Germans were sufficiently familiar with the situation within the Roman world to realize that the current frontier weakness was not a permanent condition. In fact, although the third-century invasions did cause great destruction within parts of the Empire, especially in Europe, the situation was brought under control well before the end of the third century and most of the large groups of Germanic barbarians were pushed back east of the Rhine and north of the Danube Rivers.

The Franks were among the Germans who crossed the frontier in the third century. Their origin is uncertain. Not a single nation, they were rather an agglomerate of Germanic peoples who had been living just to the east of the lower Rhine River. Their crossing was primarily a raiding expedition which carried them deep into Gaul and across the Pyrenees before the Roman defenses rallied and pushed them back across the lower Rhine.

From this time on, the Franks were more or less in constant contact with the Roman world. No large body of Franks was admitted into the Empire, but individuals and small groups did cross over the frontier. This movement was generally peaceful (although the Roman defenses rallied when too many Franks tried to cross at the same time). This peaceful Frankish penetration of Gaul was allowed primarily because it helped solve the military problems facing Rome. Individual Franks (like other Germans) readily achieved admission into the Roman army, but small groups were also admitted as military colonists (*laeti*).[1] These latter seem first to have been settled in the area immediately west of the Rhine mouth; but as time went on and the problem of defense became more acute, military colonies were spread through much of the northern part of Gaul (colonies of Franks were not, of course, the only barbarian military colonists to be settled here and in central Gaul).

So the Franks became better known to the Romans in the fourth century, especially as a few Frankish individuals (such as Ricimer and Arbogast) rose high in the imperial service. Relations between the two peoples became strained by the middle of the century, however, as Frankish pressure from the east gradually pushed some of the Frankish groups across the Rhine frontier into an area which seems to have been at least partially abandoned by Roman settlers during the upheavals of the third century. After some years of friction, in 358 the Roman Caesar Julian (later to be emperor) recognized the right of these Franks to remain where they were in part of what is now the southern Dutch Netherlands and northern Belgium: the bulk of the Franks continued to dwell east of the Rhine. In return for the right to occupy territory in northeast Gaul, the western Franks became federate allies of the Empire; that is, they undertook to protect this part of the frontier against further Germanic penetration. These Franks thus became the first barbarians to be admitted as a group into the Empire (although to be sure only a small part of the Franks was involved) and given land in return for assuming responsibility for protecting a part of the frontier.

For the next hundred years, relations between the Romans and Franks were relatively peaceful. The Franks were able to take advantage of the fact that the attention of the Roman authorities was directed toward the Danubian frontier where the Goths (first the Visigoths and later the Ostrogoths) were being pushed against and over the Danube River by the advance and retreat of the Huns. During this interval, more Franks crossed the Rhine and the Franks gradually extended the land they were occupying in northeastern Gaul. That this expansion through what is now Belgium into the northeastern part of France brought no strong Roman resistance would seem to indicate that settlement in this area was not very dense and that the Franks, as they moved west and slightly south, were not dispossessing significant numbers of people. That the Franks came to constitute a majority of the population in this area (in contrast with Germanic settlement elsewhere in Gaul) is indicated by the eventual triumph of the German language over Latin as the language of the people.

In the interval between the mid-fourth and late-fifth centuries, this gradual Frankish penetrating movement continued. During this period the Franks were undoubtedly to some degree influenced by Roman culture although, except for the evidence associated with the grave goods found in cemeteries along the frontier[2] and in the burial place of the Frankish chieftain Childeric who died in 481,[3] we have no direct evidence to indicate the nature of this influence. We do know that the Franks still did not constitute a single tribe or nation. Instead they were broken up into a number of groups under the rule of war leaders (dukes or kings [*reges*]) whose exact origin and function are uncertain—and many of the Franks still lived east of the Rhine.

The Franks in Gaul played their role as federate allies of the Empire through the middle of the fifth century and in 451 joined the other barbarian federates (Burgundians and Visigoths) and some units of the Roman army (under the commander Aetius) in defeating the Huns at the Battle of Chalons (Catalaunian Plains) in eastern France. After this defeat of the Huns, the imperial authority in Gaul rapidly disintegrated (as the Italian situation deteriorated and a Western Emperor ceased to be with the deposition of Romulus Augustulus in 476), leaving behind a province dependent on one of the Roman field armies centered on the city of Soissons not far from Letitia (Paris). It was this independent sub-Roman unit in north-central Gaul that bore the brunt of the continued Frankish push to the west.

As these developments were taking place, the various Frankish peoples under their separate dukes or kings began slowly to coalesce into two major groupings, the Salian Franks, the more westerly, and the Ripuarians, somewhat to the east and up the Rhine. (But the Rhine should not be regarded as the boundary between the two.) Frankish consolidation would be accomplished under the leadership of the rulers of a family later known as Merovingian (from the name of its semi-mythical founder, Merovech).

The first Merovingian king of whom we have clear historical proof was the Salian ruler Childeric, who died in 481 and was succeeded by his fifteen-year-old son Clovis. By 509 Clovis had eliminated his rival kings and had united all of the Franks, both Ripuarian and Salian, under his rule. In 486 he had attacked the sub-Roman state at Soissons. He defeated its commander and ruler Syagrius, and assumed his position, taking over as much as he could use of Syagrius's military force and administration, distributing at least some of the land of the imperial fisc to his followers, and retaining the rest for himself. There was also undoubtedly some redistribution of private property among the ordinary free Frankish families, but there is no evidence for how this distribution was carried out. Perhaps some of the Romans were entirely or partially dispossessed; perhaps some of the farm land had been abandoned during the disturbances of the third and fifth centuries. But large numbers of Franks now settled in the north-central part of France, and south as far as the Loire River. At the same time, large numbers of Gallo-Romans continued to live in the area, and for these people Clovis took a position at the head of the Roman administrative system.

The position of the Franks and the nature of their relations with the Gallo-Romans at this time are uncertain, although it seems clear that Clovis hoped to reassure the Gallo-Romans that he would maintain peace and security of person and property. The Franks were still mostly heathen (although there may have been some conversion to Arianism), but the Gallo-Roman bishops corresponded with and perhaps influenced Clovis, and Clovis married a Catholic Burgundian princess (although most of the Burgundians were still Arian at this time). This marriage inevitably involved Clovis in Burgundian affairs and brought him into contact with an area more highly Romanized than his own. In any event, Clovis now had available the service of men trained in the old tradition: he had succeeded to the remnants of Roman power in northern Gaul and he had established contacts with the Roman-influenced court of the Burgundians in southeastern Gaul.

Incorporation of the Ripuarian Franks into his kingdom had brought Clovis's realm into the area of the middle Rhine and into contact with the Germanic Alamanni. The Alamanni had the reputation of being strong and aggressive fighters and Clovis may well have had reason to fear that they were a threat to his new eastern frontier; he may, however, merely have wanted to increase his military reputation. In any event, increasing tension between the Franks and Alamanni led eventually to war. Clovis soon defeated the Alamanni and as a result the Alamanni living in the middle Rhine area and Alsace came under his rule; the rest of the Alamanni, living to the east and south, would not be incorporated into the Frankish kingdom until the early eighth century. The date and place of Clovis's battle with the Alamanni are not certainly known. According to a time sequence based on Gregory of Tours, it may have taken place at Strasbourg in 496; based on evidence from Cassiodorus it may have been at Tolbiac in 506.[4]

Clovis's conversion to Catholicism is associated by Gregory of Tours (in his *History of the Franks* written in the late sixth century) with Clovis's victory over the Alamanni; in return for support from the Christian God,

Clovis himself and his followers accepted baptism. There is difficulty, however, in accepting Gregory's explanation of the conversion to Christianity if the defeat of the Alamanni had actually come in 496, for the Franks were almost certainly not Christian at the time Clovis issued the first version of his code (usually dated 507–511, although it may have been earlier). The controversy over the exact date of this conversion, however, is not nearly so important as the fact that the Franks as a people became Catholic rather than Arian Christian. Even though real conversion may have taken place over an extended period of time, Clovis's formal conversion seems to have brought almost immediate sympathy from the Gallo-Roman Catholic hierarchy in Gaul, which supported him against his barbarian neighbors who remained Arian at this time.

With at least tacit support from the hierarchy, Clovis turned against the Arian Visigoths and defeated them at the battle of Vouillé (near Poitiers) in 507,[5] thereby adding the area between the Loire and the Garonne Rivers to his kingdom. By 534 Burgundy in southeastern Gaul had been added during the reigns of Clovis's sons, although the Burgundians had for the most part accepted Catholicism by this time and defense against heretics could not be used as an excuse. By the time Frankish control had been extended to the Pyrenees shortly thereafter, all of what had been Roman Gaul except the Mediterranean coast west of the Rhône (Septimania remained Visigothic) was under Frankish rule.

Although the grave goods from Childeric's tomb indicate that Childeric had assumed the trappings of a member of the Roman court and thereby considered himself to be ruling as a Roman, the literary and legal evidence suggests that Clovis inherited from his father a kingship that was essentially Germanic—the king and his followers offered the Franks a basically military leadership that was tempered with some degree of responsibility for other aspects of government. Clovis and his Merovingian successors now faced the problem of developing an acceptable rule for a large territory that included other Germans as well as Franks in addition to Gallo-Romans.[6] Except in a small area in the extreme northeast and immediately along the middle and upper Rhine frontier, the Gallo-Roman population always outnumbered the Germanic immigrants. In the southwestern and southeastern parts of Gaul, the Germanic Visigoths and Burgundians had themselves earlier established states where they developed forms of government heavily influenced by the Roman administrative system in effect when they settled there. So the Franks had a number of sophisticated models to follow. They also had the help of the personnel who had previously served the Roman rulers of Gaul and, after the Frankish conversion to Roman Christianity in the late fifth or early sixth century, they had the support and help of the Catholic hierarchy as well.

In organizing a judicial system for their state, which included peoples of such different legal backgrounds, the Franks found useful (and indeed had little choice in the matter) the Germanic and early Roman concept of personality of law—each person might claim the law of his ancestors. Therefore the Gallo-Romans and the Church might claim to be judged by Roman law, the Visigoths by Visigothic law, and the Burgundians by Burgundian law. Now if the customary unwritten Frankish law were to compete with these other legal systems, which were written,[7] Frankish judges as well as Roman magistrates in Frankish territory needed a more reliable source of law than the memories of the elders of the community. It might also be argued that Clovis felt the need to improve his image, to demonstrate that he was more than an uncivilized Germanic king, and so he engaged in a Roman imperial activity: the establishment of a text of written law.[8]

At any rate, Clovis responded to his new responsibilities by codification of the Frankish law. Presumably the customary laws of the Franks had existed in unwritten form before the time of Clovis, but to Clovis almost certainly belongs the oldest version of the written Salic law, dating from the last years of the fifth century or from the first years of the sixth (it was probably issued between 507 and 511). In issuing a written collection of laws, Clovis was following Visigothic and Burgundian precedent; also like the Visigoths and Burgundians, he almost certainly had the help of advisers trained in the Roman law. Unlike his Burgundian and Visigothic forerunners in the field of lawfinding or lawmaking, however, who issued separate Germanic and Roman codes for the two different parts of their population, Clovis confined his "legislative" activities to the issuing of a single written code. Both Franks and Gallo-Romans came under the provisions of the Salic law in areas covered by that law, superseding Roman law in these matters. Where the Salic law offered no guidance, however, the conclusion seems inescapable that the vulgar Roman law was still followed by the Gallo-Romans and members of the clergy. The specific source of this Roman law is not easy to trace, but it was there and increasingly influenced Frankish law. More will be said about the Frankish code in the section on law that follows.

Some of the success of the Merovingian Frankish rulers may be their acceptance of the personality of law policy. Not only did Roman law remain in use among Gallo-Romans and churchmen, Burgundian law among the Burgundians, and Visigothic law among the Visigoths, but the more purely Germanic peoples of the eastern frontier were allowed to retain their own "national" law. Since these laws were still unwritten, however, written codes were provided under the stimulus first of Merovingian and later of Carolingian Frankish leadership. Thus the laws of the Ripuarian Franks were codified in the early seventh century along with those of the Alamanni, and the earliest version of the Bavarian laws may go back to this period also. These laws were revised and laws issued for the Saxons, Thuringians, and Frisians in the late eighth and early ninth centuries by Charlemagne. These later "codes" (Ripuarian, Alamannian, Bavarian, Saxon, Thuringian, and Frisian) are alike, however, in that they were prepared under Frankish leadership and reflect significant Salic influence. The Frankish kings who succeeded Clovis still commanded the service of men learned in the law.

The unity of the Frankish realm established under Clovis did not last. Clovis had achieved unity not only by defeating the Romans and the Visigoths and laying the foundations for defeat of the Burgundians, but also by defeating the rival Frankish kings, including some within his own family. It is usually assumed that Clovis's division of his realm at death (as well as continued division under succeeding Merovingian and Carolingian monarchs) followed Frankish inheritance custom treating the kingdom essentially as heritable property. On the other hand, it is possible that the political situation at the time of Clovis's death (the presence of an older son of age who was not the son of his Burgundian queen Clotilda along with the three younger sons of Clotilda) may have encouraged division of the kingdom as a means of satisfying the various political factions within the royal family.[9] This, however, does not seem a very satisfactory explanation of later Merovingian and Carolingian history, for division into four parts appears with some regularity: Austrasia (in the northeast), Neustria (in the north-central and northwest), Aquitaine (in the southwest), and Burgundy (in the southeast). Possibly the ethnic composition of Francia had some influence, for these four parts of Gaul are quite different in their composition. In only one of these areas (Austrasia) was there a Germanic predominance in the population; in the other three the Gallo-Romans were in the majority, with the Franks contributing the Germanic element in Neustria, Visigoths in Aquitaine, and Burgundians in Burgundy. In these last two areas (Aquitaine and Burgundy), the Roman element was very strong indeed. So ethnic and cultural considerations may play an important part in divisions of the kingdom.

Nonetheless, hereditary division must have been the predominating factor. There was a strong tendency to regard the kingdom as property to be divided among male heirs.[10] One of the main bases for such division was the royal estates (made up of original acquisitions from the imperial fisc as well as later seizures and judicial confiscations)—a fair division of such estates among male heirs frequently meant overlapping jurisdictions and widely scattered territories. Because hereditary division also had the unfortunate consequence of leading inevitably to civil war, the Merovingian period after Clovis seldom saw the kingdom undivided, the boundaries of the sub-kingdoms constantly shifting as each royal heir fought to expand his holdings at the expense of his co-heirs.

The later political history of Merovingian Gaul is of relatively little importance for the story of Frankish law. Until the eighth century, when the frontiers of the Frankish state were pushed forward in all directions, the rulers faced essentially the same problems that had existed by the mid-sixth century: to establish and maintain the rule of a population that included, in addition to the bulk of the Frankish people whom we call Salian Franks from the name of their law code, the older Gallo-Romans, some Visigoths in southwestern Gaul, Burgundians in southeastern Gaul, Ripuarian Franks in the lower and middle Rhine area (many of them living east of the Rhine), and Alamanni in the region of the middle and upper Rhine. The inevitable tendency for the land to break up into regions wherein one or more of these people predominated was intensified by the Frankish custom of dividing the realm among male heirs. This internal decay was further aggravated by friction between the ruling Merovingian dynasty and a number of powerful aristocratic families, the most important of which would be the Arnulfings or Pepinids whose power centered in the northeastern part of the county (the region called Austrasia). For a time the Arnulfings, or Pepinids, dominated the land through their hereditary position as mayor of the palace (chief of the household officials) in Austrasia. Attempts to replace the Merovingian dynasty as the royal rulers of the Franks were unsuccessful until the middle of the eighth century when a mayor of the palace by the name of Pepin III (known in history as Pepin the Younger or Pepin the Short) utilized the strength of his position among the Franks, as well as the need of the Pope for allies against the Lombards, to obtain ecclesiastical sanction for the transfer of the crown from the weak and incapable hands of the Merovingians to the strong and able hands of a new Carolingian dynasty. (The Arnulfing or Pepinid family would be known as Carolingian from the name of the second of the Carolingian rulers Charles I [768–814], better known as Charles the Great or Charlemagne.)

The disintegration of Gaul under the later Merovingians was temporarily halted during the reign of Charlemagne, who succeeded in overcoming the resistance to himself of the Frankish nobility and uniting the Franks in a series of military campaigns that extended Frankish rule down into the northeastern part of Spain (a campaign that can be regarded as the beginning of the Christian reconquest of Spain from the Muslim Moors who had overthrown the Visigothic kingdom in 711); into Italy (overthrowing the Lombard kingdom in 774); and deep into Germany by conquest of the Saxons, Thuringians, and Frisians, and establishing protectorates over some of the Germanic and Slavic peoples living even further to the east.

The Frankish unity achieved by Charlemagne was not to last. In spite of the imperial title (Charlemagne was crowned Roman Emperor at Rome in 800), Charlemagne's attitude toward his realm was ultimately little changed from that of the Merovingians: faced with the ambitions of various sons, Charlemagne planned to divide his lands among them after his death. It was only the accident of history that, when Charlemagne died in 814, a single son, Louis the Pious, survived and allowed a more apparent than real unity until 843, when the quarrels of Louis's sons ended in a division of the kingdom once again.

Charlemagne's reign may be regarded as a decisive turning point in the history of Frankish law. Not only did he carry through a thorough and final revision of the Salic law originally issued by Clovis and his sons and grandson in the sixth century, but Charlemagne began what is usually thought to be an essentially new kind of legislation: he issued numerous instructions or memoranda (usually called capitularies from the custom of dividing them into "chapters") that dealt with many aspects of law and thus created a layer of what might be called imperial law over the Salic, Visigothic, Burgundian, and east German underneath. For purposes of historical background, therefore, we can end this introductory section with the reign of Charlemagne.

II. Roman Law and Germanic Law

The Law of the Western Empire at the Time of the Invasions

By the fifth century, when the Germanic barbarians began to settle in large numbers within the Western Empire, Roman law had had many centuries of development behind it. From the law of a small republic in the central part of Italy established in the late sixth century B.C., it had grown to become the law of all Italians by the early first century B.C., to the law of all freemen in the Empire by the early third century A.D.—an empire stretching from the Atlantic Ocean in the west to the upper Euphrates River in the east, from the borders of Scotland and the North Sea in the north to the edge of the Sahara Desert in the south. In this long period of development and in this extension to such widely scattered places and peoples, the Roman law had proved itself to be an extraordinarily viable institution and one of Rome's greatest contributions to western civilizaton.

The great Roman legal contribution was made in the field of private law. This was the law in which the well-known Roman jurists were interested; criminal law was rather neglected and treated only as an aspect of public law. It was the Roman private law courts that influenced the Germans because the Germans treated all suits as private ones, where criminal suits tended to be civil suits for damages rather than the trial of public crimes. For this reason, the brief historical treatment of Roman law that follows is concerned primarily with private law.[11]

In its origin, Roman law was customary law, the unwritten traditions of the people going back to an immemorial past. This unwritten law was in the keeping of a priestly class (the *pontifices*) who came from the upper stratum of society (the patricians). Opposition from the lower class (the plebeians) led in the mid-fifth century B.C. to a first written codification known as the Law of the Twelve Tables, since the laws were recorded on twelve plaques set up in the market place for all to see and thus to know what the laws were. The Twelve Tables (which we know only from much later writings) contained only a few rules of law and brief statements about procedure: the bulk of the customary law was taken for granted and not written down. It was an interesting stage in the development of Roman law and may well parallel what would occur later when the first Germanic legislation was recorded—that which everyone knew was omitted, only the new or that which was somehow complicated or being modified was recorded.

This early Roman law was a personal law, the law of the Roman people only. Other peoples had their own law—for instance, the Athenians enjoyed Athenian law and other Italian peoples enjoyed their own. So long as the Romans remained at home and "foreigners" did not wish to come to the city or were not admitted, the question of personality had no effect on the development of Roman law.

However, once Rome began to expand beyond the limits of Latium and became involved in the Mediterranean commercial system, many foreigners flocked to Rome. The Romans did not assume that Roman law would be proper for these persons, and the necessity of providing a tribunal for foreigners where something other than Roman law would be applied had an extremely important if unplanned effect on the Roman law itself. Remedies and procedures, not originally a part of the Roman civil law, would gradually find their way into the Roman law, thereby making it a much more sophisticated and adaptable system than the narrow civil law envisaged. Furthermore, as the empire grew and there were many Roman citizens living outside of Italy, the Roman law traveled with these persons. And as Roman citizenship was gradually extended to the more Romanized provincials, these new citizens also enjoyed the benefit of Roman law. By the early third century (A.D. 212) an Edict of the Emperor Caracalla extended Roman citizenship to virtually every freeman in the Empire. By this time, Roman law was the law of all; it had ceased to be a personal law and had become a territorial law.

The fully developed Roman law, based originally on the customary *ius civile* (civil law), would grow and be formed by a number of different influences. From the late second century B.C. (when rapid growth began) to the late Republic, the most important contributions would be made by magistrates' law. At the very close of the republican period and during the early Empire (late first century B.C. to the early third century A.D.), the most important contribution to growth would be made through the opinions of the jurisconsults. And in the late Empire (beginning with the late third century), the most important source of law would be the Emperor himself.

Magistrates' law. The Roman magistrates most closely concerned with law were two praetors, an urban praetor and a peregrine (foreign) praetor. The former of these officials was concerned with the administration of justice in suits involving Roman citizens, the latter with suits involving foreigners resident in Rome or suits between a Roman and a foreigner. Since the praetorships were annually elected offices sought after by men who were pursuing political careers, the men who held these positions were not professional jurists nor did they have any special training in the law. They depended heavily on the advice of those more learned than themselves. Their work therefore showed a certain consistency insofar as it leaned heavily on professional advice, but it also showed a certain flexibility since the praetors, as amateurs, often found themselves impatient with the intricacies or inconsistencies of the civil law as known to the professionals.

The praetors contributed to the growth of Roman law by issuing edicts at the beginning of their terms of office. This was of no great importance until some time in the second century B.C. when a law (*lex Aebutia*) passed by one of the popular assemblies established what is known as the formulary system. Down to this time the praetors had little if any initiative. There had been a number of set forms of action, and if one's suit did not fall in one of these, one had no recourse at civil law. But the formulary system gave the praetor power to create new forms of action. This development came at a critical time, a time when the establishment of Roman rule over much of the territory bordering the Mediterranean Sea was creating vast economic and social changes in Roman life and bringing to the city of Rome itself an increasing number of non-Roman Italians and persons from other parts of the Mediterranean world. The praetor's ability to create new forms of action greatly facilitated the growth of the *ius civile* and made it possible for that law eventually to meet the needs of a growing empire.

At the beginning of his year of office, the praetor issued an edict which consisted of a series of statements of policy and defined the circumstances in which the praetor would exercise his power to grant new remedies. Eventually the main body of the edict was carried over from year to year, the new praetor making only such additions as he deemed desirable. And if, during his term of office, the praetor found that the facts of a particular case did not fit into his edict, he could grant a new remedy. Also, although each praetor (the urban and the peregrine) issued his own edict, the two influenced each other. The peregrine praetor's edict contained legal ideas derived from the non-Roman people living in Rome. In devising new forms of action, the urban praetor drew on this material. So from very early on in the Roman historical experience, a way was found to incorporate foreign elements into the Roman law. In this way, the Roman law grew rapidly in the last century of the Republic. Under the emperors, the discretion of the praetors became gradually more restricted, until finally by the early second century A.D., the Edict had been virtually unchanged for some time. The Emperor Hadrian (117–137) commissioned the jurist Julian to make a final revision of the Edict which thenceforth was not to be changed. But by this time the means of introducing growth in the Roman law had passed from the hands of the praetors into the hands of the jurists and the emperors themselves.

The work of the jurists. The jurists (jurisconsults) were a distinctive Roman institution. During the Republic, there were no professional judges and no regular courts in our sense of the term. The parties to a suit would approach the praetor to determine whether they had a cause of action or to select the correct formulas to establish the proper pleadings for each party. The parties then selected a judge (*iudex*) from an official list of wealthy laymen who acted as justices as part of their public duty. The judge then heard the case, the parties usually being represented or advised by advocates who were not normally trained in the law but were rhetoricians skilled in the art of persuasion. The iudex was a judge of both fact and law, but since he was a layman not a jurist, he frequently (perhaps normally) sought the advice of those who were legally trained. The judge then rendered his verdict, which was binding on the parties to the suit but had no further significance since Roman law did not grow on the basis of judicial precedent.

The Roman jurists came from the leading Roman families. Those who became expert in the law offered free advice as part of their contribution to public life. For these men (jurists) knowledge of the law was only one part of their public careers; they were primarily men of affairs and so tended to be interested in the practical application of the law rather than in the theory of the law.

Praetors consulted these jurists in the composition of their edicts, private parties and advocates consulted them in the preparation of their suits, and the judges consulted them when rendering decisions in the cases submitted to them. Although the opinion of the jurist was not binding, nonetheless a learned jurist was a very impressive person and the opinions of the most famous of them were formidable indeed. Furthermore, the jurists not only gave opinions, they accepted as pupils young men who in their turn became learned in the law. These jurists wrote extensively on the problems submitted to them in actual cases and on theoretical problems that arose in the course of their own reflections or in conversation with other jurists or with their pupils. In the early Empire, their influence was a more important source of growth in the Roman law than was the work of the praetors.

Under the Empire, the jurists tended to be more formally connected with the government than had been true during the Republic when they had offered their legal opinions as purely private citizens. The jurists whose opinions were most frequently quoted and were finally preserved in the sixth-century codification accomplished under the Emperor Justinian all held high imperial office. Lesser-known jurists may well have taught at what were now fairly well recognized schools of law, the most influential of which were at Rome in the western part of the Empire and (later) at Constantinople and Beirut in the eastern. The great jurist Julian, who prepared the final version of the Praetor's Edict, lived in the second century and served the Emperor Hadrian and his immediate successors. In the early third century, serving the Severan emperors, were the even better known jurists Papinian, Paul, and Ulpian.

By the end of the third century the increasingly powerful position of the Emperor overshadowed the jurists so completely that they lost all significance in shaping the growth of Roman law. During the late Empire, the Emperor would be the sole source of new law.

Legislation and the role of the emperor. During the Republic, Roman magistrates could not make laws (*leges*); the statutory (legislative) basis of the early Roman law rested on the Twelve Tables and such laws as were passed by one or another of the Roman popular assemblies (there were three of them), although surprisingly few such acts affecting private law were passed. These written materials plus whatever else was recognized as the customary law of Rome constituted the civil law (*ius civile*) which the praetors and jurists then proceeded to adapt and modify to meet the changing needs of the people and the time.

With the establishment of the Empire (27 B.C.), the right to make new law (which had heretofore rested in the hands of the assemblies) passed gradually into the control of the Emperor, although the early emperors found it advisable to conceal this development by utilizing the Senate as the formal source of their legislation. By the second century, however, there was little doubt that the word of the Emperor was truly law; and thereafter imperial constitutions of one form or another became the chief source of new law in the Roman Empire.

The Emperor's influence on law developed in a number of ways. Edicts set forth the Emperor's orders for a part or the whole of the Empire. *Mandata* (administrative instructions to the Emperor's officials) collectively formed a sort of addendum to imperial law. But for the growth of the private law, the most influential form of imperial guidance came through the Emperor's decisions or opinions in individual cases. These took two forms, the *decreta* and *rescripta*. The *decreta* were judicial decisions of the Emperor issued in pursuit of either his original or appellate jurisdiction. The *rescripta* were not imperial judgments, but simply an imperial statement of what his decision would be if the facts proved to be as stated in a petition or question submitted to him. In spite of the fact that imperial *decreta* and *rescripta* did not have the binding force of precedent, since this was unknown to Roman law, the immense prestige of the Emperor tended to give his written judicial decisions and legal opinions the force of law.

A change in the administration of the judicial system had taken place during the Empire. In the Republic, the administration of justice had been non-professional. The praetors were not trained in the law but were primarily politicians who briefly held the praetorship during the course of long and successful political careers. The men who acted as judges in the suits prepared with the praetors' help were also laymen who allowed their names to appear on the list from which the contestants to a suit selected the man who would judge their cause. Both initiation of the suit and acceptance of the decision were left to the parties; the state had merely provided the forum before which they could adjudicate their dispute.

In the Empire, the administration of justice became more professional. The state provided a magistrate who not only heard the case and rendered a decision (either on the basis of his own knowledge of the law after consultation with a jurist or after requesting an imperial opinion), but also enforced his decision. The role of the state had become much stronger. By the time the Germanic people came into close contact with the Empire, this professional justice would be the type of judicial system they would encounter.

Attempts at codification; the growth of the vulgar law. The great formative period of Roman law came in the last century of the Republic and in the early Principate; it culminated in the work of Julian, who issued a final version of the Praetor's Edict and composed a series of writings summing up legal developments to his time. The work of the great jurists who followed him was elaboration and exposition. Accordingly, the period from Julian to the middle of the third century is commonly called the classical period of Roman law. Virtually none of the material written by the jurists of the classical period survives unchanged, although some of it would be included in several unofficial attempts at codification and in Justinian's official one. But all of this surviving "classical" material is suspect, because Justinian was interested in eliminating everything that was obsolete or contradictory and in bringing what remained into agreement with current practice (sixth century). Thus, most of what we have from the pens of such jurists as Julian, Papinian, Paul, and Ulpian comes from the *Digest* of Justinian in a more or less vulgarized form.

The one exception to this non-survival of materials unchanged from the classical period is the *Institutes* of Gaius, a textbook of Roman law composed in the late second century by Gaius, evidently one of the lesser-known jurists (for we know of him only through his *Institutes*). When Justinian's legal commission came to that part of its assignment involving the preparation of a textbook of Roman law, it incorporated much of Gaius' *Institutes* unchanged. It is through this work alone that we know something about those early aspects of Roman law that had become outmoded by the fifth and sixth centuries.

The mass of legal materials produced by the voluminous writings of the various jurists of the classical period and by three centuries of imperial legislation had become exceedingly unwieldly by the time of the Late Empire. Few legal experts could be found who knew their way through all of this material, and it became increasingly necessary to provide summaries or anthologies or codifications. Of the summaries or epitomes, the best known is an epitome of the work of the jurist Paul known as the *Sentences*—to be of great influence in the western part of the Empire. The first of the attempts at codification that we know of were private in origin and probably prepared in the reign of Diocletian (284–305): the *Codex Gregorianus* and the *Codex Hermogenianus*. We know of these collections only from later quotations in Justinian's *Digest* and in some of the vulgar western law books.

The two great official attempts at codification were undertaken by the Emperors Theodosius II and Justinian. The work of the first of these produced a compilation known as the *Theodosian Code* (438), containing all the imperial laws issued since Constantine (311–337) that were still in effect at the time of the *Code*'s composition. Although compiled in the eastern part of the Empire, this *Code* was promulgated for both east and west.

Although the *Theodosian Code* was an extremely important compilation (especially in the western part of the Empire where it would never be effectively superseded until the twelfth century), it did not include the earlier imperial legislation before Constantine, to say nothing of the massive bulk of material produced by the jurists. Therefore in the sixth century, under the Emperor Justinian, another attempt at codification was made. This produced what was intended to be a complete statement of Roman law: the *Corpus Iuris Civilis*. A commission of experts, working under the chairmanship of the jurist Tribonian, completed its work in four parts.

(1) *Code*. This contained the whole of the imperial law still in effect at the time of the codification (it drew upon the Gregorian, Hermogenian, and Theodosian codes, the post-Theodosian laws, and Justinian's own laws).

(2) *Digest*. This part of the codification was drawn from work by legal writers of the first to fourth centuries A.D. Although the bulk of the *Digest* is drawn from the jurists of the classical period of Roman law (Julian, Papinian, Ulpian, and Paul), the result is a statement, not necessarily of the classical law, but rather of the classical law as modified through the centuries and adapted by Justinian's lawyers to the needs of the time (for Justinian had instructed his commission to eliminate everything that was obsolete or contradictory and to modify the rest to bring it up to date). Therefore to a certain extent what the *Digest* contains is a form of vulgar (as opposed to classical) law, although its re-study in the west, beginning at Bologna in the eleventh century, is usually referred to as revival of the "classical Roman law."

(3) *Institutes*. Although this was also a compilation made by Justinian's commission, it was based heavily on the earlier *Institutes* of Gaius and constituted a general introduction (textbook) to Roman law.

(4) *Novels*. The fourth part of Justinian's legal compilation was known as the *Novels*. This was the new legislation.

Justinian's work was done in the eastern part of the Empire (his capital was at Constantinople); and the jurists he employed were drawn from the best law schools of the day, which also happened to be located in Constantinople and Beirut in the east. The work of codifiction accomplished by the commission was done in Latin since the sources of Roman law to this point had been written in Latin. However, in the eastern part of the Empire the administrative language reverted more and more to Greek, and hence the *Novels* (the laws of Justinian and his successors) were issued in Greek.

The *Code*, the *Digest*, and the *Institutes* formed the *Corpus Iuris Civilis* (the body of the civil law) which was completed between 528 and 534. It was formally promulgated in the Eastern Empire almost immediately; and in 552, upon defeat of the Ostrogoths in Italy, it would be introduced into Italy. But the fate of the *Corpus Iuris Civilis* was quite different in East and West. In the East, although not always understood and epitomized a number of times (most importantly in the *Basilica* issued by the Emperor Leo the Wise [886–911]), it remained in effect to the end of the East Roman or Byzantine Empire (1453). In the West, however, the *Corpus Iuris Civilis* had hardly been introduced when Byzantine rule in Italy was challenged by the appearance of the Lombards (568). Although the *Corpus* continued to be recognized in those parts of Italy still subject to Byzantine rule, in the greater part of Italy the *Corpus* ceased to be known except in the schools where grammar was taught. Here some fragmentary knowledge of the *Code* and *Institutes* continued to be available, but as examples of the written language, not as sources of law. The *Digest*, the work of the pagan jurists, seems to have been forgotten altogether until its rediscovery in the eleventh century when it would become the subject of academic study at one of the first great medieval universities, the university of Bologna. From that date would grow a revival of Roman law that would influence the law of all of modern Europe and much of the modern world, although England and overseas territories settled by the English would resist that influence more than the rest of the continent.

Roman Law and the Germanic Barbarians

Before the Germanic barbarians entered the Roman Empire they had no written codes of law. As was true in the case of the early Romans, their law was essentially customary law—the traditions or customs of the people handed down by word of mouth from untold generations in the past. Such customs were "kept" in the memories of the elders of the community who, when needed, could be called together "to speak the law."

It is conjectural how this early customary Germanic law was applied in practice; the law was almost certainly not royal law. The shift from loosely organized Germanic confederations, whose leaders were primarily military leaders, to more closely knit groupings under the leadership of individuals who were political and judicial as well as military leaders was a development that took place largely as a result of contact with Rome. Before the evolution of such "royal power," obtaining justice resided largely in the hands of the families or kin groups; and there may have been more or less popular courts attended by the more important members of the community if not by all freemen. Since enforcement of law resided in the family and kin rather than in the state, there could hardly be such a thing as territorial law. So for the Germans law was essentially personal (i.e., a man was judged by the law of his ancestors, not by the law of the place he happened to be). What we know of early Germanic legal institutions comes largely from information provided by the Germans themselves after their entry into the Empire.[12]

By A.D. 500, the Western Roman Empire had given way to a number of Germanic kingdoms, but just how "Germanic" these kingdoms were has always been a matter of dispute. Certainly the Germans constituted a minority of the population so that the new kings found themselves ruling essentially in two guises: as kings to their own German people and as magistrates toward their Roman population, with the functions of the second role being more firmly established than those of the first.

In most of the early Germanic kingdoms, an attempt was made to reduce the customary law of the Germanic people to written form. To a certain extent this was necessary since the Germans were now living on land that had long been accustomed to a regime of written law. How would it be possible for the magistrates (many of whom remained Roman) to administer a law that not only was unfamiliar to them but also was unwritten? To maintain the peace and security of their realms, the barbarian kings had to respond. For some time, the Roman Emperors had been the primary source of law in the Empire; so issuing written law seemed a royal activity, an activity that would reassure the Roman part of the population that they were still ruled by men familiar with the way things should be done.

The various barbarian kings, however, responded in different ways. In general, the barbarians' legal response to the challenge of Roman culture varied to some degree in accordance with the time of their entry into the Empire, but it varied more in accordance with the part of the Empire in which they settled. Those nations settled in the more advanced southern sections of Europe encountered a numerous Roman population and a well-established Roman legal culture. As a result, the legislative activities of their kings reflected considerable influence by Roman law and by Roman legal practices, and they also reflected genuine concern to administer a well-recognized code of Roman law for the Roman part of the population. On the other hand, the law codes issued by the rulers of those Germanic peoples who settled in the more backward northern part of the Roman Empire reflected little if any influence by the Roman law, and the rulers of these northern kingdoms were little concerned about providing a code of Roman law or judges learned in the Roman law for the remnants of the former Roman population living in their kingdoms.

The oldest surviving barbarian laws are associated with the Visigoths who were allowed to establish a federate kingdom in the southwestern part of Gaul (Aquitaine) about the year 418 and who expanded their territory south of the Pyrenees into Spain later in the fifth century. After defeat by the Franks in 507, the Visigoths lost Aquitaine and thereafter controlled Spain and a strip of territory called Septimania that ran along the Mediterranean coast of Gaul east to the Rhône River.

The Visigothic rulers faced the problem of maintaining a rule for one of the most culturally advanced parts of the Western Empire while providing control over the relatively rude and basically illiterate Visigoths. So far as is known, the first efforts of the Visigothic kings to legislate date from about 458, during the reign of the Visigothic king Theodoric II.[13] Theodoric's statement of law, known as the *Edictum Theodorici*, was until recent years ascribed to the Ostrogothic ruler Theodoric and dated in the early sixth century; however, the *Edict* is now generally attributed to the earlier Visigothic ruler Theodoric II (although Italian scholarship still prefers the Ostrogothic adscription).[14] This *Edict* dealt primarily with the resolution of cases that had arisen between Goths and Romans. In general, its provisions were derived from Roman sources, especially from the *Theodosian Code* and the *Sentences* of the jurist Paul. But this *Edict*, whether properly ascribed to a Visigothic or Ostrogothic origin, can hardly be described as a complete code of law. It seems to be a mere collection of cases listed haphazardly as they arose with little attempt to organize the material by subject matter.

The earliest surviving laws issued by a Germanic king that can be regarded as constituting a true code are fragments of a code issued by the Visigothic king Euric (466–485) about 481. Euric's code was issued for the use of the Visigoths in their suits with each other and probably for cases that arose between Goths and Romans. Although most of this code has been lost, enough survives to indicate strong Roman influence.

For the use of their Roman subjects, the early Visigothic kings sponsored the issuance of a special collection of Roman law less complex than the *Theodosian Code* (compiled in 438). The Visigothic code for Roman provincials was issued by Alaric II (485–507) about 506; it is known as the

Lex Romana Visigothorum or the *Breviary* of Alaric.[15] The *Breviary* was compiled by a commission of jurists working under instructions from the king, who may have wanted to conciliate his Catholic Gallo-Roman subjects before the threat of the Franks. In any event, the Roman jurists who accomplished this task used many sections of the *Theodosian Code* (thus preserving the greater part of it) plus material from the *Sentences* of Paul and from a vulgar compendium of the *Institutes* of Gaius, as well as from some less important Roman law sources. The *Breviary* was thus a very respectable statement of vulgar Roman law.

So far as Visigothic Spain was concerned, the *Breviary* remained in use among the Roman provincials only until the middle of the seventh century, when a new collection of Visigothic law issued by King Recceswinth (in 654) offered a unified code for both Visigoths and Romans and prohibited the use of any other code. Thereafter the *Breviary* was not used in Visigothic Spain; nevertheless its influence did not come to an end. It remained in use among the inhabitants of southwestern Gaul (Aquitaine) and of the Rhône Valley, both of which areas came under Frankish rule in the early sixth century; it would also be known in northern Gaul as well as in northern Italy, although its use in these last two areas is more difficult to trace. It was one of the most important sources of Roman law in western Europe prior to the revival of the "classical" Roman law (the law of the *Corpus Iuris Civilis*) in the eleventh and twelfth centuries.

The revised Visigothic code, issued in the mid-seventh century and corrected and expanded thereafter by royal enactment, is commonly known as the *Leges Visigothorum* or the *Forum Iudicum*. This Visigothic law book remained in use in Spain even during the period of Moorish domination and in the thirteenth century was incorporated in Castilian translation (*Fuero Juzgo*) in a code, the *Siete Partidas*, issued by Alfonso the Wise of Castile. Through the *Siete Partidas* some elements of Visigothic law were eventually to find their way to Spanish America.

The Visigothic code is the most Romanized of the early Germanic law codes—it lacks such typically Germanic legal concepts as collective family responsibility symbolized by the threat of the blood feud and popular participation in the judicial or legislative process. In addition, most of the judicial procedure is basically Roman, depending on a strong state where the king is the source of law; and the judicial system, backed by strong state control and operated by state magistrates, has superseded private or family justice.

Almost contemporaneous with this Visigothic legal activity was that of the Burgundians, who settled in the Rhône Valley in southeastern Gaul. The Burgundians also established a federate kingdom in a very thoroughly Romanized part of the Empire; and the new Burgundian rulers also faced the problem of providing a stable rule for a population partly Germanic and partly Gallo-Roman, where the Gallo-Romans were in a majority. As in the case of the Visigoths, this effort involved a reduction to writing of the old Burgundian customary law and a modification of that law to adjust it to the more settled circumstances of the new Burgundian life. At the same time, the Burgundian rulers attempted to guarantee that the Roman part of the population would continue to enjoy its rights and its own law. Accordingly, in the closing years of the fifth century the Burgundian king Gundobad (474–516) and later his son and successor Sigismund (516–523) issued codes for both the Burgundian and Roman parts of their population. The Germanic code was issued in several parts between the years 483 and 532 and is known as the *Liber Constitutionum* or the *Lex Gundobada*. The laws for the Roman population were probably issued about the year 517, and collectively are known as the *Lex Romana Burgundionum*. The Burgundian rulers were clearly following Visigothic precedent in these affairs and, as in the case of the Visigoths, almost certainly employed Roman jurists in the preparation of their compilations.

The two Burgundian law books had markedly different fates. The Burgundian kingdom was conquered by the Franks in 534, but this conquest did not mean the end of Burgundian law. The Franks, even more than the other barbarians who entered the Empire, retained their respect for the personal concept of law; accordingly, Frankish subjects of Burgundian descent continued to claim the right to be judged by Burgundian law for centuries after they were conquered by the Franks. On the other hand, the use of the *Lex Romana Burgundionum* was very brief. When the Franks conquered the Burgundian kingdom, the *Lex Romana Burgundionum* was set aside and replaced by the more comprehensive Visigothic *Breviary*, which would be the chief source of Roman law in the Frankish empire.

Although some of the Franks were recognized as federates of the Empire as early as 358, a significant Frankish kingdom did not emerge until the late fifth century (compared with 418 for the Visigoths and 443 for the Burgundians); nonetheless, the Franks participated in the law-code making activity that characterized the earliest Germanic states. The details surrounding this Frankish activity, however, are much more obscure than that of the Visigoths and Burgundians. Roman influence in general is so nearly lacking in the Frankish code that for long it was regarded as the earliest attempt by the Germanic rulers to record the customary law of their people. The Frankish code (titled Salic law) is now, however, pretty firmly assigned in its original form to 507–511, putting it very close in time to the Visigothic and Burgundian activity but sufficiently behind to be influenced by their model. It is also now evident that the Frankish rulers had the service of a legally trained Roman bureaucracy; but the fact remains that it is hard to trace the source of legal education in northern Gaul whereas there is strong likelihood that some legal training was still available at such southern sites as Bordeaux and Arles.[16] More will be said about the Frankish legislative activity in the following section.

Two other Germanic peoples established early kingdoms: the Vandals in Africa (429–534) and the Ostrogoths in Italy (490–552). Although there is a strong possibility that both of these people (especially the Ostrogoths under their great king Theodoric) participated in the early Germanic legislative activity, their law books have not survived and the relatively brief existence of their kingdoms would mean that Ostrogothic and Vandal law would leave few traces behind.

There are two other major Germanic law codes dating from a slightly later time than the work of the Visigoths, Burgundians, and Franks: those of the Anglo-Saxons and of the Lombards. A brief word about each of these is in order.

When the various Germanic peoples known as the Anglo-Saxons settled in Britain between the middle of the fifth and the middle of the sixth centuries, they encountered an area that had been part of the Roman Empire since the mid-first century, but which had been to a degree cut off from its Roman contacts for some time (the last Roman legions had been withdrawn at the beginning of the fifth century) and had always been out on the fringes of Roman territory. As a result, Roman survivals were weaker here than in any of the other Germanic kingdoms.

Since many of the more Romanized Romano-Britons retreated before the Anglo-Saxon advance, there was no need to retain Roman-law courts or Roman law in Germanic Britain and therefore Roman legal ideas (except those associated with the church) seem to have had little if any influence on Anglo-Saxon law. So the Anglo-Saxon kings issued no laws for their Roman population, and in issuing laws for their Germanic population, the Anglo-Saxon rulers alone of the early Germanic kings employed their native Germanic tongue rather than Latin. After all, they had no Roman personnel, no Roman jurists, to employ in their administrations. As a result of these factors, the Anglo-Saxon codes more closely approach pure

Germanic custom than any other early Germanic legislation (the Frankish code is the most nearly related in this respect).

The Lombards were the last major Germanic people to invade the Empire. They entered in the second half of the sixth century, invading an Italy torn by a long-drawn-out war between the Ostrogothic kingdom and the Byzantine Empire. The Byzantines had at last won the war and established a provincial administration in Italy. But before Byzantine rule could become well established, the Lombards invaded from the north and, with relatively little difficulty, overcame the weak Byzantine garrisons that had been left in the major towns.

The experience of the Lombards was not radically different from the experience of the Visigoths and Burgundians in their attempts to rule a people more culturally advanced than themselves and to provide an administration that could protect the lives and property of both Germanic and Roman subjects. Much of the Roman provincial administration in Italy had been disturbed if not destroyed by the long Ostrogothic-Byzantine wars, but the Lombard kings undoubtedly had some Roman advisers. The form of the municipal *civitas* (urban center with surrounding region) remained the basis for the Lombard local administration.

Although the Lombard judges were learned only in the Lombard law and the Lombard courts do not seem to have offered a means of settling disputes among the Roman part of the population, it is clear from their legislation that the Lombards recognized Roman law as continuing to live in Italy and that the Roman part of the population continued to settle its disputes and regulate its legal transactions in accordance with it. It is not clear how this Roman law was administered for, unlike the situation in the Ostrogothic, Visigothic, and Burgundian kingdoms, the Lombard courts took no cognizance of Roman law.

The value of the Lombard legislation lies in the continuing legislative activity of the Lombard kings and the development of a fairly sophisticated legal reasoning revealed in the successive issues of these laws. The most important laws were issued by King Rothair (*Rothair's Edict*, 643) and by King Liutprand (between 713 and 735). *Rothair's Edict* is almost entirely Germanic custom modified only slightly by the experiences encountered by the Lombards in the process of migrating into and settling in Italy. It deserves the designation "code" more than almost any other of the Germanic issues inasmuch as it is a nearly complete statement of Lombard legal principles and is organized according to a number of general categories (e.g., offenses involving damages or violence, family law, and property law). The material added after *Rothair's Edict* adds to and modifies the original *Edict*, and accordingly there is little sense of organization here. In general, it would seem that the later Lombard kings were issuing laws inspired by specific cases that had arisen in their kingdoms. So these laws are clearly not Germanic custom but are instead new laws worked out to meet new conditions. Not surprisingly, much of this new legislation owes a great deal to the influence of Roman law, although it also owes much to the influence of the church (the once-Arian Lombards became Catholic in the seventh century).

After the conquest of the Lombards by the Franks in 775, Italy was administered as a separate kingdom by Charlemagne and his successors. Lombard law, supplemented by a number of Carolingian capitularies, continued to be the law of the greater part of the population.

Each of the early Germanic law codes is distinct from the other; and there is a vast difference between the most Romanized of them, the Visigothic, and the most Germanic, the Anglo-Saxon. Nonetheless, all were composed under roughly similar circumstances and all enjoyed certain characteristics. All were the products of a new royal power, even when nominal acknowledgment of consulting the "elders" or "the people" is given. All reflected the fact that much of the responsibility for maintaining peace and order in the community had passed from the family to the state. All envisaged a judicial system staffed by royal appointees who either conducted the proceedings alone or who presided over a court that contained representatives of the community. All handled criminal offenses as injuries against an individual or his family, and the judicial action to resolve the issue was essentially a suit for civil damages. All (except possibly the Visigothic) relied on the cooperation of the family in order to obtain justice, for the state as such merely provided a court for arbitration; it was up to the injured party (backed by his kin) to get the accused before the court. Once an issue had been settled in court, however, the injured family was liable to judicial interference if it attempted to resort to the blood feud.

III. The Franks as Seen Through Their Law Code

Background of *Lex Salica*

We know very little about the legislative activity of the early Franks. For a long time, the Frankish code was thought to be the earliest of the Germanic law codes because of its strongly Germanic flavor. It has only recently been established with some certainty that the earliest codification of Frankish law took place after the earliest Visigothic and Burgundian codes were issued. The earliest written Frankish code is attributed to King Clovis, who is thought to have issued his code (*Pactus Legis Salicae*) some time between 507 and 511.[17] What was the background of Clovis's legislative activity and what were his motives?

After the defeat of Syagrius' sub-Roman "kingdom" at Soissons in 486, Clovis had all of northern Gaul under his control and had inherited its former Roman administration there. Since Gaul had been in turmoil for some time and rule from Rome had become ineffective even before the deposition of the last Western Emperor in 476, it is difficult to know just how intact was this Roman administration. Nonetheless, some form of Roman rule must still have been in place and, since the Franks had no experienced administrative staff to substitute, the Roman staff must have been retained. In addition, the remnants of Syagrius' army were almost certainly allowed to join the Frankish army, if not the personal retinue of Clovis himself.[18] To further whatever Roman influence came through these administrative and military channels, at an early point in his reign Clovis established friendly relations with the Catholic hierarchy.

Clovis came under another form of Roman influence when he married (in 493) the Catholic niece of the Burgundian king Gundobad. With Clotilda came some Catholic influence (and pressure for Clovis's conversion to Catholic rather than to Arian Christianity), and with Clotilda came a close contact with southeastern Gaul where the Germanic Burgundians had established a kingdom in 443. The Burgundians found themselves in a thoroughly Romanized area and retained the Roman administration already in place there; further evidence of their sympathy for doing things the Roman way is indicated by the fact that their ruler Gundobad had held high office at the Roman imperial court before becoming king in 474. Furthermore, a codification of both Roman and Burgundian law had been or would be undertaken by King Gundobad and continued by his son Sigismund (the first version of the Burgundian code was issued in 483; the Roman in 517). So Clovis had the earlier Burgundian legislative example before him, as well as the even earlier example of the Visigoths, who also issued law codes for both the Roman and Visigothic portions of their population. (Although they had issued earlier law, the Visigoths issued their first Germanic "code" in 481, their Roman code in 506.)

The Frankish code issued by Clovis (probably some time between 507 and 511) is the most Germanic of the barbarian law codes (with the exception of the Anglo-Saxon); nonetheless it seems fairly certain that Clovis had the help of a Roman staff with some legal training when he came to codify the Frankish laws. The code itself does not help in determining this matter. Neither the short nor the long prologue is thought to be contemporaneous with the original issuance of the code and cannot be taken as reflecting accurately how the work was done. We are told in both prologues that the laws were issued with the agreement of the notables after selecting four men from different parts of the country who met in three courts to discuss the disputes that gave rise to the collection of law,[19] but neither the men named nor the places they came from have been identified and the statement is nearly meaningless. In effect, the issuance of the *Pactus Legis Salicae* was an aspect of the new royal power that Clovis exercised as heir to Roman rule in northern Gaul. The writing may actually have been done by Roman scribes at the dictation of Roman personnel—but the authority of the Frankish king gave legitimacy to the code.[20]

It is interesting to note that, unlike the Visigothic and Burgundian kings, Clovis made no attempt to issue a code of Roman law for the Gallo-Romans in his kingdom. Although Gallo-Romans almost certainly constituted a majority of the population in all of northern Gaul except the extreme northeastern corner, nonetheless the Gallo-Roman preponderance must not have been as great as in Aquitaine and Burgundy where formal recognition of Roman law was made by the Germanic rulers of these areas. Northern Gaul had not been as thoroughly Romanized as the southwest and southeast. In addition, it had been subject to much disturbance in the fourth and fifth centuries as a series of pretenders to the Roman throne either came from this area or moved through it and as colonies of military colonists (*laeti*—usually Germans but occasionally other barbarian peoples from eastern Europe) had been scattered through northern and central Gaul.[21] So the Roman presence in the north was not as overpowering as in the south, and the debased culture that survived in northern Gaul might even represent some Celtic resurgence.

Pactus Legis Salicae (the Frankish code) is not a well-organized code, nor is it very comprehensive. Much of its content is devoted to establishing monetary or other penalties for various damaging acts or to setting up rules of legal procedure. Such private-law concerns as marriage and the family, inheritance, gifts, and contracts—which play such a large role in the Visigothic, Burgundian, and Lombard codes—are treated very briefly if at all. Thus the very nature of the Frankish legislation goes far to explain why there is less Roman influence (considering the Roman preoccupation with private law) in the Frankish code than in any other of the early Germanic codes except the Anglo-Saxon.

Since the Salic law applied to Gallo-Romans as well as to Franks in the matters that it covered, one is tempted to conclude that Clovis's legal advisers were eager to record that part of the law which differed from the Roman. The long schedule of physical injuries, each with its designated tariff (composition) would be unfamiliar to the Gallo-Romans; Roman law would not be so minutely concerned with damages to wild and domestic animals, to orchards, vegetable gardens, and fields; Gallo-Romans would be unfamiliar with the Frankish court procedure—and these matters make up much of the Frankish code. In northern Gaul, the Salic law became a territorial code in those areas of law that it covered; however, one assumes that Frankish law did not drive out Roman law completely since there were so many areas not covered at all by the Salic law. Nor did the Salic law make any provision for the church as an institution or for the members of the clergy as persons distinct from the other members of society.[22] For the church and for the clergy, as well as for Gallo-Romans in areas not covered by the Salic law, Roman law must have continued in force in northern Gaul. The source of this law and its administration are unknown, however.

The Salic law was never extended to all parts of the Frankish kingdom nor was it extended beyond Gaul as a result of Charlemagne's conquests. It was primarily the law of the northern half of Frankish Gaul where the bulk of the Frankish settlements were concentrated. Elsewhere it was invoked only as the personal law of individual Franks, and as a result it had disappeared outside of northern France by the time of the revival of the Roman law of the *Corpus Iuris Civilis* in the eleventh and twelfth centuries. But in northern Gaul, the Frankish law was extremely tenacious. It held its own beside later feudal custom and it was strong enough to retain much of its content even after medieval French kings encouraged the study of the revived Roman law. Its continued use in modified form would account for the fact that, at the outbreak of the French Revolution in the late eighteenth century, northern France was still described as the land of customary (i.e., Germanic) law (*pays du droit coutumier*) in contrast with southern France, the land of the written (i.e., Roman) law (*pays du droit écrit*).

The Frankish State

The nature of the government established by Clovis and his Merovingian successors is a matter of some dispute, depending upon whether one emphasizes the Germanic contribution or the Roman. The most generally accepted theory holds that Clovis took over the previous Roman administration and tried to make it work (his legislative activity is an indication of his seriousness in this regard).[23] And although the Frankish administration was undoubtedly less effective than the Roman had been, nonetheless the Merovingian Franks succeeded in maintaining a reasonably impressive state through the sixth century and well into the seventh (many of the important administrative posts and virtually all of the bishoprics were originally held by Gallo-Romans). By the middle of the seventh century (when fusion of the two peoples was well advanced), decay had set in; the period between the middle of the seventh century and the middle of the eighth, when a revival took place under the new Carolingian rulers, is a period of breakdown in the central power. The royal power became ineffective, and the state itself was torn apart as ambitious powerful families attempted to assert their independence.

Although education steadily deteriorated during this interval and internecine civil wars disturbed the land, the most adequate explanation for the decline in the Frankish royal power is the economic one. When Clovis established his kingdom, he inherited the estates of the imperial fisc as well as the income from those Roman taxes still collected (the tax on commerce brought in a significant income and would continue to do so for another century).[24] Thus Clovis had the means to "run" his government, especially since it cost him less than it had the Romans. His military expenses were not as great, since he depended upon his personal military followers as well as the usual military service rendered without pay by the free Frankish man.[25] The personal retainers were maintained either in the king's household or were given grants from the lands of the fisc—in either case, they did not represent a cash outlay for the king. Administrators also were not paid regular salaries; their incomes depended on receiving various fines associated with their judicial activity or on grants of land from the king.

The early Merovingians still had some money income and would continue to mint quite respectable coinage for a time, but interest in coinage declined as the need for money was replaced by land as the major source of wealth. The early Merovingians seemed to have plenty of this—they not only had the lands of the imperial fisc but also land secured by inheritance or forfeiture or confiscation—and they were lavish in bestowing it on others. It was only after more than a century of depleting the royal estates by making grants to persons whom the king wished to reward for their services or to conciliate to his rule or by making grants to the church that the later Merovingians found themselves in a serious economic position. Depletion of the royal estates, thus depriving the kings of the means to influence others, partially explains the failure of the Merovingian dynasty. Much of the Carolingian success was owed to ceaseless military campaigns that added lands which the ruler might use to reward his own followers or to influence the notables in his favor.

But when this much is said, we still know very little about how Clovis and his successors actually ran their kingdom, and one reason for studying the Salic law is that it is one of the few contemporary sources that may tell us something about it. In the discussion of Frankish institutions that follows, an attempt has been made to take for granted as little as possible, in order to determine whether the laws themselves can tell us something about the Frankish way of doing things that we have not known before or have known about in another way. It should be kept in mind that the picture that emerges is that of the law code, and thus may present institutions as the lawgivers imagined or wished them to be rather than as they actually were.

The Frankish Judicial System

Little is known about the Germanic court system before the Germans established contact with Rome. Before the invasions, the Germanic state was weak, if not nonexistent, and whatever judicial system there was depended heavily on the cooperation of the kin groups and the threat of blood feud to maintain some semblance of peace. Once the Germans settled within the Empire, their judicial systems were immediately influenced by the Roman model; but the resulting product was different for each Germanic people. The Frankish system seems to have been less influenced than those of the Visigoths, Burgundians, or Lombards. In fact, the Frankish law code gives us more information about the Germanic elements in the early medieval administration of justice than any other barbarian code (since the Anglo-Saxon laws take the judicial system and judicial procedure pretty much for granted and have little to say on these subjects). The Frankish code has a lot to say about the courts and about judicial procedure.

The chief judicial officers of the kingdom were the count and his subordinate, the hundredman (*centenarius*) or *thunginus*.[26] Counts and hundredmen (or *thunginii*) were royal appointees and part of a centralizing force in the kingdom, but unlike late Roman judges, the Frankish judges had little to do with determining what the law was or in interpreting the law. The Frankish judges presided over and administered the courts; matters of law were determined by men from the community specifically designated to speak the law—the rachimburgi (usually seven to a court). So the Frankish courts retained a strong popular representation in the rachimburgi, although we do not know how the rachimburgi were chosen. We assume they came from the more suitable families of the area where the court was held and that they continued to serve for some time, thus gaining considerable experience in the law.

If this popular justice did not work, the matter went to the king, who was the head of the judicial system and (insofar as he might ignore, interpret, or modify the written law) the ultimate source of law. The king's role in the administration of justice was an important one and, if he played his judicial role properly, must have constituted a major part of his activities. It also necessitated his traveling around the kingdom on a regular basis since the time allowed for appeal to the king was relatively short. Perhaps the heavy judicial responsibilities of the Frankish king contributed to the tendency to divide the kingdom among several rulers.

Frankish law, like the law of the other Germanic peoples, did not distinguish between what we might call civil and criminal causes. The Franks did not have a police force to bring criminals before police courts (as did the Romans); instead, what we would call criminal cases were handled as civil suits for damages. A person who had sustained an injury (or his family) was responsible for bringing the person who had injured him before the court. The state did not intervene in the matter—in essence, the state merely provided a tribunal before which the parties involved could have their dispute (over violence or property or anything else) adjudicated.

In court, proof was determined by oath (compurgation) or by the ordeal. Compurgation was a method of judicial proof whereby both accuser and accused offered oath and supported their statements with a number of oathtakers or oathhelpers, the number depending upon the seriousness of the matter involved. The oathhelpers were not witnesses—they were not giving sworn evidence. They were swearing their willingness to support the oath of their principal, whether accuser or defendant. The entire procedure was very formal. If at any point in the process the oathhelper hesitated or refused to take the oath, the oath was said to be broken and the accused "proved" to be guilty (if the oath were for the defendant); the accuser lost his case (if the oath were on his behalf). Compurgation was the most widely used form of proof in the Frankish courts.

Use of the ordeal was a means of appealing to divine intervention in the establishment of proof. The Franks normally used the ordeal of boiling water (in the case of freemen), but they also used an ordeal involving the casting of lots (primarily in the case of slaves). In the case of the water ordeal, the person being sent to the ordeal was required to plunge his hand into a cauldron of boiling water and pick out a stone or some other object. If the wound that resulted from the scalding turned out "clean," the deity had demonstrated the individual's innocence (or the truth of his accusation). If the wound turned out to be a "dirty" one, guilt or falseness was demonstrated (Cap. V, CXXXII).[27]

In the case of Frankish freemen, it is not clear how it was determined whether proof by compurgation or proof by the ordeal would be used in a particular cause. Most of the Germanic peoples allowed the man of good birth and/or good reputation to defend himself by presenting oathhelpers who swore to support the oath of their principal, whereas the lesser man and/or the man of suspicious reputation was sent to the ordeal. This may have been true for the Franks also, but there is some indication in the laws that oaths were used for the less serious offenses, the ordeal for the more serious (LXXIII). There is also some indication that the question of whether compurgation would be allowed or the ordeal required was decided by the rachimburgi (LVI, 2–3). And further, some persons sent to the ordeal were allowed to redeem their hands from the ordeal by making a money payment. Such redemption was allowed in cases involving compositions up to and including the amount of the wergeld (LIII, 1–7). This ability to buy out of the ordeal seems to have been limited to the Franks and Anglo-Saxons. In any event, the ordeal by boiling water was not an entirely irrational way to establish proof since there was a certain amount of prejudgment exercised by the court.[28]

We do not know how frequently people were able to "pass" the boiling water ordeal, but there are certainly enough references in literature to such an event to indicate that sometimes indeed the hand did come out clean, and people in the early Middle Ages do not seem to have had difficulty in believing that this was indeed divine intervention.

In the case of slaves, the question of prejudgment by the court does not arise. The slave must either confess through the application of torture or be sent to the ordeal (whether it was torture or the ordeal was determined by the law, not by the court). Slaves obviously could not be allowed proof by compurgation (how could they provide oathhelpers?), but instead of sending them to the ordeal of boiling water they were sent to the ordeal by lot. It would seem to us that passing the ordeal by lot would be more difficult than passing the ordeal by water, since the possibility of choosing rightly by random choice would not be very great. But of course if one expects divine intervention, then a slave could hope to prove himself innocent; in the meantime, he had not suffered the appalling pain of plunging his hand into a cauldron of boiling water and had not damaged his lord's property.[29]

Whatever form of proof was employed, if the accused party were determined to be guilty, the rachimburgi then "spoke" the law—that is, the rachimburgi announced the penalty (a penalty set out in the code). The penalty in all but the most serious offenses (discussed later) consisted in the assessment of a monetary payment, a payment called composition in the case of injuries less than death and wergeld in the event of homicide. Composition was an amount fixed by the laws, which were very detailed in this regard. Wergeld was an amount that varied with the individual; it was a man's (or woman's) value. These payments were made to the injured party (or to his family in the case of homicide); with the acceptance of payment, the injured party had to be content. This Germanic method of judicial redress of grievances was a method to maintain the peace worked out in the dim past. Behind it lay the threat of the blood feud: if an injured party or his family were unrecompensed, he or they would wreak vengeance on the offender or his family. The blood feud had not entirely disappeared among the Franks, as it had not yet among the other Germans, but it was to a large extent regulated by the Germanic practice of substituting money payments for vengeance.[30] The compositions and wergelds were very high, in the case of serious offenses, and most families must have preferred to receive money (or some other form of wealth) in compensation rather than resort to costly feud. The state was likewise recompensed for its efforts to maintain the peace. The man who had been "proved" guilty of a particular offense not only paid composition to the injured party, he also paid a fine to the court (LXVg and Cap. VII, V); or, when the court helped a man to collect a debt, two-thirds went to the creditor, one-third to the count as a fine (L, 3). This was one of the main forms of income for the presiding officer of the court. The rachimburgi, as respected members of the community, served as a public duty without pay. We do not know what was the source of the legal knowledge of the rachimburgi. In some cases a copy of the Salic code may have been available for consultation, but in most cases the rachimburgi must have acted on the basis of personal knowledge accumulated from years of serving on the court.

The usual court (*mallus*) was a court convened by the hundredman or thunginus either on a regular basis or at the request of suitors (this court could also be presided over by a superior, the count). The same procedure was used for instituting property disputes as suits for damages: the accuser, with witnesses, went to the defendant and summoned him to court; if the man did not come, he was assessed a penalty (I, 1–5). In the case of disputed property the accuser, with witnesses, must summon his opponent not once but three times, at seven-day intervals, although a penalty was added to the property in dispute for each summons that was necessary. If the defendant ignored all three summonses, he lost the property in dispute in addition to paying the added penalties (LII; L, 3). Frankish law thus provided the defendant with a number of delays.

If a man refused to come to court or ignored the procedures noted above or refused to give security for carrying out a judgment entered by the rachimburgi, he was summoned before the king. The procedure whereby this was accomplished was for the plaintiff to have twelve witnesses present at the court where judgment was rendered in his favor. A date forty days thereafter was set for the defendant to appear in court in order to pay the judgment against him or to offer security for payment of the judgment. On that court day the witnesses to the judgment were present and, if the defendant did not appear, the witnesses on oath testified that the court had been held, the judgment rendered, and a court date for payment set. Then the defendant was summoned to appear before the king in fourteen days.

At that time, plaintiff and his witnesses appeared before the king; the witnesses stated on oath that all of the above procedures had been complied with and, if the defendant again had not appeared, another court day was set for him. On that final court day, if he still had not responded, the defendant was outlawed and forfeited all his property to the fisc. After this anyone, even the man's wife, who fed or offered hospitality to him was liable to a fine of fifteen solidi.[31] The condition of outlawry lasted permanently or until the judgment was paid (LV, 4; LVI, 5–6).[32]

A man's witnesses could be challenged, but at considerable risk. The man bringing a charge against witnesses must submit to the ordeal of boiling water. If his hand came out clean, the witnesses were proved to have perjured themselves and each paid a fine of fifteen solidi. If, however, the hand sustained a dirty burn, the challenger paid a fine of fifteen solidi to each of the witnesses (CXXXII).

If the rachimburgi were asked to render judgment in a suit (to "speak the Salic law," as the code says) and refused to do so and continued to refuse after a second request, each of the seven was fined three solidi and another court day set. If they refused to speak the law at the second court, each was fined fifteen solidi. If the rachimburgi rendered judgment and the party decided against did not think that the judgment was in accordance with the law, he could challenge the decision in court. If his pleading was able to establish that the rachimburgi had not rendered justice according to law, each of the rachimburgi was fined fifteen solidi. If, however, the challenging party was unable to sustain his accusation, he must pay each of the rachimburgi fifteen solidi. We have no indication how the evidence for such a challenge was obtained; perhaps copies of the law code were more accessible than one might think (LVII), or, more likely, the challenger underwent the ordeal.

Once the rachimburgi had spoken the law and thereby indicated the amount of the property judgment or the amount of the composition, the defendant offered security or a pledge for his eventual payment of the decree. How long an interval was allowed for the final payment is not clear; but should the payment not be made, the offender was placed outside the law so that all of his property and even his person were ultimately responsible for the debt (L; LVI, 6).

Outlawry was used in other cases. For example, if a man dug up and despoiled a dead body, he was placed outside the law until the relatives of the dead man agreed that he might be allowed to "come among men again." In the meantime, anyone who provided food or lodging for the outlaw, even a wife or other relative, was subject to a fifteen-solidi fine (LV, 4). Two laws from one of the capitularies also provided for outlawry. In one case, where a woman married her own slave, she was outlawed and the fisc acquired her property—and again, the fine for giving her food or shelter was fifteen solidi (Cap. III, LXLVIII). Another law (from the Decree of King Chilperic for keeping the peace) provided that in the case of an evil man who has fled to the forest, if the man whom he has injured accused him before the king, the king would outlaw him "so that whoever finds him can kill him without fear" (CXV). And in one of the laws issued by King Childebert, the person guilty of rape who sought refuge in a church was outlawed (if he was captured before he reached sanctuary, he suffered death or outlawry) (Cap. VI, II, 2).

A man was normally expected to plead his own case in court, but evidently he could call upon others to help him. A relative (a member of one's kin group or parentela) could speak on one's behalf without a formal request. No one else, however, was allowed to do so unless requested; the fine for doing so without a request was fifteen solidi (CV).

Twelve seems to have been the age of majority—to kill a boy before he was twelve (the long-haired boys) meant payment of a six-hundred-solidi wergeld instead of two hundred (XXIV, 1, 4; XLI, 18); to cut his hair without the consent of his relatives (and thereby indicate his majority and make him liable to fines for criminal actions or competent to control his property) involved a forty-five-solidi composition (LXLVII, 1). A child's inheritance could not be challenged until he was twelve and therefore of legal age. The same age probably applied to girls and was just as symbolic (LXLVII, 2). Before a girl could bear children her wergeld was two hundred solidi. During the childbearing years, a woman's wergeld was six hundred solidi, and two hundred thereafter (XXIV, 8–9; XLI, 17–19; LXVe; Cap. VI, Seven Types of Cases, VII).

It would seem that each man had twelve designated oathhelpers who could be called upon without delay to support his oath. But such oathhelpers—obviously very close to the individual involved—could support their principal's oath in suits involving only three different matters: the marriage gift, property lost in the army, or a man recalled into slavery. In all other cases, a man had to find other oathhelpers. If the twelve offered oath in types of suits other than the three named, they were fined—the three oldest each paying fifteen solidi, the other nine five solidi each (LXIX). This kind of oathhelper, used in specified cases only, is out of character with most other Germanic legislation and seems to be a peculiarly Frankish institution.

In cases other than the three noted above, the number of oathhelpers required depended on the amount of composition involved in a case. The following scale is given in a law involving antrustions (members of the king's *trustis* or retinue) who brought suit against one another, but the relative number of oathhelpers involved was likely the same for all freemen. In this case, if the offense involved was a minor one (where the composition would be less than thirty-five solidi), the plaintiff brought the charge supported by six oathhelpers and the defendant supported himself with twelve oathhelpers.[33] If the composition involved were between thirty-five solidi and forty-five solidi, the charge was supported by nine oathhelpers and the defense by eighteen oathhelpers. If the composition were forty-five solidi or more—up to the amount of the wergeld[34]—the charge was brought with the support of twelve oathhelpers and the defense with twenty-five (rather than twenty-four as one would expect). If the composition involved was the amount of the wergeld or more, the charge was supported by twelve oathhelpers and the defendant must go to the ordeal (LXXIII, 1–5).[35] If the antrustion accused was unable to defend himself by oath and would not pay composition or refused to go to the ordeal, he was summoned before the king. At the king's court, the plaintiff presented nine witnesses who took oaths in groups of three that the defendant had been properly summoned on three occasions at seven-day intervals and still had not complied with the law. Thereafter the defendant was placed outside the law, his property and his person liable for the debt—anyone who fed him or offered him hospitality, even his wife, paid a composition of fifteen solidi (LXXIII, 6).

The Family and Kin Group

The Frankish family was the small family usually found among the other Germanic barbarians: it consisted of husband, wife, minor sons, unmarried daughters, and other dependents including half-free dependents (*lidi*) and slaves. However, although the basic family group was the same for the Franks as for most of the other Germanic barbarians who settled within the territory of the Roman Empire, the Franks relied more heavily on the larger kin group than did the Burgundians, Visigoths, or Lombards (it is difficult to know about the Anglo-Saxons, for the early Anglo-Saxon laws are uninformative on this subject).

The kin group was important because the individual alone, or even with his immediate family, was in a precarious position in Frankish society. One needed the support of a wider kin to help him bring offenders against his peace before the courts, and one needed kin to help provide the oathhelpers that a man might be required to present in order to make his case or to establish his own innocence before the court. These roles of the kin are familiar to all the Germans. But the Frankish kin group had further responsibilities and privileges. For example, if a man were killed, his own children collected only half of the composition due, the remaining half being equally divided between those members of his kin group who came from his father's side and those who came from his mother's side (LXII, 1). It is interesting to note that the wife did not share in this composition since she was not a member of her husband's kin group. Furthermore, should there be no members of the father's kin group on either the mother's or father's side available, that share went to the royal fisc, or to whomever the fisc granted it (LXII, 2).[36]

The right of the kin group to share in the receipt of composition involved also the responsibility for helping members of the group to pay composition. If a man by himself did not have sufficient property to pay the entire composition assessed against him, he could seek help from his closest kin, father and mother first, then brothers and sisters. If sufficient help was still not forthcoming, more distant members of the maternal and paternal kin (up to the sixth degree, i.e., second cousins [XLIV, 11–12]), could be asked to help. This responsibility of the kin to aid their kinsmen is known in Frankish law as *chrenecruda* (LVIII). This arrangement protected the wife's property from being used to satisfy her husband's debts. It was his kin group that was responsible, not she or hers; in the reverse instance, of course, the husband's property was protected against calls upon his wife to aid her kinsmen.

The importance of the kin group should thus be obvious, and added importance derived from the fact that one shared in the inheritance of one's kin up to the sixth degree should closer heirs be lacking. Normally the advantages and disadvantages of belonging to a kin group (legally related in an association known as parentela) evened themselves out, and the security of association plus the opportunity to inherit well justified the potential liability of the kin. However, on occasion the liabilities overshadowed the advantages. The debts of an uncontrollable relative might endanger a man's property, or movement away from the area in which the kin group lived might have made the operation of parentela awkward if not impossible. So the law provided the means whereby a man could remove himself from his kin's parentela, thereby avoiding responsibility for his kin—but in return he forfeited his position in the line of inheritance of that kin group (LX).

But just as it was possible to remove oneself from one's kin, so it was also possible to bring someone else in. Presumably this occurred when there were no heirs in the kin group and the adoption of an heir was the means to prevent the property from going to the fisc. This procedure was called *afatomiae* in the Frankish law (XLVI). This is a very obscure law to translate and the procedure described archaic, but the meaning is clear. The individual wishing to transfer his property to someone not related to him threw a stick into the grantee's lap; this ritual was followed by the grantee's formally entertaining a number of men at the grantor's board. Reliable witnesses to these acts were necessary to protect the claims of the new heir.

Marriage

The Frankish laws contain little direct information about the institution of marriage. A legal marriage could be contracted between an adult freeman and an adult free woman (the laws do not set a minimum age), subject to the consent of their relatives and provided the two parties were not related within the prohibited bonds of relationship. The Frankish laws specifically prohibit marriage between an uncle and niece or grandniece (and so by implication between an aunt and nephew and grandnephew), or marriage with the former wife of a brother or of a mother's brother (and by implication marriage with the former husband of a sister or with the former husband of a mother's sister) (XIII, 11). Note here that the mother's brothers and sisters were evidently held to be more closely related than the father's brothers and sisters since it is marriage with the former spouse of mother's brother or sister that is prohibited, not that of father's brother or sister. Admittedly the church councils of Merovingian Gaul interpreted consanguinity more broadly than here defined, but these added restrictions were not enforced in the civil courts, just as among the Franks neither Christian non-dissolubility of marriage nor monogamy was enforced in the courts. A late law issued by King Childebert in 594 provided death for the man who married his father's wife (one of the very few instances for the death penalty in the code). In the case of marriages that had already taken place and now were designated incestuous (e.g., marriage with the wife of brother, or sister of wife, or wife of uncle), they were to be corrected by proclamation of the bishop. If this was ignored, the parties were to be excommunicated and their property passed to their relatives (Cap. VI, I, 2).

As in the case of the other Germans, the offspring of a Frankish illegal marriage was illegitimate and could not inherit (XIII, 11). There are no provisions for the offspring of unions not recognized as marriage.

In the case of the Franks, betrothal preceded marriage, as among the other Germans. The betrothal seems to have been arranged by the man and woman in the presence of the relatives of both. It was symbolized by the groom-to-be giving a bride-price for his bride-to-be which became part of the wife's dos after marriage (her father also gave her a gift—Cap. I, LXVII), and remained in her possession after her husband's death until she remarried, when part of it was given up (see below). If the man withdrew from the betrothal agreement, he paid a composition of sixty-two and one-half solidi (LXVa) (there is no provision for the woman who withdrew).

The married woman's endowment was made up of gifts from her husband and from her father. This property could not be alienated by her husband and normally passed to their children. If the husband predeceased his wife, the woman kept the entire dos her husband had given for her unless she remarried. If she wished to remarry and there had been children, she was to give one solidus for each ten solidi of the husband's dos to her husband's closest relatives (see inheritance table below) to release her *mundium* (right of legal representation) to the new husband. For example, if the husband had given thirty solidi for her dos, the woman must give three solidi to his relatives. After the woman's death, the remainder of the dos went to the children she had had by her first husband (Cap. III, C, 1–2).

If a woman predeceased her husband, her dos went to her children—it could not be used as a dos for a second wife. If the children were minors, the father administered the property until they came of age—but he could not sell or give away any of this property (Cap. III, CI, 1). If there were no children, the dead wife's relatives could claim two-thirds of her dos—provided they left "two beds, two covered benches, and two armchairs" (CI, 2).[37] The married woman was transferred from her family's legal control (*mundium*) to that of her husband. On his death, her *mundium* must have passed to his relatives, hence the payment to them when she remarried. How strong this legal control was seems doubtful. The laws certainly do not openly state that either the bride's parents or the relatives of a dead husband had the right to veto a second marriage should the property payments be forthcoming. In many ways, the Frankish woman seems almost legally self-competent. She was able to own and inherit property (as among the other Germans), and this property was kept separate from her husband's property. Among the other Germans, however (with the exception of the Visigoths), the husband administered his wife's property even though he could not dispose of it without the consent of his wife or her relatives. Among the Franks, the wife may have administered her own property. At least she could be assessed composition separately from her husband, which implies that she had an independent control (LV, 4). And as a widow, a woman might receive the payment that allowed a widowed daughter-in-law to go to a second husband, implying that she had held her daughter-in-law's *mundium* after her son's (the first husband) death (Cap. III, C, 1).

Since the wife enjoyed such a strong position where her own property was concerned, it should not be surprising that there is no indication (as occurred among most of the other Germans) that a widow was guaranteed an inheritance from her husband nor the enjoyment of the usufruct of a portion of his property. The woman did, of course, keep her marriage portion (dos) consisting of her bride-price and whatever additional gift her father might make to her and she did retain her position as heir in her own kin group (and, as we shall note, in some cases the female line may have enjoyed some slight preference over the male). But if the female line enjoyed some slight preference in inheritance, it also suffered the liability that a wife and her children were called on to help pay composition for the penalties incurred by persons from her side of the family (LVIII, 3), another proof that a wife held and managed her own property if she had to help her own kin group. In any event, the female connection is very strong among the Franks—stronger than among the Burgundians, the Visigoths, and the Lombards.[38]

Inheritance

The basic inheritance laws of the Salian Franks provided for the passing of family land (called allodial land in the laws) as follows (LIX). A man's heirs in descending order of preference were:

1. Children (and their descendants).
2. Mother and father.
3. Brothers and sisters.
4. Father's sisters.
5. Mother's sisters.
6. Father's relatives (to sixth degree).

The problem of inheritance of land in the Frankish kingdom is complicated by the concluding statement in this law, that "concerning Salic land (*terra Salica*) no portion or inheritance is for a woman but all the land belongs to members of the male sex" (LIX, 6). Most commentators have taken this last provision to mean that women did not inherit land in the Merovingian kingdom, the argument being that the first five sections of this law refer to movable property and only the last provision to land. But this is surely a mistake since the term *alodis* in the title of this law almost certainly refers to allodial land.[39] Allodial land is land that is not held as a benefice—in other words, it is land referred to here as family land. Family land among the Germans was not normally alienable; it was preserved for the family. Among the Franks, a man's children (both boys and girls equally) were his first heirs, followed by his mother and father (equally), and then his brothers and sisters (equally). If there were no heirs available in these ranks, the aunts and uncles came next, but the aunts (first on the paternal side, and then on the maternal) took precedence over the uncles. So there is here a slight preference for the female line in the inheritance of family property. After the aunts and uncles, inheritance passed to the more distant kin in the paternal line and then perhaps in the maternal line.

In the distinction between allodial land (*de alode*) which was inherited by heirs of both sexes, and *terra Salica* which could be inherited only by males, we enounter an interesting indication that not all land was held as a result of a partition among family groups at the time of the original Frankish occupation. Sufficient land was held by grant or beneficial tenure (from king or other lord) that *terra Salica* is recognized in the law. Since these lands were granted normally in return for past or future services, it would be expected that this land could only be inherited by someone who could render similar services. In essence, this is the way the inheritance of the Merovingian kingdom was handled—as a benefice divisible among male heirs, the female heirs not being considered.

After having made this strong statement about the female heir's equal right to inherit family land, it should be noted that a later addition (Cap.

IV) issued by King Chilperic (some of the sections are very obscure) indicated that daughters succeeded to landed property only if there were no
sons. However, there is no indication that this reference is to family (allodial) land (Cap. IV, CVIII)—but at least it is clear that a woman could
inherit land. And since this law referred to the inheritance by sons "as the
Salic law provides," the reference is to an earlier law which must be the one
about Salic land (*terra Salica*) going only to male heirs (LIX, 6). In that
case, the later law improves the position of women, giving them the right
even to inherit land held by grant in the absence of male heirs.

Social Classes

If there were different classes of freemen among the Franks, if there was
even a class of nobles, the laws tell us nothing about them other than the
references to "notables" in the prologue that was added to the code later
in the sixth century, or a very obscure reference to "better persons" (*meliores*) and "lesser persons" (*minofledis*) that appears in Capitulary III
(CII—undated), or Chilperic's statement (also undated) that he agreed
with his highest-born optimates and antrustions when he issued Capitulary
IV.[40] But although the laws do not support the existence of different social
classes based on birth in the Frankish kingdom, they nonetheless make it
clear that some people were worth more than others. This difference in
value was indicated by a person's wergeld, the amount at which that life
was valued.

The basic Frankish wergeld was 200 solidi for both freemen and free
women (XV, 1), but this amount could be modified by age or sex, service
to the king, military service, or place where the person happened to be
when he was killed. For example, boys under twelve years of age enjoyed a
wergeld of 600 solidi rather than the usual 200 (XXIV, 1, 4; XLI, 18), indicating that in the years before a boy could be expected to protect himself
with arms the higher wergeld protected him against death by violence.
During the time that she was able to bear children, a woman's wergeld was
600 solidi (XXIV, 8; XLI, 19; LXVe, 1); before and after her childbearing
years, a woman's wergeld was 200 solidi (XXIV, 9; XLI, 17; LXVe, 2–4;
XLI, 15). To kill a pregnant woman involved a wergeld of 700 solidi—600
solidi for the woman and 100 solidi for her fetus (XXIV, 5 and 6), although
elsewhere this amount is stated to be 600 for the woman plus 600 solidi
for a male fetus (LXVe).[41] The adult male's wergeld was normally 200

solidi (XLI, 1); however, this increased to 600 solidi if a man were killed in his own house (XLI, 21) or while he was serving in the army (LXIII, 1). Also to kill a person and conceal the crime (e.g., burn the body) required a payment three times the normal wergeld (Cap. I, LXX).

Royal service also increased a man's wergeld. The count's wergeld was 600 solidi (LIV, 1), the wergeld of a royal antrustion (or retainer) was 600 solidi (XLI, 5),[42] increasing to 1,800 solidi if the man were killed while serving in the army (LXIII, 2). The sagibaron's (a royal judicial assistant) wergeld was also 600 solidi (LIV, 3) (if the sagibaron were a royal servile dependent [*puer*], however, his value was only 300 solidi, and the same if a count were a servile dependent [LIV, 2]).

As stated earlier, the Frankish laws applied to Gallo-Romans in northern Gaul as well as to Franks. The position of the Roman was protected at law, but some curious differences in treatment emerged—his "value" was approximately one-half that of a Frank. Accordingly, the wergeld of the Roman landholder (equivalent to the Frankish freeman?) was 100 solidi (XLI, 9) (instead of the Frankish 200); the wergeld of the Roman who was a "table companion of the king" (equivalent to an antrustion?) was 300 solidi (XLI, 8) (instead of 600); and the wergeld of a Roman soldier[43] (equivalent to the ordinary Frankish freeman) was 100 solidi (CXVII, 2) (instead of 200). It is specifically stated that the payment for a Roman killed by a *contubernium* (band of men) was one-half that for a Frank (XLII, 4); and in speaking of injuries to women, the amount for half-free women (*lidae*) and Roman women was one-half that for free Frankish women (CIV, 9).

There were other discrepancies in treatment. The Frank who robbed a Roman defended himself with twenty oathhelpers or paid thirty solidi as composition (XIV, 3), whereas the Roman who robbed a Frank had to have twenty-five oathhelpers or paid a composition of sixty-two and one-half solidi (XIV, 2). If a Frank or a Roman tied up a Frank, the composition was thirty solidi; whereas if a Frank tied up a Roman, the composition was only fifteen solidi (XXXII, 1–4).

Presumably the king's value was more than that of any others, but the laws do not say what it was. Nor did the original collection of laws (by Clovis) have anything to say about the wergeld of members of the clergy. A post-Clovis law (the Seven Types of Cases, VIII, 5) assigns bishops a wergeld of 600 solidi (the same as that of a count, an antrustion, or a sagibaron). The Carolingian revision of the laws gave deacons a wergeld of 300 solidi (S.V. VI).

In addition to freemen, the laws make reference to persons in other status: freedmen, half-free men (*lidi*), and slaves. Only for the slaves is there enough information to offer much description.

Although the Frankish laws demonstrate that slavery was a very important institution in Frankish society, we are not given a very clear picture of it. Almost all the laws concerning slaves were interested in the slave only insofar as he was property, and an injury to a slave or the theft of a slave was a property loss to the slave's lord. Slaves were valued between fifteen and twenty-five solidi (X, 6–7). Specific occupations named are as follows: household slaves, both male and female; agricultural slaves such as swineherds, vinedressers, grooms, and stablehands; and skilled workers such as metal workers, millers, carpenters, craftsmen, and ironsmiths (X, 6–7; XXXV, 9).

The king's slaves were obviously valued more highly than the slaves of other persons. To steal or sell an ordinary person's slave involved payment of a composition of seventy-two solidi (X, 6) or thirty-five solidi (X, [6]), whereas to kill a slave or freedman of the king involved payment of a composition of 100 solidi (Cap. V, CXVII). The king might employ his servile dependents (*pueri*) in positions of very high rank: the value of a sagibaron (royal judicial official) or of a count who were royal servants was 300 solidi (LIV, 2).

In addition to the normal acquisition of slaves by conquest in war, purchase, or birth, the Frankish laws indicate that an individual could become a slave through inability to pay property judgments or compositions judicially assessed against him (LVIII), or a man or woman might voluntarily place himself or herself in servitude (Cap. VII, VI), or a man became a slave if he married someone else's female slave (XIII, 9; XXV, 3; Cap. VII, III), or a woman became a slave if she married someone else's male slave (XXV, 4) (if a woman married her own slave, her property went to the fisc, she was outlawed, and the slave was tortured [LXLVIII]). A man was also reduced to slavery if he were taken in theft in a man's locked house (Cap. II, LXXXV). If one became a slave through the operation of the debtor or criminal laws, it may have been possible to become free again if the debt or composition was finally paid off. The laws do not say this about the slave, but they do provide that if an individual were outlawed for failure to pay a debt or fine, his outlawry could be ended by eventual payment of that debt or fine (LVI)—and outlawry and slavery would seem to have quite a bit in common (with slavery probably being preferable since it offered security of food and shelter that outlawry did not).

A slave might be emancipated by his lord. This could be accomplished by setting the slave free "with a denarius before the king" (XXVI, 2) or by charter (Cap. VII, XI). Whether emancipation could be accomplished by other means (e.g., by testament or in church) is not stated in the laws.

The laws do not indicate what the status of an emancipated slave was. There are, however, references to "freedmen" and half-free men (*lidi*), but these references are so vague that it is difficult to say just what the position of a freedman or *lidus* might be except that he was still regarded as the dependent of his lord (XXVI, 1; Cap. V, CXVII; Cap. V, CXXIV). On the other hand, the value of a *lidus* was the same as that of a Roman, half the value of a free Frank (see the discussion on Romans above). Perhaps on the basis of the evidence of the Frankish laws, all we can say with certainty about these two types of persons is that they enjoyed a status about halfway between slave and free.

Since the slave was essentially property, he was not treated as a person at law. On the other hand, the slave was obviously something more than property and the courts took cognizance of this fact. If a slave was killed or injured, the courts obviously assigned damages to his lord and the offender (if a freeman) paid, or the offender's lord (if a slave) paid (XXXV). But what of the criminal slave: how was he treated?

If a slave were accused of an offense, he was sent to the ordeal by lot[44] or tortured (XL, 2, 4, 7; Cap. II, LXXXII, 1–2); if proved guilty, his lord paid composition for the offense and the slave was punished (lashes, castration, or death) (XII; XXV, 5–7; XL, 1–5, 11; Cap. II, LXLVIII, 2). This is severe treatment and, if always enforced, might have reduced the slave population. However, the laws offered a means of mitigating both the proof and the punishment—not so much because the slave might deserve better treatment but because the torture and/or physical punishment of a slave would be a heavy loss to his lord—especially if the lord were convinced of his slave's innocence. Therefore, if a slave's lord wished to do so, he could pay to "spare his slave's back"—three solidi took the place of 120 lashes; six solidi took the place of castration (XII). In somewhat more serious thefts, the lord might take the blame on himself—that is, he paid the value of the object involved plus whatever composition a freeman might pay in such a case—up to forty-five solidi (XL, 9). But in the event that the accusation were of a still more serious nature, the lord must produce his slave for torture after having been summoned to court three times (XL, 10), although he might require a pledge (presumably another slave) from the torturer (who seems to be the accuser) which he might keep in place of the slave if the slave did not confess under torture (and presumably had died or was reduced in value as a result of the torture) (XL, 4).

The Frankish Economic Scene

The economic scene revealed in the Frankish laws is basically rural and agricultural, with glimpses of the forests and rivers—there is not a single urban reference.

The laws imply several different kinds of agricultural organization, from the freestanding property held as allodial land and worked as a "farm" by the free Frankish family together with its slaves and other dependents (and this seems to be the principal type of holding that the laws have in mind) to the agricultural village or estate where the land was held on some basis other than ownership. We are given no name for this latter holding but there are vague references to a kind of village organization or community; for instance, if a vacancy developed in a village and some of the inhabitants wanted a newcomer to come in, the objections of only one of the other inhabitants could keep him out (XLV, 1–2). On the other hand, if the newcomer moved in and no one objected for a period of twelve months, he could remain there secure (XLV, 4).

A considerable portion of the laws is involved with the agricultural scene. Domesticated animals were valuable, and the care taken with various types indicates a hierarchy of importance. Pigs (II; CXIX, 4) were evidently the most common farm animal, with cows and oxen (III), and horses (XXIII; XXXVIII; LXV) coming next; thereafter sheep (IV), goats (V), dogs (VI), birds (geese, chickens, doves, etc., VII), and bees (VIII). In a somewhat different category were animals that had been trained for special purposes, as were dogs trained for hunting and guarding (VI), deer trained for hunting (CXVIII), and birds (hawks and falcons) for hunting (XXXIII). Perhaps the horse as well as the cow and ox should be listed here as well as above.

Fences, locked enclosures, bells, hobbles, barns, granaries, pig sties, pruning knives, scythes, grafted trees, gardens, orchards, meadows, grain, flax, wine, mills all add further emphasis to the importance of the agricultural economy, as do laws dealing with other aspects of the rural scene: woods (XXXIV), rivers and boats (XXI; CXIX, 1–2), and fishing nets (XXVII, 28; CXIX, 1).

Violence, Theft, Homicide

A significant portion of the Frankish laws deal with crimes of violence, theft, and homicide. In the case of freemen, the penalty involved was almost invariably composition—the payment of money compensation to the injured person or his family. In the case of the more serious offenses, the compositions are very high (200 solidi is the wergeld of the ordinary Frankish freeman, and this amount could increase to 1,800 solidi in special circumstances). It is difficult to know how many Frankish families could pay such sums, but it must have often been the case that the money penalties could not be paid. The Frankish laws are clear on this point—a man's entire property and his person were the final security for payment. In the long run then, a man's person must frequently have paid for his offense—in effect, he became a slave to the injured party (perhaps the injured party could inflict death but, given the emphasis on compensation, slavery must have been the usual effect of the law).

The first version of the code as presumably issued by Clovis imposes no penalty other than money compensation (or ultimately slavery or outlawry) on freemen, but some of the capitularies issued later in the sixth century by Clovis's sons and grandson indicate that crime had become a more serious concern and therefore occasionally physical penalties were imposed on freemen. Capitulary IV (Decree of King Chilperic for Keeping the Peace) seems to refer to the notorious offender without resources who has fled to the forest to escape being brought into court. The injured party should institute an accusation before the king who will then place the offender "outside of our protection so that whoever finds him can kill him" (Cap. IV, CXV). The death penalty is provided in three cases in Capitulary VI: if a man marries his father's wife he is to lose his life (Cap. VI, I, 2); the man who commits rape will be killed or outlawed (Cap. VI, II, 2); and the "man who kills another man without cause" shall lose his life (Cap. VI, II, 3). That the death penalty was applied in other instances can be assumed, however, from several references to penalties for taking down a man (living or dead) from a gibbet (Cap. III, LXLV and LXLVI). In any event, death by hanging must have been the usual means of carrying out the death penalty when it was imposed.

Some of the major Frankish institutions revealed in the laws have been discussed here, but many others would emerge from a careful analysis. As in the case of the other Germanic codes, however, the laws are annoyingly incomplete: many of the things that would bring the lives of the Franks alive for us have been omitted simply because they were too well known to need recording. Of course, even if the code were complete we would still be left with the difficult problem of reconciling life as seen in the laws with life as it was actually lived; nonetheless the Salic laws offer evidence that cannot be overlooked.

IV. Transmission of *Lex Salica* and This Translation

The main purpose of this translation is to make available in English a representative version of the Salic law. Unfortunately, it is difficult to do this since the laws survive in so many manuscripts of differing order and content that it has been impossible for the various learned editors who have tackled the problem to establish a single critical text. There are many versions of the laws and numerous varying texts of each of these versions.

Disentangling the intricate scheme of relationship among the various versions of the law and their variants would be impossible in a short introduction. However, a brief discussion of the manuscript tradition is essential and is offered here.

The Salic law survives in over eighty manuscripts. None of these manuscripts is contemporary with the original issue of the written law, which is with fair certainty ascribed to the time of Clovis and usually dated between 507 and 511. To the laws originally issued by Clovis, other "capitularies" and a brief prologue were added later in the sixth century by Clovis's sons (Childebert I and Chlotar I) and his grandson (Chilperic I). This cumulative sixth-century version of the law is usually known as *Pactus Legis Salicae*.

Evidently the Salic law underwent other modifications in the sixth and seventh centuries as the Germanic Frankish law encountered the influence of Roman law and of Christianity. It was modified not only by such influences but also by use. Early Frankish custom recorded in Latin—which frequently did not have an equivalent word or concept for the Frankish custom—caused problems for both the scribes and the judges. As the knowledge of classical Latin declined, the uncertainty of the scribes in transcribing the laws increased. Barbarisms crept in and were handed on to other scribes. To explain the Germanic phrases (some of which were undoubtedly still Germanic in form but others hardly more than garbled transcriptions), the so-called Malberg glosses were added and handed down in some of the manuscript traditions. So the original issue of Clovis (in 65 titles) expanded by the capitularies issued by Childebert I, Chlotar I, and Chilperic I presumably existed in a number of versions, all more or less barbarized, by the late Merovingian period.

The new Carolingian dynasty undertook a thorough reform of all aspects of Frankish political and cultural life, including reform of the laws. Pepin I's reform of the laws (763–64) produced a lawbook in 100 titles (or 99 in some versions) of the entire corpus of Frankish law, including the 65 titles of Clovis, plus the additions of Childebert I, Chlotar I, and Chilperic I, and retained the glosses. This version was reissued in slightly revised form by Charlemagne, probably in 798 (*Lex Salica Emendata*).

Charlemagne's second version is in less barbarous Latin than the others and presents a clearer picture of Salic law. Nonetheless, although *Lex Salica Karolina* provided the Franks with a better and more comprehensible version of the law, it did not replace the earlier versions—all seem to have been acceptable. And so the older versions continued to be recopied—passing on old errors of transcription and introducing others. Today *Lex Salica* exists in many versions—there are many "families" of manuscripts; none of the manuscripts dates earlier than the mid-eighth century.

Charlemagne's second revision of the laws (which we know as *Lex Salica Karolina*) is a puzzling work. It is a revision of the 65-title code almost exclusively with only one or two laws added from the later sixth-century capitularies. What was the purpose of this revision? An up-grading of the barbarous Latin that had come to characterize the surviving manuscripts as well as elimination of the virtually meaningless Malberg glosses could be expected from a court interested in a revival of "classical" learning. But why were the efforts confined to the 65-title text? The language of the capitularies is much more barbarous than that of the 65-title text—why were these additions and modifications not incorporated in what was a major revision of Salic law? And just as puzzling was the failure to bring the monetary system in line with early ninth-century practice: *Lex Salica Karolina* reads as if no major numismatic reforms had taken place between the sixth and ninth centuries. So there are many puzzling features of *Lex Salica* in addition to the continued recopying of old versions of the law.

Although there are other versions of *Lex Salica*, these three seem the most important: the 65-title version (presumably Clovis's issue or as close to it as we can come); the 100-title version (containing the Malberg glosses and incorporating the Merovingian capitularies of Childebert I, Chlotar I, and Chilperic I); and the 70-title version of Charlemagne (*Lex Salica Karolina*).[45] But it must be remembered that there are other versions of *Lex Salica* and that future scholarship may identify still more. The student interested in this problem (and in the linguistic difficulties posed by the Malberg glosses) should consult a number of works to which the following will offer guidance:

1. J. M. Pardessus. *Loi Salique, ou Recueil contenant les anciennes rédactions de cette loi et le texte connu sur le nom de lex emendata avec des notes et dissertations.* Paris, 1843. Pardessus describes 65 different manuscripts, most of which he had examined himself. He also notes a number of others that seem to have disappeared. Pardessus offers five different main texts of the laws, in addition to a few variants that he regards as important enough to include as appendices.

2. J. H. Hessels. *Lex Salica: the ten texts with the glosses and the lex emendata.* With notes on the Frankish words in the *Lex Salica* by H. Kern. London, 1880. Hessels identifies five different "families" of manuscripts—one of which relies solely on the edition of *Lex Salica* by B. J. Herold (*Originum ac Germanicarum antiquitatum libri* [Basel, 1557]), which was evidently based on one or more manuscripts now lost that differed from any in the other four families. Hessels presents the ten major versions of the laws (with variants) in parallel columns. He makes no attempt to develop a critical text. The material on Frankish words by H. Kern is very helpful (although not all of his interpretations are accepted by modern scholars).

3. Karl August Eckhardt, ed. *Lex Salica 100 Titel-Text. Germanenrechte Neue Folge.* Weimar, 1953. In this volume Eckhardt reviews the manuscript tradition and justifies his selection of texts for this volume (the 100-title version) as well as for subsequent volumes on the 80-title version (in the same series, 1954), the 65-title text (1955), and the 70-title version (1956). Eckhardt's editions in the *Germanenrechte* series (which also appear in slightly different form in the *Monumenta Germaniae Historica* editions noted below), are now the standard editions of *Lex Salica* and provide the texts for the translations presented here.

4. Karl August Eckhardt, ed. *Pactus Legis Salicae. Monumenta Germaniae Historica, Legum Sectio I, Leges Nationum Germanicarum*, Vol. IV, Part I. Hanover, 1962. This volume contains an edition of the main 65- and 70-title versions of the *Pactus*, plus the capitularies. Eckhardt presents a single version of the text with the major variants in eight parallel columns.

5. Karl August Eckhardt, ed. *Lex Salica. Monumenta Germaniae Historica, Legum Sectio I, Leges Nationum Germanicarum*, Vol. IV, Part II. Hanover, 1969. In this volume of the *Monumenta* Eckhardt presents a text of the 100-title version, with the major variants again in 8 parallel columns, and then he offers an edition of that version of the 70-title *Lex Salica Karolina* known as the "Systematic Version." This volume also contains a glossary and a synopsis indicating the relationship among the various main versions of the laws.

6. J. F. Niermeyer. *Mediae Latinitatis Lexicon Minus (A Medieval Latin-French/English Dictionary)*. Leiden, 1976. Niermeyer's examples are taken primarily from the *Monumenta Germaniae Historica* editions and are mostly from the period A.D. 550–1150. This dictionary contains numerous examples taken from the Salic law.

The present work offers a translation of two versions of the Salic law. The first is that usually called the *Pactus Legis Salicae* which contains the 65-title *Pactus* issued by Clovis in the early sixth century plus the prologue and capitularies issued later in the sixth century by Clovis's sons and grandson, Childebert I, Chlotar I, and Chilperic I, and containing the Malberg glosses. The second version is the code as corrected and reissued without the Malberg glosses in the early ninth century by Charlemagne—the *Lex Salica Karolina*—but in the rearranged "Systematic Version," a private compilation from north Italy that rearranged the laws in a more systematic fashion than the official version.

Pactus Legis Salicae

The 65-Title Version of the Code
Ascribed to Clovis Plus the Later
Sixth-Century Additions

The Pactus Legis Salicae Begins[1]

1. With the aid of God, it was decided and agreed among the Franks and their notables in order that peace be established among themselves, that all increase of litigation be curtailed so that just as the Franks stand out from other peoples living around them by the strength of their arms so also they shall excell them in the authority of their laws. Thus they [the Franks] will provide an end to criminal actions according to the nature of the cause.[2]

2. Therefore from among many men four were chosen who were named as follows: Wisogast, Arogast, Salegast, and Widogast from places beyond the Rhine named Botheim, Saleheim, and Widoheim.[3] These men, meeting together in three different courts and discussing the causes of all disputes, gave judgment in each case in the following fashion.

The Titles of the Pactus Legis Salicae

CAPITULARIES

CAPITULARY I

Book I Ends. II Begins

CAPITULARY II

THE PACT ISSUED BY KINGS CHILDEBERT AND CHLOTAR FOR KEEPING THE PEACE

THE DECREE OF KING CHILDEBERT

Book III

THE DECREE OF KING CHLOTAR

In the Name of the Lord the Pactus Legis Salicae Begins

I

CONCERNING A SUMMONS TO COURT [S.V. I]⁴

1. If a man has been summoned to court in accordance with the king's laws and does not come, and if a lawful excuse (*sunnis*) has not detained him (called *reaptena* in the Malberg gloss),⁵ he shall be liable to pay six hundred denarii (i.e., fifteen solidi).⁶
2. If he who summoned another man [to court] does not come himself, and if a lawful excuse has not detained him (called *reaptena* in the Malberg gloss), he who summoned shall likewise be liable to pay six hundred denarii (i.e., fifteen solidi).
3. He who summons another man should go with witnesses to that man's house and summon him thus or, if the man summoned is not present, he should deliver the charge to that one's wife or to some other member of his family so he or she will make known to him [the accused] that he has been summoned to court.
4. If a man is occupied in the king's service, he cannot be summoned to court.
5. But if the man is in the district on his own business, he can be summoned, as said above.

II

CONCERNING THE THEFT OF PIGS [S.V. LI]

1. He who steals a suckling pig from the first or middle enclosure (*chranne*) and it is proved against him (called *chrannechaltio leschalti* in the Malberg gloss), shall be liable to pay one hundred twenty denarii (*unum tualepti sunt*) (i.e., three solidi) [in addition to return of the animal or its value plus a payment for the time its use was lost].
2. If he steals it from the third enclosure (called *chrannechaltio* in the Malberg gloss), he shall be liable to pay six hundred denarii (i.e., fifteen solidi) in addition to return of the animal stolen [or its value] plus a payment for the time its use was lost (*excepto capitale et dilatura*).⁷

3. He who steals a piglet from a sty (*sute*) that is locked shall be liable to pay eighteen hundred denarii (i.e., forty-five solidi)[8] [in addition to return of the animal or its value plus a payment for the time its use was lost].

4. He who steals from the field a young pig that can live without its mother [a weaned piglet] and it is proved against him (called *hymnisfith* or *tertega* in the Malberg gloss), shall be liable to pay forty denarii (i.e., one solidus) in addition to return of the animal stolen [or its value] plus a payment for the time its use was lost.

5. He who strikes a breeding sow so that she loses her young and it is proved against him (called *narechalti* in the Malberg gloss) shall be liable to pay two hundred eighty denarii (i.e., seven solidi) in addition to a payment for the value of the animals as well as for the time their use was lost.

6. He who steals a sow with piglets (called *focichalte* in the Malberg gloss) shall be liable to pay seven hundred denarii (i.e., seventeen and one-half solidi) [in addition to the return of the animals or their value plus a payment for the time their use was lost].

7. He who steals a one-year-old pig and it is proved against him (called *ingimus hataria* in the Malberg gloss) shall be liable to pay one hundred twenty denarii (i.e., three solidi) in addition to return of the animal [or its value] plus a payment for the time its use was lost.

8. He who steals a two-year-old pig (called *ingimus suaini* in the Malberg gloss) shall be liable to pay six hundred denarii (i.e., fifteen solidi) in addition to return of the animal [or its value] plus an indemnity for the time its use was lost.

9. The same penalty shall be imposed for each of two animals.

10. He who steals three or more pigs—up to six animals (called *ingimus texaga* in the Malberg gloss)—shall be liable to pay fourteen hundred (twice seven hundred—*tua septun chunna*) denarii (i.e., thirty-five solidi) in addition to return of the animals stolen [or their value] plus a payment for the time their use was lost.

11. He who steals a small pig from among other pigs when a swineherd is in attendance and it is proved against him (called *suainechalte* in the Malberg gloss) shall be liable to pay six hundred denarii (i.e., fifteen solidi) in addition to return of the animal [or its value] plus a payment for the time its use was lost.

12. He who steals a pig still fed at home up to one year old (called *drache* in the Malberg gloss) shall be liable to pay one hundred twenty denarii (i.e., three solidi) in addition to return of the animal [or its value] plus a payment for the time its use was lost.

13. He who steals a pig more than one year old (called *drache* in the Malberg gloss) shall be liable to pay six hundred denarii (i.e., fifteen solidi) in addition to return of the animal [or its value] plus a payment for the time its use was lost.

14. He who steals a boar and it is proved against him (called *christiau* in the Malberg gloss) shall be liable to pay seven hundred denarii (i.e., seventeen and one-half solidi) in addition to return of the animal [or its value] plus a payment for the time its use was lost.

15. He who steals a leader sow (*scrovam ducarium*) and it is proved against him (called *chredunia* in the Malberg gloss) shall be liable to pay seven hundred denarii (i.e., seventeen and one-half solidi) in addition to return of the animal [or its value] plus a payment for the time its use was lost.

16. He who steals a sacrificial gelded boar and it can be proved with witnesses that it had been consecrated (called *barcho anomeo chamitheotho* in the Malberg gloss) shall be liable to pay seven hundred denarii (i.e., seventeen and one-half solidi) in addition to return of the animal [or its value] plus a payment for the time its use was lost.

17. Likewise concerning another's gelded boar that has not been consecrated: he who steals it and it is proved against him (called *barcho* and *in alia mente bagine* in the Malberg gloss) shall be liable to pay six hundred denarii (i.e., fifteen solidi) in addition to return of the animal [or its value] plus a payment for the time its use was lost.

18. He who steals twenty-five pigs from a herd where there are no more and it is proved against him (called *sonista* in the Malberg gloss) shall be liable to pay twenty-five hundred (two thousand five hundred—*tua zymis fitmiha chunna*) denarii (i.e., sixty-two and one-half solidi) in addition to return of the animals [or their value] plus a payment for the time their use was lost.

19. If more than twenty-five pigs were stolen but others remain, he who stole them and it is proved against him (called *texaga* in the Malberg gloss) shall be liable to pay fourteen hundred denarii (i.e., thirty-five solidi) in addition to return of the animals [or their value] plus a payment for the time their use was lost.

20. If fifty pigs were stolen and others still remain in that herd, he against whom it is proved (called *sonista* in the Malberg gloss) shall be liable to pay twenty-five hundred denarii (i.e., sixty-two and one-half solidi) in addition to return of the animals [or their value] plus a payment for the time their use was lost.

III

CONCERNING THE THEFT OF CATTLE [S.V. L]

1. He who steals a nursing calf and it is proved against him (called *podero* or *freodo* in the Malberg gloss) shall be liable to pay one hundred twenty denarii (i.e., three solidi) in addition to return of the animal [or its value] plus a payment for the time its use was lost.

2. He who steals a yearling calf (called *ochstiorci* in the Malberg gloss) shall be liable to pay six hundred denarii (i.e., fifteen solidi) in addition to return of the animal [or its value] plus a payment for the time its use was lost.

3. He who steals a two-year-old animal and it is proved against him (called *scolo* in the Malberg gloss) shall be liable to pay six hundred denarii (i.e., fifteen solidi) in addition to return of the animal [or its value] plus a payment for the time its use was lost.

4. He who steals a cow with calf and it is proved against him (called *inzymis podero malia* in the Malberg gloss) shall be liable to pay fourteen hundred denarii (i.e., thirty-five solidi) in addition to return of the animals [or their value] plus a payment for the time their use was lost.

5. He who steals a cow without a calf (called *malia* in the Malberg gloss) shall be liable to pay twelve hundred denarii (i.e., thirty solidi) in addition to return of the animal [or its value] plus a payment for the time its use was lost.

6. He who steals a cow broken to the yoke (called *chanzyn podero* in the Malberg gloss) shall be liable to pay fourteen hundred denarii (i.e., thirty-five solidi) in addition to return of the animal [or its value] plus a payment for the time its use was lost.

7. He who steals an ox and it is proved against him (called *ohsino* in the Malberg gloss) shall be liable to pay fourteen hundred denarii (i.e., thirty-five solidi) in addition to return of the animal [or its value] plus a payment for the time its use was lost.

8. He who steals a bull that rules a herd and has never been yoked and it is proved against him (called *chariocheto* in the Malberg gloss) shall be liable to pay eighteen hundred denarii (i.e., forty-five solidi) in addition to return of the animal [or its value] plus a payment for the time its use was lost.

9. He who steals a two-year-old bull (called *trasilo* in the Malberg gloss) shall be liable to pay thirty-five solidi [in addition to return of the animal or its value plus a payment for the time its use was lost].

10. If the bull services the cows of a three-village common, that is, he is a *trespellius*, he who steals it and it is proved against him (called *chamicheto* in the Malberg gloss) shall be liable to pay eighteen hundred denarii (i.e., forty-five solidi) in addition to return of the animal [or its value] plus a payment for the time its use was lost.

11. He who steals a royal bull (called *chamicheto* in the Malberg gloss) shall be liable to pay thirty-six hundred denarii (i.e., ninety solidi) in addition to return of the animal [or its value] plus a payment for the time its use was lost.

12. He who steals twelve head of cattle and no more remain (called *sonista* in the Malberg gloss) shall be liable to pay twenty-five hundred denarii (i.e., sixty-two and one-half solidi) in addition to return of the animals [or their value] plus a payment for the time their use was lost.

13. If there are more than these twelve cattle (called *inzymis texaca* in the Malberg gloss), [he who stole them] shall be liable to pay fourteen hundred denarii (i.e., thirty-five solidi) in addition to return of the animals [or their value] plus a payment for the time their use was lost.

14. He who steals more [than twelve] up to twenty-five and others remain that were not stolen (called *sonista* in the Malberg gloss) shall be liable to pay twenty-five hundred denarii (i.e., sixty-two and one-half solidi) in addition to return of the animals [or their value] plus a payment for the time their use was lost.

IV

CONCERNING THE THEFT OF SHEEP [S.V. LII]

1. He who steals a nursing lamb and it is proved against him (called *lammi* in the Malberg gloss)⁹ shall be liable to pay seven denarii (i.e., one-half a triens [one-third of a solidus]) in addition to return of the animal [or its value] plus a payment for the time its use was lost.

2. He who steals a one- or two-year-old wether and it is proved against him (called *lamilam* in the Malberg gloss) shall be liable to pay one hundred twenty denarii (i.e., three solidi) in addition to return of the animal [or its value] plus a payment for the time its use was lost.

3. He who steals three or more [wethers] and it is proved against him (called *lamp* in the Malberg gloss) shall be liable to pay fourteen hundred

denarii (i.e., thirty-five solidi) in addition to return of the animals [or their value] plus a payment for the time their use was lost.

4. This composition should be observed up to forty wethers.

5. But he who steals forty or fifty or sixty or more wethers and it is proved against him (called *sonista* in the Malberg gloss) shall be liable to pay twenty-five hundred denarii (i.e., sixty-two and one-half solidi) in addition to return of the animals [or their value] plus a payment for the time their use was lost.

V

CONCERNING THE THEFT OF GOATS [S.V. LIII]

1. He who steals three goats and it is proved against him (called *lau scimada* in the Malberg gloss) shall be liable to pay one hundred twenty denarii (i.e., three solidi) in addition to return of the animals [or their value] plus a payment for the time their use was lost.

2. He who steals more than three goats (called *muro scimada* in the Malberg gloss) shall be liable to pay six hundred denarii (i.e., fifteen solidi) in addition to return of the animals [or their value] plus a payment for the time their use was lost.

VI

CONCERNING THE THEFT OF DOGS [S.V. XLVII]

1. He who steals a trained hunting dog and it is proved against him (called *leodardi* in the Malberg gloss) shall be liable to pay six hundred denarii (i.e., fifteen solidi) in addition to return of the animal [or its value] plus a payment for the time its use was lost.

1a. He who steals a trained hunting dog (called *trocuuithien uano* in the Malberg gloss) shall be liable to pay twice nine hundred (*tue ne chunne*) or eighteen hundred denarii (i.e., forty-five solidi) in addition to return of the animal [or its value] plus a payment for the time its use was lost.

2. He who steals a dog that is a tracking hound (*canem agutorium*) (called *chunnouano* in the Malberg gloss) shall be liable to pay six hundred denarii (i.e., fifteen solidi) in addition to return of the animal [or its value] plus a payment for the time its use was lost.

3. He who after sunset kills a dog that is usually tied up (called *repouano* in the Malberg gloss) shall be treated as stated above: he shall be liable to pay six hundred denarii (i.e., fifteen solidi) in addition to payment of the dog's value plus a payment for the time its use was lost.

4. He who steals or kills a herd dog and it is proved against him (called *leodardi* or *theouano* in the Malberg gloss) shall be liable to pay one hundred twenty denarii (i.e., three solidi) in addition to return of the animal [or its value] plus a payment for the time its use was lost.

VII

CONCERNING THE THEFT OF BIRDS [S.V. XLIX]

1. He who steals a hawk from a tree and it is proved against him (called *ortfocla* in the Malberg gloss) shall be liable to pay one hundred twenty denarii (i.e., three solidi) in addition to return of the bird [or its value] plus a payment for the time its use was lost.

2. He who steals a hawk from its perch and it is proved against him (called *uueiape ortfocla* in the Malberg gloss) shall be liable to pay six hundred denarii (i.e., fifteen solidi) in addition to return of the bird [or its value] plus a payment for the time its use was lost.

3. He who steals a hawk kept under key and it is proved against him (called *ortfocla* or *uueiano antedio* in the Malberg gloss) shall be liable to pay eighteen hundred denarii (i.e., forty-five solidi) in addition to return of the bird [or its value] plus a payment for the time its use was lost.[10]

4. He who steals a sparrow hawk (called *socelino* in the Malberg gloss) shall be liable to pay one hundred twenty denarii (i.e., three solidi) in addition to return of the bird [or its value] plus a payment for the time its use was lost.

5. He who steals a rooster (called *chanasuuido* in the Malberg gloss) shall be liable to pay one hundred twenty denarii (i.e., three solidi) in addition to return of the bird [or its value] plus a payment for the time its use was lost.

6. He who steals a hen (called *solampinam* in the Malberg gloss) shall be liable to pay one hundred twenty denarii (i.e., three solidi) in addition to return of the bird [or its value] plus a payment for the time its use was lost.

7. He who steals a domesticated crane or swan (called *ortfocla* in the Malberg gloss) shall be liable to pay one hundred twenty denarii (i.e., three solidi) [in addition to return of the bird or its value plus a payment for the time its use was lost].

8. He who steals a domesticated goose or duck and it is proved against him (called *sundolino* in the Malberg gloss) shall be liable to pay one hundred twenty denarii (i.e., three solidi) in addition to return of the bird [or its value] plus a payment for the time its use was lost.

9. He who steals a turtle dove from another man's net shall be liable to pay three solidi [in addition to return of the bird or its value plus a payment for the time its use was lost].

10. He who steals a little bird from a trap (called *acfalla* in the Malberg gloss) shall be liable to pay three solidi [in addition to return of the bird or its value plus a payment for the time it use was lost].

11. He who cuts down or steals a domesticated apple tree or pear tree inside or outside an enclosed yard (*curte*)[11] shall be liable to pay one hundred twenty denarii (i.e., three solidi) [in addition to the value of the tree plus a payment for the time its use was lost].

12. He who cuts down or steals [a fruit tree] from a garden shall be liable to pay six hundred denarii (i.e., fifteen solidi) [in addition to the value of the tree plus a payment for the time its use was lost].

13. He who steals a ploughshare (called *leodardi* in the Malberg gloss) shall be liable to pay six hundred denarii (i.e., fifteen solidi) [in addition to return of the share or its value plus a payment for the time its use was lost].

VIII

CONCERNING THE THEFT OF BEES [S.V. LIV]

1. He who steals one swarm of bees—i.e., one hive—kept locked and under a roof and it is proved against him (called *antedio olechardis* in the Malberg gloss) shall be liable to pay eighteen hundred denarii (i.e., forty-five solidi) in addition to return of the swarm [or its value] plus a payment for the time its use was lost.

2. He who steals one swarm or one hive where there are no more and it is proved against him shall be held liable as in the case above.

3. He who steals up to six swarms that are not under a roof where more remain and it is proved against him (called *leodardi* in the Malberg gloss) shall be liable to pay six hundred denarii (i.e., fifteen solidi) in addition to return of those stolen [or their value] plus a payment for the time their use was lost.

4. He who steals seven or more and still others remain there under lock and it is proved against him (called *antedio texaga olechardis* in the Malberg gloss) shall be liable to pay eighteen hundred denarii (i.e., forty-five solidi) in addition to returning them [or their value] plus a payment for the time their use was lost.

IX

CONCERNING DAMAGE TO A CULTIVATED FIELD OR SOME OTHER ENCLOSURE [S.V. LXI]

1. He who finds a cow or horse or other animal in his field should do it no grievous harm. If he does do so and confesses it, he must restore the full value of the animal to its owner and keep for himself the weakened animal that he had struck. But if he does not confess it and it is proved against him (called *leodardi* in the Malberg gloss), he shall be liable to pay six hundred denarii (i.e., fifteen solidi) in addition to return of the animal [or its value] plus a payment for the time its use was lost.

2. He who brands an animal, horse, or mare that he has stolen (called *stalachia* in the Malberg gloss) shall be liable to pay six hundred denarii (i.e., fifteen solidi) in addition to return of the animal [or its value] plus a payment for the time its use was lost.

3. He who finds in his field another man's animals that do not have a herder and shuts them up by force and makes it known to no one, and some of the animals die (called *texaga* in the Malberg gloss), must restore the full value of the animals to their owner and in addition be liable to pay fourteen hundred denarii (i.e., thirty-five solidi) [plus a payment for the time their use was lost].

4. He who through neglect harms [another man's] cow or other animal and confesses it shall pay the full value of the animal to its owner and take

and keep the injured animal for himself. But if he denies this and it is proved against him (called *leodardi* in the Malberg gloss), he shall be liable to pay six hundred denarii (i.e., fifteen solidi) in addition to return of the animal [or its value] plus a payment for the time it use was lost.

5. If a man's pigs or other animals that are being watched run into someone else's field and, although he denies it, it is proved against him (called *andesito* or *leodardi* in the Malberg gloss), he shall be liable to pay six hundred denarii (i.e., fifteen solidi).

6. If the animals have been shut up to keep them from causing damage, he who attempts to remove them by force (called *scuto* in the Malberg gloss) shall be liable to pay six hundred denarii (i.e., fifteen solidi).

7. If he whose field was being wasted leads them away from further damage [and shuts them up], anyone who presumes to release them (called *scuto* in the Malberg gloss) shall be liable to pay six hundred denarii (i.e., fifteen solidi).

[6,7.[12] If he whose work was being destroyed shuts up the animals or leads them to his house to keep them from further damage and someone presumes to release them or drive them out by force (called *schoto* in the Malberg gloss), he [the latter] shall be liable to pay six hundred denarii (i.e., fifteen solidi).]

8. If the animals have been shut up because they have caused damage, he whose animals they are must pay the estimated value of the damage and in addition be liable to pay ten denarii.

9. If anyone through malice or arrogance opens another man's fenced enclosure and sends his animals into that field or meadow or vineyard or other cultivated area, and if he whose worked land it is convicts him [the former] with witnesses, he [who opened the enclosure] must pay the estimated value of the damage caused (called *leodardi* in the Malberg gloss) and in addition be liable to pay twelve hundred denarii (i.e., thirty solidi).

X

CONCERNING STOLEN SLAVES OR OTHER CHATTELS (*mancipii*) [S.V. XLII]

1. He who steals another man's male or female slave, horse or mare, and this is proved against him (called *theotexaca* in the Malberg gloss), shall be

liable to pay fourteen hundred denarii (i.e., thirty-five solidi) in addition to returning the chattel stolen [or its value] plus a payment for the time its use was lost.

2. If the male or female slave has carried some property of his or her lord with him or her, the thief shall restore the bondsman and the property (called *theobardi* in the Malberg gloss) and is liable to pay six hundred denarii (i.e., fifteen solidi) [for the property] [in addition to thirty-five solidi for the slave plus a payment for the time his/her use was lost].

3. He who steals or kills or sells or sets free another man's male slave, and it is proved against him (called *meotheo* in the Malberg gloss), shall be liable to pay fourteen hundred denarii (i.e., thirty-five solidi) [in addition to return of the slave or his value plus a payment for the time his use was lost].

4. He who steals a female slave (called *theotexaca* in the Malberg gloss) shall be liable to pay twelve hundred denarii (i.e., thirty solidi) [in addition to return of the slave or her value plus a payment for the time her labor was lost].

5. The freeman who takes another man's slave with him while committing a theft (*in texaca*) or conducts any business with him (called *theolasina* in the Malberg gloss) shall be liable to pay six hundred denarii (i.e., fifteen solidi).

6. He who loses [i.e., steals and sells][13] a female slave worth fifteen or twenty-five solidi or a swineherd, vine dresser, metalworker, miller, carpenter, or groom (*stratore*), or any other craftsman worth twenty-five solidi (called *theoducco* in the Malberg gloss) and it is proved against him shall be liable to pay twenty-eight hundred eighty denarii (i.e., seventy-two solidi)[14] in addition to return of the slave [or his/her value plus a payment for the time his/her labor was lost].

[6. He who steals or kills or sells an overseer (*maiorem*), steward (*infertorem*), butler (*scancionem*), horsekeeper (*mariscalcum*), groom (*stratorem*), a metalworker, goldworker, or carpenter or swineherd or household servant (*ministerialem*) worth twenty-five solidi (called *theuca texaca* in the Malberg gloss) shall be liable to pay fourteen hundred denarii (i.e., thirty-five solidi) in addition to return of the slave [or his value] plus a payment for the time his labor was lost. If it is a female overseer (*maiorissama*) or female household servant (*ministerialem*) worth twenty-five solidi, the above provisions should be observed.]

7. He who steals a young male or female household slave (called *horogauo*, *horogania* in the Malberg gloss) shall return the twenty-five solidi value of

the slave and in addition shall be liable to pay fourteen hundred denarii (i.e., thirty-five solidi) and return of the slave [or his/her value] plus a payment for the time his/her labor was lost.

[7. He who steals a slave who keeps young horses (*puledrum*) (called *uuadredo* in the Malberg gloss) shall be liable to pay eighteen hundred denarii (i.e., forty-five solidi) [plus return of the slave or his value in addition to a payment for the time his labor was lost].]

XI

CONCERNING THEFTS OR HOUSEBREAKING COMMITTED BY FREEMEN [S.V. XXXIX]

1. The freeman who outside a house steals something worth two denarii and it is proved against him (called *leodardi* in the Malberg gloss) shall be liable to pay six hundred denarii (i.e., fifteen solidi) in addition to return of the object stolen [or its value] plus a payment for the time its use was lost.

2. He who outside a house steals something worth forty denarii and it is proved against him (called *texaga* in the Malberg gloss) shall be liable to pay fourteen hundred denarii (i.e., thirty-five solidi) in addition to return of the object stolen [or its value] plus a payment for the time its use was lost.

3. If a freeman makes an entry [into a house] and steals something worth two denarii and it is proved against him (called *antedio* in the Malberg gloss) he shall be liable to pay twelve hundred denarii (i.e., thirty solidi) in addition to return of the object stolen [or its value] plus a payment for the time its use was lost.

[3. If a freeman breaks in and steals something worth two denarii inside a house (called *antidio* in the Malberg gloss) he shall be liable to pay eighteen hundred denarii (i.e., forty-five solidi) in addition to return of the object stolen [or its value] plus a payment for the time its use was lost.]

4. He who steals something worth more than five denarii from a locked enclosure and it is proved against him (called *antedio* in the Malberg gloss) shall be liable to pay fourteen hundred denarii (i.e., thirty-five solidi) in addition to return of the object stolen [or its value] plus a payment for the time its use was lost.

5. He who cuts or duplicates a key and then enters a house and takes something therefrom in theft, and it is proved against him (called *anorchlot antedio* in the Malberg gloss), shall be liable to pay eighteen hundred denarii (i.e., forty-five solidi) in addition to return of the object stolen [or its value] plus a payment for the time its use was lost.

6. But if he breaks in and takes nothing but escapes fleeing, for the breaking in alone he shall be liable to pay twelve hundred denarii (i.e., thirty solidi).[15]

XII

CONCERNING THEFTS OR BREAKING-IN COMMITTED BY SLAVES [S.V. XL]

1. The slave who steals something worth two denarii outside a house and it is proved against him (called *falcono* in the Malberg gloss) shall, in addition to return of the object stolen [or its value] plus a payment for the time its use was lost, receive stretched out one hundred twenty lashes or shall pay one hundred twenty denarii (i.e., three solidi) to spare his back.[16]

2. The slave who steals something worth forty denarii shall be castrated or pay two hundred forty denarii (i.e., six solidi). The lord of the slave who committed the theft shall return the object stolen [or its value] to its owner plus a payment for the time its use was lost.

XIII

CONCERNING THE ABDUCTION OF FREEMEN OR FREE WOMEN [S.V. XXIII][17]

1. If three men take a free girl from her house or workroom (called *ambahtonia* in the Malberg gloss), the three shall be liable to pay twelve hundred denarii (i.e., thirty solidi).

2. If there are more than three involved, each one of them [over three] shall be liable to pay two hundred denarii (i.e., five solidi).

3. Each one of those who carried arrows shall [in addition] be liable to pay one hundred twenty denarii (i.e., three solidi).

4. The abductor shall be liable to pay twenty-five hundred denarii (i.e., sixty-two and one-half solidi).

5. If the girl was taken from a locked room or workroom (called *alteofaltheo* in the Malberg gloss), the penalty should be imposed as in the previous case.

6. If the girl who was seized had been placed in the king's protection, the fine (*fredus*) to be exacted is twenty-five hundred denarii (i.e., sixty-two and one-half solidi).

7. If it was a servant (*puer*)[18] of the king or a half-freeman (*letus*) who abducted the free girl, he shall make composition with his life [i.e., he shall be given as a slave to the family of the girl].

8. But if the free girl voluntarily followed one of these she shall lose her freedom.

9. The freeman who takes another man's female slave shall suffer likewise (*paciatur*).

[9. The freeman who takes another man's female slave in marriage (called *honema* in the Malberg gloss) shall remain in servitude with her.]

10. He who associates another man's half-free woman (*litam*) with himself in marriage (called *ambahtonia* in the Malberg gloss) shall be liable to pay twelve hundred denarii (i.e., thirty solidi).

11. He who joins to himself in profane marriage the daughter of his sister or brother, or a cousin of further degree [i.e., daughter of a niece or nephew or of a grandniece or grandnephew], or the wife of his brother, or of his mother's brother, shall be subjected to this punishment: the couple shall be separated from such a union and, if they had children, these will not be legitimate heirs but will be marked with disgrace.

12. He who takes a woman betrothed to someone else and joins her to himself in marriage (called *andrastheo* in the Malberg gloss) shall be liable to pay twenty-five hundred denarii (i.e., sixty-two and one-half solidi) [to her family or guardian].

13. He shall be liable to pay fifteen solidi to the man to whom she was betrothed.

14. He who attacks on the road a betrothed girl with her bridal party being led to her husband and forcefully has intercourse with her (called *gangichaldo* in the Malberg gloss) shall be liable to pay eight thousand denarii (i.e., two hundred solidi) [to her family or guardian or to her betrothed husband?].

XIV

CONCERNING WAYLAYING OR PILLAGING [cf. S.V. XVIII and IX]

1. He who robs a freeman by waylaying him and it is proved against him (called *mosido* in the Malberg gloss) shall be liable to pay twenty-five hundred denarii (i.e., sixty-two and one-half solidi) [plus return of the objects taken in addition to a payment for the time their use was lost].
2. If a Roman robs a Salic barbarian (*barbarum Salicum*) and it is not certainly proved against him, he can clear himself with twenty-five oathhelpers, half of whom he has chosen. If he cannot find the oathhelpers (called *mosido* in the Malberg gloss) he shall go to the ordeal of boiling water or it should be observed as in the case preceding [i.e., pay sixty-two and one-half solidi in addition to return of the objects taken or their value plus a payment for the time their use was lost].
3. If a Frank robs a Roman and it is not certainly proved, he shall clear himself with twenty oathhelpers, half of whom he has chosen. If he cannot find the oathhelpers (called *mosido* in the Malberg gloss), if it is proved, he shall be liable to pay twelve hundred denarii (i.e., thirty solidi) [in addition to return of the objects taken or their value plus a payment for the time their use was lost].
4. If anyone contrary to the king's command presumes to halt (*testare*) or attack a man who is trying to move somewhere (*migrare*) and has a permit from the king [to do so] and can identify himself (*abundivit*) in public court (called *alachtaco* in the Malberg gloss), he shall be liable to pay eight thousand denarii (i.e., two hundred solidi) [to the man attacked].
5. If anyone attacks a man moving (*migrantem*) somewhere and it is proved against him (called *via lacina* in the Malberg gloss), he shall be liable to pay [him] eight thousand denarii (i.e., two hundred solidi).
6. If a man's place (*villam*) is attacked, each one of those in the band of men (*contubernio*)[19] proved to be among those attacking (*superventi*) (called *turpefalthio* in the Malberg gloss) shall be liable to pay twenty-five hundred denarii (i.e., sixty-two and one-half solidi).
7. He who attacks another man's place (*villam*) and there breaks down doors, kills dogs, or wounds men or carries off anything thence in a cart

(called *turpefalthio* in the Malberg gloss) shall be liable to pay eight thousand denarii (i.e., two hundred solidi) [in addition to returning the objects taken or their value, plus a payment for the time their use was lost].

8. Whatever he took from there he shall restore to its place. As many as are proved to be in his band (*contubernium*) or among those attacking (*superventi*), each of them shall be liable to pay twenty-five hundred denarii (i.e., sixty-two and one-half solidi).

9. He who stealthily robs a dead body before it is put in the earth and it is proved against him (called *chreomosido* in the Malberg gloss) shall be liable to pay four thousand denarii (i.e., one hundred solidi) [in addition to returning those things taken plus a payment for the time he held them].

10. He who digs up a dead body and robs it and it is proved against him (called *turnechale* or *odo carina* in the Malberg gloss) shall be liable to pay eight thousand denarii (i.e., two hundred solidi) [in addition to returning those things taken plus a payment for the time he held them].

11. He who stealthily robs a sleeping man and it is proved against him (called *friomosido* in the Malberg gloss) shall be liable to pay four thousand denarii (i.e., one hundred solidi) in addition to return of the objects stolen [or their value] plus a payment for the time their use was lost.

XV

CONCERNING HOMICIDE OR THE MAN WHO TAKES ANOTHER MAN'S WIFE WHILE HER HUSBAND STILL LIVES [not in S.V.]

1. He who kills a freeman or takes another man's wife while her husband lives, and it is proved against him (called *affalthecha* in the Malberg gloss), shall be liable to pay eight thousand denarii (i.e., two hundred solidi).

2. He who rapes a free girl and it is proved against him (called *uueruanathe* in the Malberg gloss) shall be liable to pay twenty-five hundred denarii (i.e., sixty-two and one-half solidi).[20]

3. He who secretly has intercourse with a free girl with the consent of both and it is proved against him (called *firilasia* in the Malberg gloss) shall be liable to pay eighteen hundred denarii (i.e., forty-five solidi).

XVI

CONCERNING ARSON [S.V. X]

1. He who sets fire to another man's house while men are sleeping therein and it is proved against him (called *seolandouefa* in the Malberg gloss) shall pay sixty-two and one-half solidi to him whose house it is, and as many men as were in the house should summon him to court concerning the *seolandouefa* and to each of them he is liable to pay sixty-two and one-half solidi. And if anyone was burned inside (called *leode seolandouefa* in the Malberg gloss), he shall be liable to pay sixty-two and one-half solidi plus the composition *(leode)* of eight thousand denarii (i.e., two hundred solidi); and to him whose house it is (called *alfathio* in the Malberg gloss) he shall be liable to pay twenty-five hundred denarii (i.e., sixty-two and one-half solidi).

[1. He who sets fire to someone else's house while men are sleeping inside shall be liable to pay twenty-five hundred denarii (i.e., sixty-two and one-half solidi) to him whose house it is (called *andebau* in the Malberg gloss). Those who escaped therefrom should each call him to court for the Malberg *seulandeueuas* and he is liable to each of them for four thousand denarii (i.e., one hundred solidi). If some remain therein [i.e., do not escape] (called *leudi* in the Malberg gloss), he shall be liable to pay eight thousand denarii (i.e., two hundred solidi) in addition to restoration of the value involved plus a payment for the time its use was lost.]

2. He who sets fire to a building *(salina)* made of wattling *(cletem)* and it is proved against him (called *althifathio* in the Malberg gloss) shall be liable to pay twenty-five hundred denarii (i.e., sixty-two and one-half solidi).

3. He who sets fire to a barn *(spicarium)* or granary *(machalum)* with grain in it and it is proved against him (called *leodeba* in the Malberg gloss) shall be liable to pay twenty-five hundred denarii (i.e., sixty-two and one-half solidi) [plus the value of the grain involved].

4. He who sets fire to a sty with pigs in it or a stable with cattle or hay in it and it is proved against him (called *sundeba* in the Malberg gloss) shall be liable to pay twenty-five hundred denarii (i.e., sixty-two and one-half solidi) in addition to restoration of the value involved plus a payment for the time their use was lost.

5. If a Roman inflicts one of these things on another Roman and proof is not certain, he may clear himself with twenty oathhelpers, half of whom he has chosen. If he cannot find the oathhelpers, then he must go to the

ordeal of boiling water (called *leodeba* in the Malberg gloss). If he is judged guilty, he should pay twelve hundred denarii (i.e., thirty solidi).

6. He who sets fire to another man's fence or hedge and it is proved against him (called *bila* in the Malberg gloss) shall be liable to pay six hundred denarii (i.e., fifteen solidi) [plus the value of the hedge or fence].

7. He who cuts down another man's fence or hedge (called *bicha biggeo* in the Malberg gloss) shall be liable to pay six hundred denarii (i.e., fifteen solidi) in addition to restoration of the value involved plus a payment for the time its use was lost.

XVII

CONCERNING WOUNDS [S.V. XV]

1. He who wounds or tries to kill another man and the blow misses him, and it is proved against him (called *seolandouefa* in the Malberg gloss), shall be liable to pay twenty-five hundred denarii (i.e., sixty-two and one-half solidi).

2. He who tries to shoot another man with a poisoned arrow and the arrow misses him, and it is proved against him (called *seolandouefa* in the Malberg gloss), shall be liable to pay twenty-five hundred denarii (i.e., sixty-two and one-half solidi).

3. He who hits another man on the head so that his blood falls to the ground, and it is proved against him (called *seolandouefa* in the Malberg gloss), shall be liable to pay six hundred denarii (i.e., fifteen solidi).

4. He who strikes another man on the head so that the brain shows, and it is proved against him (called *chiesiofrit* in the Malberg gloss), shall be liable to pay six hundred denarii (i.e., fifteen solidi).

5. If the three bones that lie over the brain protrude (called *chicsiofrit* in the Malberg gloss), he shall be liable to pay twelve hundred denarii (i.e., thirty solidi).

6. If the wound penetrates between the ribs or into the stomach so that it reaches the internal organs (called *gisifrit* in the Malberg gloss), he shall be liable to pay twelve hundred denarii (i.e., thirty solidi).

7. If the wound runs continuously and never heals (called *freobleto* in the Malberg gloss), he shall be liable to pay twenty-five hundred denarii (i.e., sixty-two and one-half solidi). For the cost of medical attention (called *andechabinus* in the Malberg gloss), he shall pay three hundred sixty denarii (i.e., nine solidi).

8. If a freeman strikes another freeman with a stick but the blood does not flow, for up to three blows (called *uuadfalt* in the Malberg gloss), he shall be liable to pay three hundred sixty denarii (i.e., nine solidi), that is, for each blow he shall always pay one hundred twenty denarii (i.e., three solidi).

9. If the blood flows (called *uuadfalt* in the Malberg gloss) he shall pay composition as if he had wounded him with an iron weapon, that is, he shall be liable to pay six hundred denarii (i.e., fifteen solidi).

10. He who strikes another three times with a closed fist (called *uuadfalt* in the Malberg gloss) shall be liable to pay three hundred sixty denarii (i.e., nine solidi)—that is, he renders three solidi for each blow.

11. If a man attacks another man on the road and tries to rob him but that one evades him by flight, if it is proved against him (called *urtifugia* in the Malberg gloss), he shall be liable to pay twenty-five hundred denarii (i.e., sixty-two and one-half solidi).

12. But if he robs him (called *harauuano* in the Malberg gloss) [and does not attack him] he shall be liable to pay thirty solidi [in addition to returning what he took plus a payment for the time the use of whatever was stolen was lost].

XVIII

CONCERNING HIM WHO ACCUSES BEFORE THE KING AN INNOCENT MAN WHO IS ABSENT [S.V. V]

He who accuses before the king an innocent man who is absent (called *seolandouefa* in the Malberg gloss) shall be liable to pay twenty-five hundred denarii (i.e., sixty-two and one-half solidi).

XIX

CONCERNING MAGIC PHILTERS OR POISONED POTIONS [S.V. XXXII]

1. He who casts a magic spell over another man or gives him an herbal potion to drink so that he dies, and it is proved against him (called *touuerfo* in the Malberg gloss), shall be liable to pay eight thousand denarii (i.e., two hundred solidi).[21]

2. If a man gives an herbal potion to another man or casts a magic spell over him but that one does not die, the author of the crime who is proved to have committed this or has been convicted (called *seolandouefa* in the Malberg gloss) shall be liable to pay twenty-five hundred denarii (i.e., sixty-two and one-half solidi).

3. He who casts a magic spell over another wherever he is (called *thouuerphe* in the Malberg gloss) shall be liable to pay twenty-five hundred denarii (i.e., sixty-two and one-half solidi).

4. The woman who casts a magic spell over another woman so that she cannot have children shall be liable to pay twenty-five hundred denarii (i.e., sixty-two and one-half solidi).

XX

CONCERNING THE MAN WHO TOUCHES THE HAND OR ARM OR FINGER OF A FREE WOMAN [S.V. XXII]

1. The freeman who touches the hand or arm or finger of a free woman or of any other woman, and it is proved against him (called *chamin* in the Malberg gloss) shall be liable to pay six hundred denarii (i.e., fifteen solidi).

2. If he touches her arm [below the elbow] (called *chamin* in the Malberg gloss), he shall be liable to pay twelve hundred denarii (i.e., thirty solidi).

3. But if he places his hand above her elbow and it is proved against him (called *chamin malicharde* in the Malberg gloss), he shall be liable to pay fourteen hundred denarii (i.e., thirty-five solidi).

4. He who touches a woman's breast or cuts it so that the blood flows (called *de bruchte* in the Malberg gloss) shall be liable to pay eighteen hundred denarii (i.e., forty-five solidi).

XXI

CONCERNING STOLEN BOATS [S.V. LXIII]

1. If anyone without the consent of its owner moves another man's boat and crosses a river in it (called *fimire* in the Malberg gloss), he shall be liable to pay one hundred twenty denarii (i.e., three solidi).

2. But if he steals the boat and it is proved against him (called *fimire* in the

Malberg gloss), he shall be liable to pay six hundred denarii (i.e., fifteen solidi) [in addition to return of the boat plus a payment for the time its use was lost].

3. He who steals a boat or skiff (*ascum*) kept under lock and key (called *ciasco* in the Malberg gloss) shall be liable to pay fourteen hundred denarii (i.e., thirty-five solidi) in addition to return of the object stolen [or its value] plus a payment for the time its use was lost.

4. If anyone steals a skiff kept under lock and key and hung carefully suspended, and it is proved against him (called *chanciasco* in the Malberg gloss), he shall be liable to pay eighteen hundred denarii (i.e., forty-five solidi) [in addition to return of the boat or its value plus a payment for the time it use was lost].

XXII

CONCERNING THEFTS COMMITTED IN A MILL [S.V. LVI]

1. If a freeman steals another man's grain from yet another man's mill and it is proved against him (called *antedio* in the Malberg gloss), he shall pay six hundred denarii (i.e., fifteen solidi) to the owner of the mill for the use of his mill and to the owner of the grain he shall likewise pay another six hundred denarii (i.e., fifteen solidi) in addition to return of the grain stolen [or its value] plus a payment for the time its use was lost.

2. He who steals an iron piece from another man's mill (called *antedio* in the Malberg gloss) shall be liable to pay eighteen hundred denarii (i.e., forty-five solidi) [in addition to return of the piece or its value plus a payment for the time its use was lost].

3. He who breaks into the enclosure of another man's mill (called *urbis via lacina* in the Malberg gloss) shall be liable to pay six hundred denarii (i.e., fifteen solidi).

XXIII

ON MOUNTING A HORSE WITHOUT THE CONSENT OF ITS OWNER [S.V. XLV]

He who mounts another man's horse without the consent of its owner and rides it around, and it is proved against him (called *leudardi* or in another form *burgositto* in the Malberg gloss), shall be liable to pay twelve hundred denarii (i.e., thirty solidi).

XXIV

ON KILLING CHILDREN AND WOMEN [S.V. XXXIII]

1. He who kills a free boy less than twelve years old up to the end of his twelfth year, and it is proved against him (called *leode* in the Malberg gloss), shall be liable to pay twenty-four thousand denarii (i.e., six hundred solidi).
2. He who cuts the hair of a long-haired free boy without the consent of his relatives, and it is proved against him (called *uuerdade* in the Malberg gloss), shall be liable to pay eighteen hundred denarii (i.e., forty-five solidi).[22]
3. If he cuts the hair of a free girl without the consent of her relatives, and it is proved against him (called *theuischada* in the Malberg gloss), he shall be liable to pay eighteen hundred denarii (i.e., forty-five solidi).[23]
4. He who kills a long-haired boy, and it is proved against him (called *leode* in the Malberg gloss), shall be liable to pay twenty-four thousand denarii (i.e., six hundred solidi).[24]
5. He who strikes a pregnant free woman, and it is proved against him (called *anouaddo* or, if she dies, *anouaddo leode* in the Malberg gloss), shall be liable to pay twenty-eight thousand denarii (i.e., seven hundred solidi).[25]
6. He who kills an infant in its mother's womb or within nine days of birth before it has a name, and it is proved against him (called *anouuado* in the Malberg gloss), shall be liable to pay four thousand denarii (i.e., one hundred solidi).
7. If a boy under twelve years old commits some offense, a fine (*fredus*) will not be required of him.[26]
8. He who kills a free woman after she has begun to bear children, if it is proved against him (called *leodinia* in the Malberg gloss), shall be liable to pay twenty-four thousand denarii (i.e., six hundred solidi).[27]
9. He who kills a woman after she is no longer able to bear children, if it is proved against him (called *leodinia* in the Malberg gloss), shall be liable to pay eight thousand denarii (i.e., two hundred solidi).

XXV

ON HAVING INTERCOURSE WITH SLAVE GIRLS OR BOYS [S.V. LXVII]

1. The freeman who has intercourse with someone else's slave girl, and it is proved against him (called *theualasina uuertico* in the Malberg gloss), shall be liable to pay six hundred denarii (i.e., fifteen solid) to the slave girl's lord.

2. The man who has intercourse with a slave girl belonging to the king and it is proved against him (called *theualasina* in the Malberg gloss), shall be liable to pay twelve hundred denarii (i.e., thirty solidi).

3. The freeman who publicly joins himself with (i.e., marries) another man's slave girl, shall remain with her in servitude.

4. And likewise the free woman who takes someone else's slave in marriage shall remain in servitude.[28]

5. If a slave has intercourse with the slave girl of another lord and the girl dies as a result of this crime, the slave himself shall pay two hundred forty denarii (i.e., six solidi) to the girl's lord or he shall be castrated; the slave's lord shall pay the value of the girl to her lord.[29]

6. If the slave girl has not died (called *balemundio* in the Malberg gloss), the slave shall receive three hundred lashes or, to spare his back, he shall pay one hundred twenty denarii (i.e., three solidi) to the girl's lord.

7. If a slave joins another man's slave girl to himself in marriage without the consent of her lord (called *anthamo* in the Malberg gloss), he shall be lashed or clear himself by paying one hundred twenty denarii (i.e., three solidi) to the girl's lord.

XXVI

CONCERNING BONDSMEN SET FREE WITHOUT THE CONSENT OF THEIR LORDS [S.V. LXVIII]

1. The freeman who sets free with a denarius before the king without the consent of his lord another man's half-free man (*letum*) who was in the army with his lord, and it is proved against him (called *maltho thi atomeo leto* in the Malberg gloss), shall be liable to pay four thousand denarii (i.e., one hundred solidi) [in addition to the value of the half-free man]. The property of the half-free man shall be restored to his lord.

2. He who sets free with a denarius before the king another man's slave, and it is proved against him (called *maltho thi atomeo theo* in the Malberg gloss) shall be liable to pay eighteen hundred denarii (i.e., thirty-five solidi) and in addition return the value of the slave to his lord. Let his lord receive the property of the slave.

XXVII

CONCERNING VARIOUS KINDS OF THEFTS [S.V. LVII]

1. He who steals the bell from another man's troop of pigs, if it is proved against him (called *leodardi* in the Malberg gloss), shall be liable to pay six hundred denarii (i.e., fifteen solidi) in addition to return of the bell [or its value] plus a payment for the time its use was lost.
2. He who steals the bell from a cow and it is proved against him (called *leodardi* in the Malberg gloss) shall be liable to pay one hundred twenty denarii (i.e., three solidi) [in addition to return of the bell plus a payment for the time its use was lost].
3. He who steals the bell (*schillam*) from a horse (called *campania* in the Malberg gloss) shall be liable to pay six hundred denarii (i.e., fifteen solidi) [in addition to return of the bell plus a payment for the time its use was lost].
4. He who steals the hobble from a horse and it is proved against him (called *leodardi* in the Malberg gloss), shall be liable to pay one hundred twenty denarii (i.e., three solidi) in addition to return of the hobble [or its value] plus a payment for the time its use was lost.
5. If the horses are lost, he shall pay their full value.
6. He who enters another man's field and in theft takes something away and has been found (called *leodardi* in the Malberg gloss), shall be liable to pay six hundred denarii (i.e., fifteen solidi) [in addition to returning what he took plus a payment for the time its use was lost].
7. He who furtively enters another man's garden to steal something, or his turnip patch, or bean patch, or pea patch, or lentil patch, and it is proved against him (called *leodardi* in the Malberg gloss), shall be liable to pay six hundred denarii (i.e., fifteen solidi) in addition to return of the objects stolen [or their value] plus a payment for the time their use was lost.
8. He who takes away the grafted twigs from an apple or pear tree (called

leodardi in the Malberg gloss) shall be liable to pay one hundred twenty denarii (i.e., three solidi) [in addition to return of the grafts or their value plus a payment for the time their use was lost].

9. If they were in a garden (called *ortopondo* in the Malberg gloss), he shall be liable to pay six hundred denarii (i.e., fifteen solidi) [in addition to return of the grafts or their value plus a payment for the time their use was lost].[30]

10. He who strips the bark from (*exceruicauerit*) an apple tree or pear tree (called *leodardi* in the Malberg gloss) shall be liable to pay one hundred twenty denarii (i.e., three solidi).

11. If it was in a kitchen garden (called *ortobaum* in the Malberg gloss), he shall be liable to pay six hundred denarii (i.e., fifteen solidi).

12. He who enters with intent to steal into a turnip patch, a bean patch, a pea patch, a lentil patch, or other similar place, if it is proved against him (called *leodardi* in the Malberg gloss), shall be liable to pay one hundred twenty denarii (i.e., three solidi).[31]

13. He who steals flax from another man's field and carries it home on a horse or in a cart and it is proved against him (called *leodardi* in the Malberg gloss) shall be liable to pay six hundred denarii (i.e., fifteen solidi) in addition to return of the flax [or its value] plus a payment for the time its use was lost.

[13. He who steals something from another man's field and takes it away in a cart or on his horse (called *leudardi* in the Malberg gloss) shall be liable to pay eighteen hundred denarii (i.e., forty-five solidi) [in addition to returning that which he stole or its value plus a payment for the time its use was lost].]

14. But if he takes away only as much as he can carry on his back (called *leodardi* in the Malberg gloss), he shall be liable to pay one hundred twenty denarii (i.e., three solidi) in addition to return of the material stolen [or its value] plus a payment for the time its use was lost.

[14. If indeed he takes away only as much as he can carry on his back (called *leudardi* in the Malberg gloss) he shall be liable to pay six hundred denarii (i.e., fifteen solidi) [in addition to returning that which he took or its value plus a payment for the time its use was lost].]

15. He who cuts down a tree planted in another man's field (called *ortobaum* in the Malberg gloss), shall be liable to pay twelve hundred denarii (i.e., thirty solidi) [in addition to paying the value of the tree plus a payment for the time its use was lost].

16. He who prevents a plow from entering another man's field or throws [it off] or raises an objection (*testaverit*) against him (called *achuuerpho* in the Malberg gloss), shall be liable to pay six hundred denarii (i.e., fifteen solidi).

17. He who cuts another man's meadow shall lose the fruit of his work and in addition shall be liable to pay fifteen solidi; and if he takes the hay thence by cart to his own house and unloads it and it is proved against him (called *leodardi* in the Malberg gloss), he shall be liable to pay eighteen hundred denarii (i.e., forty-five solidi) in addition to return of the material stolen [or its value] plus a payment for the time its use was lost.

18. But if he takes only so much as he can carry on his back and it is proved against him (called *leodardi* in the Malberg gloss), he shall be liable to pay one hundred twenty denarii (i.e., three solidi) [in addition to return of the hay or its value plus a payment for the time its use was lost].

19. He who reaps the harvest of another man's vineyard by theft and is discovered (called *leodardi* in the Malberg gloss) shall be liable to pay six hundred denarii (i.e., fifteen solidi) [in addition to return of the harvest or its value plus a payment for the time its use was lost].

20. If he takes the wine away to his house on a horse or in a cart and it is proved against him (called *leodardi* in the Malberg gloss), he shall be liable to pay eighteen hundred denarii (i.e., forty-five solidi) in addition to return of the stolen wine [or its value] plus a payment for the time its use was lost.

21. The same provisions should be observed concerning the grain harvest.

22. He who breaks into another man's enclosure (called *urbis via lacina* in the Malberg gloss) shall be liable to pay fifteen solidi.

23. He who steals or cuts down or burns wood or other material from another man's forest and it is proved against him (called *leodardi* in the Malberg gloss) shall be liable to pay six hundred denarii (i.e., fifteen solidi) [in addition to paying the value of the material plus a payment for the time its use was lost].

24. But if he presumes to take by theft another man's material hewn by an axe (called *leodardi* in the Malberg gloss), he shall be liable to pay one hundred twenty denarii (i.e., three solidi) [in addition to returning that which he took or its value plus a payment for the time its use was lost].

25. He who steals wood from another man's forest shall be liable to pay three solidi [in addition to returning the wood or its value plus a payment for the time its use was lost].

26. He who takes a tree after the year that it was marked for cutting shall bear no blame. If he cuts it down during that year (called *leodardi* in the Malberg gloss), he shall be liable to pay three solidi [in addition to paying the value of the tree plus a payment for the time its use was lost].

27. He who steals a net for catching eels from a river and it is proved against him (called *obdobbo* in the Malberg gloss) shall be liable to pay eighteen hundred denarii (i.e., forty-five solidi) in addition to return of the object stolen [or its value] plus a payment for the time its use was lost.

28. He who steals a fishing net (*statuam*) or a trammel net (*tremaclem*) or a fish weir (*vertevolum*) from a river and it is proved against him (called *naschus texaca* in the Malberg gloss) shall be liable to pay six hundred denarii (i.e., fifteen solidi) [in addition to returning that which he stole or its value plus a payment for the time its use was lost].

29. He who breaks into a workroom that is not locked and it is proved against him (called *obdo* in the Malberg gloss) shall be liable to pay six hundred denarii (i.e., fifteen solidi).

30. He who breaks into a workroom that is locked (called *streonas antedio* in the Malberg gloss) shall be liable to pay eighteen hundred denarii (i.e., forty-five solidi) in addition to return of the material stolen [or its value] plus a payment for the time its use was lost. And if he takes nothing away (called *leodardi* in the Malberg gloss), he shall be liable to pay fifteen solidi for the breaking in.

31. He who plows another man's field and does not sow it (called *leodardi* in the Malberg gloss) shall be liable to pay six hundred denarii (i.e., fifteen solidi).

32. He who plows and sows another man's field (called *obrepo andre scrippas* in the Malberg gloss) shall be liable to pay eighteen hundred denarii (i.e., forty-five solidi).

33. He who conducts business with another man's slave and his lord does not know about it (called *theolasina* in the Malberg gloss) shall be liable to pay six hundred denarii (i.e., fifteen solidi).

34. He who steals a woman's girdle-belt (*brachilem*) (called *subto* in the Malberg gloss) shall be liable to pay one hundred twenty denarii (i.e., three solidi) [in addition to return of the girdle-belt plus a payment for the time its use was lost].

35. He who passes through another man's house without the consent of its owner (called *alachiscido* in the Malberg gloss) shall be liable to pay twelve hundred denarii (i.e., thirty solidi).

XXVIII

CONCERNING SECRET HIRINGS [S.V. LXIV]

1. He who secretly tries to hire someone to kill a man and that one accepts the price for this but does not kill [the one intended] and this is proved against him [i.e., the hirer] (called *morter* in the Malberg gloss), he [the hirer] shall be liable to pay twenty-five hundred denarii (i.e., sixty-two and one-half solidi).

[1. He who secretly tries to hire someone to kill a man and that one accepts the price for this (called *auuena* in the Malberg gloss) shall be liable to pay four thousand denarii (i.e., one hundred solidi).]

2. If he who was hired accepts the money and tries to kill the man designated but does not do it and it is proved against him (called *morter* in the Malberg gloss), he [the man hired] shall be liable to pay twenty-five hundred denarii (i.e., sixty-two and one-half solidi).

3. If he who was hired transfers the job to a third man and it is proved against that one (called *morter* in the Malberg gloss), that man shall be liable to pay twenty-five hundred denarii (i.e., sixty-two and one-half solidi): thus the giver, the receiver, and the transferer shall each of them be liable to pay sixty-two and one-half solidi.

XXIX

CONCERNING DISABLING INJURIES[32] [S.V. XVI]

1. He who maims another man's hand or foot or gouges out or strikes out his eye or cuts off his ear or nose and it is proved against him (called *sicti* in the Malberg gloss) shall be liable to pay four thousand denarii (i.e., one hundred solidi).

2. If he has cut the hand and the hand remains hanging there (called *chaminus* in the Malberg gloss), he shall be liable to pay twenty-five hundred denarii (i.e., sixty-two and one-half solidi).

[1,2. He who cuts another man's hand or foot and the hand [or foot] cut hangs from the man (called *sichte* in the Malberg gloss) shall be liable to pay twenty-five hundred denarii (i.e., sixty-two and one-half solidi).]

3. If the hand is pierced through (called *secthe* in the Malberg gloss) he who did this shall be liable to pay twenty-five hundred denarii (i.e., sixty-two and one-half solidi).

[3. If the hand has been struck off (called *chamin* in the Malberg gloss), he shall be liable to pay four thousand denarii (i.e., one hundred solidi).]

4. He who cuts off another man's thumb or big toe and it is proved against him (called *alachtamo* in the Malberg gloss) shall be liable to pay two thousand denarii (i.e., fifty solidi).

5. If the cut thumb or big toe hangs on (called *alachtamo chaminis* in the Malberg gloss), he who did this deed shall be liable to pay twelve hundred denarii (i.e., thirty solidi).

6. He who cuts off a man's second finger that is used to release arrows (called *alachtamo briorotero* in the Malberg gloss) shall be liable to pay fourteen hundred denarii (i.e., thirty-five solidi).

7. He who cuts off the other remaining fingers—all three equally with one blow (called *chaminis* in the Malberg gloss)—shall be liable to pay eighteen hundred denarii (i.e., forty-five solidi).

8. If he cuts off two of these, he shall be liable to pay thirty-five solidi.

9. If he cuts off one of them, he shall be liable to pay thirty solidi. He who cuts off a following finger [the middle] (called *taphano* in the Malberg gloss) shall be liable to pay six hundred denarii (i.e., fifteen solidi). If he strikes off a fourth finger (called *melachano* in the Malberg gloss), he shall be liable to pay nine solidi. If he strikes off the little finger (called *minecleno* in the Malberg gloss) he shall be liable to pay six hundred denarii (i.e., fifteen solidi).

10. If a foot has been cut and hangs on injured (called *chuldachina chamin* in the Malberg gloss), he who did this shall be liable to pay eighteen hundred denarii (i.e., forty-five solidi).

11. If the foot has been struck off (called *chuldachina sichte* in the Malberg gloss), he who did this shall be liable to pay twenty-five hundred denarii (i.e., sixty-two and one-half solidi).

12. He who puts out another man's eye (called *lichauina* in the Malberg gloss) shall be liable to pay twenty-five hundred denarii (i.e., sixty-two and one-half solidi).

13. He who cuts off another man's nose (called *frasito* in the Malberg gloss) shall be liable to pay eighteen hundred denarii (i.e., forty-five solidi).

14. He who cuts off another man's ear (called *channichleora* in the Malberg gloss) shall be liable to pay six hundred denarii (i.e., fifteen solidi).

15. He who cuts out another man's tongue so that he is not able to speak (called *alchaltea* in the Malberg gloss) shall be liable to pay four thousand denarii (i.e., one hundred solidi).

16. He who knocks out another man's tooth (called *inchlauina* in the Malberg gloss) shall be liable to pay six hundred denarii (i.e., fifteen solidi).

17. He who castrates a freeman or cuts into his penis so that he is incapacitated (called *gaferit* in the Malberg gloss) shall be liable to pay one hundred solidi.

18. But if he takes the penis away entirely (called *alacharde* in the Malberg gloss) he shall be liable to pay eight thousand denarii (i.e., two hundred solidi) in addition to nine solidi for the doctor.

XXX

CONCERNING ABUSIVE TERMS [S.V. LXX]

1. He who calls someone else a pederast (*cinitum*) (called *quintuc* in the Malberg gloss) shall be liable to pay six hundred denarii (i.e., fifteen solidi).

2. He who claims that someone else is covered in dung (*concagatum*) shall be liable to pay one hundred twenty denarii (i.e., three solidi).

3. He who calls a free woman or man a prostitute and cannot prove it (called *strabo* in the Malberg gloss) shall be liable to pay eighteen hundred denarii (i.e., forty-five solidi).

4. He who calls someone else a fox (*vulpem*) shall be liable to pay one hundred twenty denarii (i.e., three solidi).

5. He who calls someone else a rabbit (*leporem*) shall be liable to pay one hundred twenty denarii (i.e., three solidi).

6. The freeman who accused another man of throwing down his shield and running away, and cannot prove it (called *austrapo* in the Malberg gloss), shall be liable to pay one hundred twenty denarii (i.e., three solidi).

7. He who calls someone else an informer or liar and cannot prove it (called *leodardi* in the Malberg gloss) shall be liable to pay six hundred denarii (i.e., fifteen solidi).

XXXI

ON BLOCKING THE ROAD[33] [S.V. XXXVIII]

1. He who blocks the road to a freeman or strikes him (called *via lacina* in the Malberg gloss) shall be liable to pay six hundred denarii (i.e., fifteen solidi).

2. He who blocks the road to a free woman or girl or strikes her (called *urbis via lacina* in the Malberg gloss) shall be liable to pay eighteen hundred denarii (i.e., forty-five solidi).

3. He who blocks the road that leads to a mill (called *urbis via lacina* in the Malberg gloss) shall be liable to pay six hundred denarii (i.e., fifteen solidi).

XXXII

ON THE TIEING-UP OF FREEMEN [S.V. XIX]

1. He who ties up a freeman without cause (called *obrepus andrepus* in the Malberg gloss) shall be liable to pay twelve hundred denarii (i.e., thirty solidi).

2. He who ties up someone else and takes him bound to another place (called *andrepus* in the Malberg gloss) shall be liable to pay eighteen hundred denarii (i.e., forty-five solidi).

3. If a Roman ties up a Frank without cause, he shall be liable to pay twelve hundred denarii (i.e., thirty solidi).

4. If a Frank ties up a Roman without cause, he shall be liable to pay six hundred denarii (i.e., fifteen solidi).

5. He who through arrogance or force takes a bound man away from the count (called *mithio frastatitho* in the Malberg gloss) must pay composition for his life [i.e., the amount of his wergeld].[34]

XXXIII

ON STOLEN GAME [S.V. XLVIII]

1. He who steals and hides anything from the bird or fish hunt (called *leudardi* in the Malberg gloss) shall be liable to pay eighteen hundred denarii (i.e., forty-five solidi) in addition to return of the objects stolen [or their value] plus a payment for the time their use was lost. It is fitting to observe the same law for the hunting of birds or for fishing.

2. He who steals or kills a domesticated stag bearing a brand, one which has been trained for hunting, and it can be proved by witnesses that its owner has had it on the hunt and has killed two or three animals with it

(called *trouuidio* in the Malberg gloss), shall be liable to pay eighteen hundred denarii (i.e., forty-five solidi) [in addition to paying the value of the animal plus a payment for the time its use was lost].

3. He who steals or kills a domesticated stag which has not yet been on a hunt, and it can be proved (called *trouuidio chamstala* in the Malberg gloss) shall be liable to pay twelve hundred denarii (i.e., thirty solidi) [in addition to paying the value of the animal plus a payment for the time its use was lost].

4. He who steals or hides another man's exhausted stag that the dogs of someone else have chased and tired (called *trochuuido* in the Malberg gloss) shall be liable to pay six hundred denarii (i.e., fifteen solidi) [in addition to return of the animal or its value plus a payment for the time its use was lost].

5. He who kills a tired boar which the dogs have chased (called *harossina* in the Malberg gloss) shall be liable to pay six hundred denarii (i.e., fifteen solidi) [in addition to paying the value of the animal plus a payment for the time its use was lost].

XXXIV

CONCERNING STOLEN FENCES [S.V. LXII]

1. He who steals or cuts three branches that bind or hold a fence together or steals or cuts through the crossbars or cuts the twist of osier twigs (*retorta*) that holds the stakes of the fence, and this is proved against him (called *leodardi* in the Malberg gloss), shall be liable to pay six hundred denarii (i.e., fifteen solidi) [in addition to returning that which he took plus a payment for the time their use was lost].

2. He who burns another man's coppice-wood (*concisa*) hedge (called *bila* in the Malberg gloss) shall be liable to pay six hundred denarii (i.e., fifteen solidi) [in addition to paying for the hedge plus a payment for the time its use was lost].

3. He who draws a harrow through another man's field after it has sprouted or crosses it with a cart outside of the path (called *leodardi* in the Malberg gloss) shall be liable to pay one hundred twenty denarii (i.e., three solidi).

4. He who crosses another man's field where the stalks have already grown with a cart outside the path or tracks (called *leodardi* in the Malberg gloss) shall be liable to pay six hundred denarii (i.e., fifteen solidi).

5. He who with evil intent puts a stolen object into another man's enclosure or house or other place and the owner of the enclosure or house does not know it and the stolen object is found there (called *ferthebero* in the Malberg gloss) shall be liable to pay twenty-five hundred denarii (i.e., sixty-two and one-half solidi) [to the owner of the house or other place in addition to the usual payments to the owner of the stolen property].

XXXV

CONCERNING THE KILLING OR ROBBING OF SLAVES [S.V. LXVI]

1. If a slave kills a male or female slave like himself and it is proved against him (called *theoleodi* or *theoleodinia* in the Malberg gloss), their lords shall divide the killer [i.e., divide his work?] between themselves.
2. If a freeman attacks and robs another man's slave and he is convicted of having taken something worth more than forty denarii from him (called *rencusmosido* in the Malberg gloss), he shall be liable to pay twelve hundred denarii (i.e., thirty solidi) [to the slave's lord in addition to return of the property stolen plus a payment for the time its use was lost].
3. If what he took is worth less than forty denarii (called *theomosido* in the Malberg gloss) he shall be liable to pay six hundred denarii (i.e., fifteen solidi) [in addition to return of the property stolen plus a payment for the time its use was lost].
4. He who beats another man's slave so that he is kept from his work for more than forty days (called *daudinario* in the Malberg gloss) shall be liable to pay one solidus and one triens [to the slave's lord].
5. The freeman who robs another man's half-free man (*letum*) and it is proved against him (called *letosmosido* in the Malberg gloss) shall be liable to pay fourteen hundred denarii (i.e., thirty-five solidi) [to the lord of the half-free man in addition to return of the property stolen plus a payment for the time the property's use was lost].
6. He who secretly robs another man's dead slave and takes from him that which is worth more than forty denarii (called *theofriomosido* in the Malberg gloss) shall be liable to pay fourteen hundred denarii (i.e., thirty-five solidi) [to the slave's lord in addition to return of the property taken plus a payment for the time its use was lost].

7. If he takes that which is worth less than forty denarii (called *theofriomosido* in the Malberg gloss), he shall be liable to pay six hundred denarii (i.e., fifteen solidi) [to the slave's lord in addition to return of the property taken plus a payment for the time its was lost].

8. If another man's slave or half-free man (*letus*) kills a freeman, the killer shall be handed over to the relatives of the dead man as half of the composition for that one; the slave's lord shall know that he must pay the other half of the composition. And if he knows how, he can legally summon himself to court (*se obmallare*) [on behalf of his slave] so that he does not have to pay [if it is proved that the slave is not at fault].[35]

[But if the slave knows the law, his lord can summon himself to court so that he does not pay the wergeld (*leudem*).]

9. He who steals or kills a male household slave (*vassum ad ministerium*) (that is a *horogauo*), a female household slave (*puellam ad ministerium*), or an ironsmith, or a goldsmith, or a swineherd, or vintner, or stablehand, and it is proved against him (called *texaga* or *ambahtonia* in the Malberg gloss), shall be liable to pay twelve hundred denarii (i.e., thirty solidi). For breach of the peace (*fredo*) and composition (*faido*) he shall be liable to pay eighteen hundred denarii (i.e., forty-five solidi) in addition to return of the slave [or his/her value] plus a payment for the time his/her use was lost. In sum, he pays seventy-five solidi.

XXXVI

CONCERNING FOUR-FOOTED ANIMALS THAT KILL A MAN [S.V. LXV]

If a man has been killed by a domesticated four-footed animal and it is proved by witnesses that the owner of the animal had not fulfilled the law beforehand [by taking proper care of his beast], the owner of the animal shall pay half of the composition; and let him hand over the animal that caused the offense to those demanding it to count for the other half-composition.

[. . . let him [the owner] pay half of the wergeld (*leudi*) and give up his animal to the men [the relatives] for the other half. But if the owner does not acknowledge the fault of his animal, he may defend himself according to law and pay nothing for the animal.]

XXXVII

ON FOLLOWING TRACKS (*de vestigio minando*) [S.V. LVIII]

1. If anyone loses in theft an ox or cow, a horse, or any other animal and he finds it within three days after following its track, if he who leads the animal says or declares that he bought or traded for it, the man who followed its track should take possession (*achramire*) through a third party.

2. If he who was seeking his property finds it after three days have passed, he with whom it was found, if he says that he bought or traded for it, shall be permitted to retain possession (*achramire*).

3. But if he who was following the track says that he recognizes his property and although the other denies it he [the tracker] does not wish to take possession through a third party nor does he go to court according to law (*solem secundum legem culcaverit*) and he is convicted of taking his property by force (called *mithio frastatitho* in the Malberg gloss), he shall be liable to pay twelve hundred denarii (i.e., thirty solidi) [in addition to return of the animal in dispute plus a payment for the time its use was lost].

XXXVIII

CONCERNING THE THEFT OF HORSES OR MARES [S.V. XLIV]

1. He who steals a horse that pulls a cart and it is proved against him (called *chanzacho* in the Malberg gloss) shall be liable to pay eighteen hundred denarii (i.e, forty-five solidi) in addition to return of the animal [or its value] plus a payment for the time its use was lost.

2. He who steals a stallion (*admissarium*) from a Frank, and it is proved against him (called *wadredo* in the Malberg gloss), shall be liable to pay eighteen hundred denarii (i.e., forty-five solidi) [in addition to return of the animal plus a payment for the time its use was lost].

3. He who steals a gelded horse (called *chanzisto* in the Malberg gloss) shall be liable to pay fourteen hundred denarii (i.e., thirty-five solidi) in addition to return of the animal [or its value] plus a payment for the time its use was lost.

4. He who steals a stallion (*waranionem*) belonging to the king (called *scelho* in the Malberg gloss) shall be liable to pay ninety solidi in addition

to return of the animal [or its value] plus a payment for the time its use was lost.

5. He who steals a stallion (*admissarium*) with its herd—that is, with between seven and twelve mares—and it is proved against him (called *sonista* in the Malberg gloss) shall be liable to pay twenty-five hundred denarii (i.e., sixty-two and one-half solidi) in addition to return of the animals [or their value] plus a payment for the time their use was lost.

6. But if the herd was smaller—up to seven head including the stallion—and it is proved against him, in addition to return of the animals [or their value] plus a payment for the time their use was lost he shall be liable to pay twenty-five hundred denarii (i.e., sixty-two and one-half solidi).

7. He who steals a pregnant mare and it is proved against him (called *marthi* in the Malberg gloss) shall be liable to pay eighteen hundred denarii (i.e., forty-five solidi) in addition to return of the animal [or its value] plus a payment for the time its use was lost.

8. He who steals a one- or two-year-old colt, and it is proved against him (called *marfolen* in the Malberg gloss), shall be liable to pay six hundred denarii (i.e., fifteen solidi) in addition to return of the animal [or its value] plus a payment for the time its use was lost.

[8. He who steals a colt (called *wadredo* in the Malberg gloss) shall be liable to pay eighteen hundred denarii (i.e., forty-five solidi) in addition to return of the animal [or its value] plus a payment for the time its use was lost.

He who steals a one- or two-year-old colt (called *napodero* in the Malberg gloss) shall be liable to pay six hundred denarii (i.e., fifteen solidi) in addition to return of the animal [or its value] plus a payment for the time its use was lost.]

9. He who steals a foal following its mother and it is proved against him (called *nare* in the Malberg gloss) shall be liable to pay one hundred twenty denarii (i.e., three solidi) in addition to return of the animal [or its value] plus a payment for the time its use was lost.

10. He who drives off another man's mare (*iumentum*) (called *stalachia* in the Malberg gloss) shall be liable to pay twelve hundred denarii (i.e., thirty solidi) in addition to return of the animal [or its value] plus a payment for the time its use was lost.

11. He who steals a horse or a mare (*iumentum*) (called *azisto* in the Malberg gloss) shall be liable to pay fourteen hundred denarii (i.e., thirty-five solidi) in addition to return of the animal [or its value] plus a payment for the time its use was lost.

12. He who gelds another man's stallion (*admissarium*) without the consent

of its owner (called *andecalbina* in the Malberg gloss) shall be liable to pay six hundred denarii (i.e., fifteen solidi), and for each mare (*iumento*) [that the stallion serviced] let him compound one triens.

13. He who through arrogance or hate strikes or injures another man's horses or mares (*iumenta*) (called *stalachia* in the Malberg gloss) shall be liable to pay twelve hundred denarii (i.e., thirty solidi).

14. He who cuts off the tail of another man's horse without the consent of its owner (called *leodardi* in the Malberg gloss) shall be liable to pay one hundred twenty denarii (i.e., three solidi) in addition to return of the value of the animal plus a payment for the time its use was lost.

XXXIX

ON THOSE WHO INSTIGATE SLAVES TO RUN AWAY [S.V. LXVI]

1. If a man entices away the bondsmen of another man and this is proved against him (which is called *obscult* in the Malberg gloss), he shall be liable to pay six hundred denarii (i.e., fifteen solidi) [in addition to return of the bondsmen plus a payment for the time their labor was lost].

2. If someone entices away another man's slave and takes him overseas and there he is found by his lord, [the slave's lord] should name in public court him who enticed [the slave] away from his homeland, and he [the lord] should have three witnesses there [in court]. When the slave has been re-called from overseas, [his lord] should name [the enticer] before a second court, and he should have there three witnesses who are suitable men; and the same should be done before a third court so that there will be nine witnesses in all who can attest that they heard the slave speaking at three courts, and afterwards he who enticed him away (called *uuiridarium* in the Malberg gloss) shall be liable to pay fourteen hundred denarii (i.e., thirty-five solidi) in addition to return of the slave plus a payment for the time his labor was lost. If the confession of the slave is admitted [and indicates] that there were up to three enticers, he [the slave's lord] should always name the names of the men and their villages in the same way.

3. If anyone entices away a freeman and sells him and afterward he is re-turned to his own native land (called *chalde ficho* in the Malberg gloss), he shall be liable to pay one hundred solidi [in addition to return of the man plus a payment for the time the man was held].

4. If anyone sells a freeman and afterward he is not returned to his own native land and there is no certain proof, let him [who is charged with selling him] offer oathhelpers as if for death; if he cannot find oathhelpers (called *frio falcono* in the Malberg gloss), he shall be liable to pay eight thousand denarii (i.e., two hundred solidi).

5. If a man entices away a Roman, he shall be liable to pay twenty-five hundred denarii (i.e., sixty-two and one-half solidi).[36]

XL

CONCERNING THE SLAVE ACCUSED OF THEFT [S.V. XLI]

1. In the case where a slave is accused of theft, if [it is a case where] a freeman would pay six hundred denarii (i.e., fifteen solidi) in composition, the slave stretched on a rack shall receive one hundred twenty blows of the lash.

2. If he [the slave] confesses before torture and it is agreeable to the slave's lord, he may pay one hundred twenty denarii (i.e., three solidi) for his back [i.e., to avoid the lashes]; and the slave's lord shall return the value of the property stolen to its owner.

3. If it is a crime where a freeman should pay fourteen hundred denarii (i.e., thirty-five solidi), let the slave receive the same one hundred twenty lashes.

4. If he [the slave] does not confess under torture, then he who tortured him, if he still wishes to torture him even though his lord objects, ought to give a pledge to the lord of the slave. Afterwards the slave may be subjected to further torture, and if he confesses nothing is to be believed from him concerning his lord. Indeed, he who tortured the slave shall keep him in his power. The slave's lord, who had already received a pledge, should accept that price for his slave. If indeed he [the slave] confessed in the earlier torture, i.e., before the one hundred twenty lashes were completed, let him [the slave] be castrated or pay two hundred forty denarii (i.e., six solidi); the lord should restore the value of the property stolen to its owner.

5. If he [the slave] is guilty of a crime for which a freeman or a Frank would be liable to pay eight thousand denarii (i.e., two hundred solidi), let the slave compound fifteen solidi (i.e., six hundred denarii). If indeed the slave is guilty of a more serious offense—one for which a freeman would be liable to pay eighteen hundred denarii (i.e., forty-five solidi)—and the slave confessed during torture, he shall be subjected to capital punishment.[37]

6. If the slave is guilty of such a crime that he who charged ought to require that he [the slave's lord] should hand over his slave to torture, he who charged should have rods prepared which are the size of the little finger and he should have a rack prepared where the slave can be stretched out.

7. If the slave's lord delays in handing over his slave for torture and if the slave is present, he who is bringing the charge ought immediately to set a court day for the slave's lord. He should then set a court day for seven days so that the slave can be handed over for torture.

8. If the lord delays in handing over his slave after the seven days have been completed, then let another court day be set with witnesses, and let the court be set for another seven days, so that fourteen days will be completed after the first warning.

9. But if after fourteen days have been completed he [the lord] still does not wish to hand his slave over to torture, let the slave's lord take upon himself the whole cause or composition, that is, if it were a cause where a freeman would compound six hundred denarii (i.e., fifteen solidi), let the lord pay that amount. And if it is a more serious offense where a freeman would have to pay fourteen hundred denarii (i.e., thirty-five solidi), let the lord likewise compound that. But if it is a still more serious offense where a freeman would pay eighteen hundred denarii (i.e., forty-five solidi) and the lord has not presented his slave [for torture], let him [the lord] be held to that number and pay the value of the slave plus the value of his work lost to the injured party. But if he [the slave] is guilty of a still more serious offense, the slave's lord may not free his slave by taking the whole blame on himself as a freeman.

10. If the slave accused is absent, then [the accuser] should warn the slave's lord with three separate witnesses present that he should present his slave within seven days. If he [the slave's lord] does not do it, then let him [the injured party] again set a day for him with witnesses, and if he has not presented his slave in this further seven days, then [the accuser] ought to give him the space of seven days for a third time, that is, a total of twenty-one days. But if after three court days have been set he [the slave's lord] still does not wish to present his slave bound for torture after the court day has been repeatedly set, then the lord must pay such composition for every repetition made for his slave as if it had been a freeman who committed the offense.

11. If indeed it is a female slave accused of an offense for which a male slave would be castrated, then she should be liable to pay two hundred forty

denarii (i.e., six solidi)—if it is agreeable for her lord to pay this—or she should be subjected to two hundred forty lashes.

[11. If indeed it is a female slave guilty of an offense for which a male slave would be castrated or receive two hundred forty lashes, let her receive the full number of lashes or compound two hundred forty denarii (i.e., six solidi).]

12. If a slave commits a theft together with a freeman, let him [the slave] pay double that which he shared in addition to return of the object stolen plus a payment for the time its use was lost; indeed, let the freeman pay fourfold damages.

XLI

ON THE KILLING OF FREEMEN [S.V. XI]

1. He who kills a free Frank or other barbarian who lives by Salic law, and it is proved against him (called *leodi* in the Malberg gloss), shall be liable to pay eight thousand denarii (i.e., two hundred solidi).

2. If he throws him into a well or holds him under water (called *mathleodi* in the Malberg gloss), he shall be liable to pay twenty-four thousand denarii (i.e., six hundred solidi). And for concealing it, he shall be liable as we have said before.

3. If he does not conceal his crime (called *moantheuthi* in the Malberg gloss), he shall be liable to pay eight thousand denarii (i.e., two hundred solidi).

4. If he covers him over with sticks or bark or hides him with something to conceal him and it is proved against him (called *matteleodi* in the Malberg gloss), he shall be liable to pay twenty-four thousand denarii (i.e., six hundred solidi).

5. He who kills a man who is in the king's trust (*in truste dominica*) or a free woman[38] and it is proved against him (called *leodi* in the Malberg gloss) shall be liable to pay twenty-four thousand denarii (i.e., six hundred solidi).

6. If he throws him into the water or into a well, he shall be liable to pay seventy-two thousand denarii (i.e., eighteen hundred solidi).

7. If he covers him over with sticks or bark or hides him with something to conceal him (called *matteleodi* in the Malberg gloss), he shall be liable to pay seventy-two thousand denarii (i.e., eighteen hundred solidi).

8. He who kills a Roman who is a table companion of the king[39] and it is proved against him (called *leudi* in the Malberg gloss) shall be liable to pay twelve thousand denarii (i.e., three hundred solidi).

9. If a Roman landholder who is not a table companion of the king is killed, he who is proved to have killed him (called *walaleodi* in the Malberg gloss) shall be liable to pay four thousand denarii (i.e., one hundred solidi).

10. He who kills a Roman who pays tribute[40] and it is proved against him (called *walaleodi* in the Malberg gloss) shall be liable to pay twenty-five hundred denarii (i.e., sixty-two and one-half solidi).

11. He who finds a freeman without hands or feet whom his enemies have left at a crossroad and kills him and it is proved against him (called *wasbuco* in the Malberg gloss) shall be liable to pay four thousand denarii (i.e., one hundred solidi).

[11a. He who takes a freeman down from a gibbet (*barco*) without permission shall be liable to pay eighteen hundred denarii (i.e., forty-five solidi).]

[11b. He who without permission of the other man [who put it there] takes down the head of a man which his enemies have put on a stick (called *rabanal* in the Malberg gloss) shall be liable to pay six hundred denarii (i.e., fifteen solidi).][41]

12. He who throws a freeman into a well and that one escapes alive therefrom (called *callissolio* in the Malberg gloss) shall be liable to pay four thousand denarii (i.e., one hundred solidi).

[12. He who throws a man into a well or water (*uipida*) and he escapes therefrom alive (called *chalips ubdupio* in the Malberg gloss) shall be liable to pay sixty-two and one-half solidi).]

13. He who throws a freeman into the sea (called *phimarina* in the Malberg gloss) [and he escapes therefrom] shall be liable to pay four thousand denarii (i.e., one hundred solidi).

[13. He who throws another man into the sea and he escapes therefrom (called *piomarina* in the Malberg gloss) shall be liable to pay sixty-two and one-half solidi.]

14. He who [unjustly] accuses a freeman of some crime for which he was then killed (called *agoepha* in the Malberg gloss) shall be liable to pay four thousand denarii (i.e., one hundred solidi).

15. He who kills a free girl before she is able to bear children (called *hismala* in the Malberg gloss) shall be liable to pay eight thousand denarii (i.e., two hundred solidi).[42]

[15. He who kills a free girl (called *nuchala* in the Malberg gloss) shall be liable to pay eight thousand denarii (i.e., two hundred solidi).]

16. He who kills a free woman after she begins to bear children shall be liable to pay twenty-four thousand denarii (i.e., six hundred solidi).[43]

17. He who kills her past middle age and no longer able to bear children shall be liable to pay eight thousand denarii (i.e., two hundred solidi).[44]

18. He who kills a long-haired boy shall be liable to pay twenty-four thousand denarii (i.e., six hundred solidi).[45]

19. He who kills a pregnant woman shall be liable to pay six hundred solidi.[46]

20. He who kills an infant in its mother's womb or before it has a name shall be liable to pay one hundred solidi.[47]

21. He who kills a freeman inside his house (called *amestalio leode* in the Malberg gloss) shall be liable to pay six hundred solidi.

XLII

CONCERNING HOMICIDES COMMITTED BY A BAND OF MEN (*contubernio*)[48] [S.V. XII]

1. He who with a band of men attacks a freeman in his house and kills him there (called *chambistalia* in the Malberg gloss) shall be liable to pay twenty-four thousand denarii (i.e., six hundred solidi). And if the man killed was one of the king's sworn antrustions, he who is proved to have killed him shall be liable to pay eighteen hundred solidi.

2. If he who was killed was not an antrustion of the king, he [who did it] shall be liable to pay twenty-four thousand denarii (i.e., six hundred solidi).

[1,2. He who with a band of men attacks a freeman in his house and kills him there (called *bistolio* in the Malberg gloss), if the man who was killed was an antrustion of the king, he [who did it] shall be liable to pay eighteen hundred solidi; if he was not an antrustion of the king, he shall be liable to pay six hundred solidi.]

3. If the body of the dead man had received three or more blows, three of those charged who are proved to have been in that band of men shall each be required to pay as set forth above. Another three members of the band (called *druchtelimici* in the Malberg gloss) shall each pay thirty-six hundred denarii (i.e., ninety solidi). And thirdly, three more of that band shall each of them be liable to pay eighteen hundred denarii (i.e., forty-five solidi) (called *seolasthasia* in the Malberg gloss).

[3. If the body of the man killed received three or more blows, it is fitting that three of those involved who were in the band, if it appears proved, should observe the rule set forth above; another three of the band shall each pay ninety solidi in composition; and further in the third place [another three shall each] pay forty-five solidi.]

4. Concerning Romans or half-free men (*letis*) or servants (*pueri*) who have been killed [by a band of men], half the amount involved in the rule above shall be paid.

[4. If a Roman or half-free man (*litus*) was killed by such a band of men, one-half this amount shall be paid.]

5. If a man robs another man's villa and seizes property there, but nevertheless there is no certain proof, he may absolve himself of the crime with twenty-five oathhelpers, half of whom have been selected by himself. If he cannot find the oathhelpers (called *alachfalthio* in the Malberg gloss), he shall be liable to pay twenty-five hundred denarii (i.e., sixty-two and one-half solidi).

XLIII

CONCERNING THE KILLING OF ONE OF A BAND OF MEN (*contubernio*) [S.V. XIII]

1. If at a banquet where there are four or five men present one of these is killed (called *seolandestadio* in the Malberg gloss), those who remain must give up one of their number to be convicted or all will pay for the death of that man. This rule should be observed where there are up to seven men at a banquet.

2. If indeed there were more than seven men at that banquet, not all of them shall be held liable to punishment; but those against whom the crime is proved must pay according to this rule.

[1,2. If there are five or more men at a banquet and one of them is killed (called *seolandistadio* in the Malberg gloss), those who remain must surrender one of their number to be convicted or all of them must pay composition for the death of that one. This rule should be observed in those cases where there are up to seven men present at a banquet, but if there were more than seven, not all shall be held guilty but those shall pay composition against whom the crime is proved.]

3. If a man has been killed by a band of men (*contubernio*) while he is out-

side of his house or making a journey or standing in a field, if he has suffered three or more wounds (called *druchteclidio* in the Malberg gloss), then
three members of that band against whom it was proved shall each pay
composition for the death of that one. And if there were more members of
that band against whom it was not proved, three of them shall each pay
twelve hundred denarii (i.e., thirty solidi), and three more from the band
shall each be liable to pay six hundred denarii (i.e., fifteen solidi).
[3. If a man has been killed by a band of men while outside his house or
making a journey or standing in a field and he received three or more
wounds (called *druchtiflido* in the Malberg gloss), three members who are
proved to be in the band shall each pay the composition for the dead man,
and three more from the band shall pay thirty solidi, and still another three
from the band shall pay fifteen solidi.]

XLIV

CONCERNING THE WIDOW'S BETROTHAL FINE (*reipus*)[49]
[S.V. XXIV]

1. If it happens that a man dies and leaves a widow, he who wishes to marry
her should take her before a thunginus (*thunginum*) or hundredman (*cente-
narium*) so that the thunginus or hundredman may convene a court, and
in that court he [the man who wishes to marry the widow] should have a
shield and three men should demand three causes.
2. And then the man who would marry the widow should have three solidi
of equal weight and a denarius. And there should be three men who should
weigh or hold or appraise his solidi; and when this is done and everything
is in order, the man to whom she [the widow] is promised may marry her.
[1,2. If it happens that a man dies and leaves a widow, [a second husband]
may not take her until he gives three solidi before the thunginus or
hundredman so that the thunginus or hundredman may convene a court
and have there a shield, and three men should demand three causes; then
the man who would take the widow in marriage should offer three solidi
of equal weight; and there should be three men to weigh or appraise these
solidi and if this is done and it is agreeable to them, then he who seeks the
widow may marry her.]
3. If he does not do this and marries her anyway (called *reipus nichalesinus*
in the Malberg gloss), he shall be liable to pay twenty-five hundred denarii

(i.e., sixty-two and one-half solidi) to him to whom the betrothal fine is owed.

4. If he carries out all of these things according to law as stated above, he to whom the betrothal fine (*reipi*) is owed shall receive the three solidi and a denarius.

5. It should be noted to whom the betrothal fine is due.

6. If there is a nephew, the oldest son of a sister [of the dead husband], he should receive it.[50]

7. If there is no nephew, the oldest son of a niece, if there is one, should receive the betrothal fine.

8. If there is no son of a niece, the cousin who is the son of a maternal aunt shall receive it. And if there are no cousins, the son of a cousin who comes from the maternal side shall receive it.

9. If there is no son of a cousin, then an uncle, the brother of the mother [i.e., the dead husband's mother] shall receive it.

10. If indeed there is no mother's brother, then the brother of him who had been married to the woman, if he will not come into the inheritance, shall have the betrothal fine (*reipus*).

11. And if there is no brother, then he who is closest up to the sixth degree after those named above, who are named individually according to the degree of their kinship, if he does not come into the inheritance of the dead husband, shall receive the widow's betrothal fine.

12. And if there is no one within the sixth degree, the betrothal fine or the proceeds of any suit that has arisen from it shall be collected by the fisc.[51]

XLV

CONCERNING THOSE WHO MOVE [S.V. XXVI]

1. The man who wishes to move into another village (*villa*) in place of someone else, and one or more of those who live in the village wish to receive him but there is one of them who objects, he may not have the right to move there.

2. If against the objection of one or two men from that village he still presumes to settle there, then he [who objects] should give testimony (*testare*) against him. And if he is not willing to leave, then he who is giving testimony against him should with witnesses say to him thus: "Sir, I declare (*testo*) to you, as the Salic law provides, that on the next day after you took

up residence I have made declaration to you that you should depart from this village within ten days." And after the ten days he should come again to the same place and declare to him again that he should depart within ten days. And if after the ten days he still will not leave, then the complainant should add a third period of ten days to his deadline so that there are thirty days in all. And if he still is not willing to go away, then the complainant should summon him to court and he should have with him those witnesses who were present at each declaration. And if that one who was testified against does not come and no lawful excuse detains him and he has been testified against in all those ways according to law as stated above, then he who is declaring against him may lay hands on his property and request the count (*grafionem*) of that place to go to the village and expel his opponent from it. And because that one did not obey the law, he shall lose the fruit of his labor there and in addition (called *widrisittolo* in the Malberg gloss) he shall be liable to pay twelve hundred denarii (i.e., thirty solidi).

3. If one man invites another man to move into someone else's village before an agreement has been reached (called *andwitheocho* in the Malberg gloss), he shall be liable to pay eighteen hundred denarii (i.e., forty-five solidi).

4. If a man has moved [into another village] and no one has protested against him for twelve months, let him remain where he has settled and let him be secure just as the other neighbors are.

XLVI

CONCERNING *ACFATMIRE* (THE TRANSFERENCE OF PROPERTY BY DONATION OR THE ADOPTION OF AN HEIR) [S.V. XXVII]

1. It should be done thus. The thunginus or hundredman should convene a court. In the court he should have a shield, and there three men should state the case three times. And afterward let a man appear who is not related to him [who wishes to transfer his property], and he [the transferer] should throw a stick (*festuca*) thus into his lap. And he should say to the man into whose lap he threw the stick how much he wishes to give him [the selected donee]—if he wishes to give him all or half of his property.

2. And afterward the man in whose lap the transferer threw the stick ought to stay in that one's house and receive there three or more guests and have

in his control as much of the property as was given to him. And he to whom it was given should do all these things in the presence of assembled witnesses.

3. Afterward within twelve months he [the transferer] should in the presence of the king hand over his property to him whom he designated or who received the stick in legitimate court—neither more nor less than the amount he gave to him he named as heir and into whose lap he threw the stick.

4. And if anyone wishes to contest this, the three witnesses should declare under oath that they were present in the court that the thunginus or hundredman convened and that they saw in what manner that man, who wished to give his property, threw the stick into the lap of him whom he had chosen. And they should name by name the man who threw his property into someone else's lap, and they should likewise name him in whose lap it was thrown and publicly called heir.

5. And three other witnesses should state under oath that he in whose lap the stick was thrown remained there in the house of that one who had given. him his property and that he assembled there three or more guests and fed them and these three or more guests offered thanks to him in accepting and ate porridge (*pultes*) at his table (*beode*) and the three were together as witnesses.

6. And three other witnesses should declare on oath all these things that it was in court in the presence of the king or in a legitimate public court that he who received the property in his lap—either in the presence of the king or in legitimate public court (called *anttheoda* or *thungino* in the Malberg gloss)—he [who was giving the property] threw the stick into the lap of that one publicly in the presence of all and thus [threw] his property into the lap of the man whom he called heir. The nine witnesses should affirm all these things in their testimony.

XLVII

CONCERNING THOSE WHO LIVE BY SALIC LAW AND RECOGNIZE THEIR PROPERTY IN THE POSSESSION OF SOMEONE ELSE (*filtortus*) [S.V. LIX]

1. He who recognizes his male or female slave, or horse, or cow, or mare, or any other property in the possession of another man should place it [his property] in the hands of a third party. And the man in whose possession

the property was recognized should acknowledge the charge (*achramire*). If both live between the Loire River and the Carbonaria Forest, both he who recognizes his property and he in whose possession it is recognized, should come to court (*placitum faciant*) within forty days. Those involved should be present at the hearing—he who sold or traded or perhaps gave the horse or other property in payment—all these should come to the court, that is, each one of those involved should summon the rest.

2. If the man who was summoned refuses to come to the hearing and a legitimate excuse does not detain him, then he who did business with him should offer three witnesses to the means whereby he summoned the first man to court and he should offer three other witnesses to the fact that he had done business with him publicly and properly. If he does this, he escapes from the charge of theft. And the man who does not come, against whom three witnesses have offered sworn testimony, will be known as the robber of that man who recognized his property, and he must return the price to him with whom he did business and he must pay composition according to law to the man who recognized his property. All these things should be done in that court where the party (*gamallus*) lives in whose possession the property was recognized or placed in the hands of a third party.

3. But if both live beyond the Loire River or the Carbonaria Forest or [just him] with whom the property was recognized, then eighty days is the time period to be observed in all of these matters.[52]

XLVIII

CONCERNING FALSE TESTIMONY [S.V. XXVIII]

1. He who offers or swears false testimony (called *calistanio* in the Malberg gloss) shall be liable to pay six hundred denarii (i.e., fifteen solidi).

2. If a man has been charged with swearing falsely to something and it is proved against him, each of his three oathhelpers shall be liable to pay fifteen solidi.

[2. He who charges another man with committing perjury and cannot prove it shall be liable to pay six hundred denarii (i.e., fifteen solidi).]

3. If there were more than three oathhelpers, each of them shall pay five solidi each.

4. The man against whom it [the perjury] was proved shall be liable to pay

six hundred denarii (i.e., fifteen solidi) in addition to payment of the value of the matter in dispute plus a payment for the time the use of the object involved was lost.

XLIX

CONCERNING WITNESSES [S.V. LX]

1. He who needs witnesses and has them to offer, and these witnesses do not want to come to court, should with witnesses summon them to court so that under oath they may state those things that they know.

[XLIX. ON COMPELLING (*adhibendis*) WITNESSES]

[1. He who needs a witness and has a suitable one, and that witness does not want to come to court, should with witnesses call him to court so that he may offer testimony about what he saw.]
2. If they do not want to come and a suitable excuse does not detain them (called *widridarchi* in the Malberg gloss), each of them shall be liable to pay six hundred denarii (i.e., fifteen solidi).
3. If those sworn and called for testimony are present and, when ordered (*ferbanniti fuerint*) to do so, do not wish to say under oath what they know [and those do not wish to offer testimony about what they saw], each of them shall be liable to pay six hundred denarii (i.e., fifteen solidi).

L

ON THE MAKING OF AGREEMENTS (*fides factas*) [S.V. XXIX]

1. If a freeman or half-free man (*letus*) makes an agreement (*fidem*) with another man and will not carry it out, then that one to whom the promise (*fides*) was given shall in fourteen or forty or whatever number of days was agreed upon call a hearing (*placitum*); he shall come to the house of the man who made the promise with the witnesses who were present when the agreement was made and with those who will evaluate the amount in dispute. And if he [who gave the promise] is not willing to fulfill the agree-

ment (called *thalasciasco* in the Malberg gloss), then he who made the agreement shall be liable to pay six hundred denarii (i.e., fifteen solidi) over and above the debt.

2. And if he [who made the promise] does not wish to pay what he owes, he [who received the promise] should call the other to court and address the court urgently (*nestigans thigius*) thus: "I ask you, judge (*thungine*), that you summon to court (*nestigan thigius*) my adversary (*gasachio*) who gave me his promise and owes me a legitimate debt." And he ought to state how much the debt was that was covered in the agreement. Then the thunginus should say, "I summon him to court (*nestigan thigio*) [I summon (*nestigantio*) your adversary (*gasachio*) to this court] which is under Salic law." Then that one to whom the promise was given should testify that the other had not paid nor given a pledge for payment nor fulfilled in any way that which he had promised. Then he should go quickly to the house of that one who gave him the promise to pay: he should go with witnesses on a day before the day in court is set and demand that he pay his debt. And if he still is not willing to pay, then the creditor shall formally set a day for him to come to court. If a day for court has been set, he [the creditor] may add one hundred twenty denarii (i.e., three solidi) to the earlier debt. He should do this three times for three summonses (*mandinas*); if he has done all these things three times and the debtor still will not pay, then the debt shall be increased three hundred sixty denarii (i.e., nine solidi), that is, for each demand and setting of a court day three solidi shall be added to the debt.

3. If he who gave the promissory note still will not pay in legitimate court, then he to whom the promise was given should go to the count (*grafionem*) of the place in whose district he lives, and he should carry a stick (*festucam*) and say these words: "Count, that is the man who gave a pledge to me and whom I have legally called to court as the Salic law provides; I place myself and my fortune in your hands that they may be held secure [i.e., I place myself and my fortune in your hands as security for the property you are being asked to seize]." And let him say for what cause and for how much the pledge was given. Then the count should collect together seven suitable rachimburgi and with them go to the house of him who gave the pledge and say to him, if he who gave the pledge is present, speaking thus: "You who are present ought voluntarily to repay this man what you have promised to pay and for this purpose you should choose two of these suitable rachimburgi, whom you wish, to appraise the debt and establish a just price." But if he does not wish to hear, whether he is present or absent, the

rachimburgi should exact the amount of the debt from his property as the amount has been appraised and its value established. And in this case, two parts of the debt shall revert to him whose cause it is and the third part shall be collected by the count as a fine, provided nevertheless that a fine has not already been paid in this case.

4. If the count has been summoned and does not come and no lawful delay or royal business detains him, and if he hesitates either to go there or to send someone else to exact justice for him according to law, he [the count] shall be liable to pay with his life or shall redeem himself for as much as he is worth [i.e., with a payment equal to his wergeld].

LI

CONCERNING THE MAN WHO UNJUSTLY REQUESTS A COUNT TO TAKE SOMEONE ELSE'S PROPERTY [S.V. III]

1. If anyone asks a count to go and requests him to seize the property of someone else and he has not legitimately called that defaulting man (*iactivum*) to court, he who asked the count to take something unjustly before he has legally called him [his adversary] to court or before a promise to pay has been given to him (called *anthomito* in the Malberg gloss) shall be liable to pay eight thousand denarii (i.e., two hundred solidi).

2. That man who unjustly asks the count to confiscate something shall be liable to pay eight thousand denarii (i.e., two hundred solidi).

3. The count who, having been asked by one of the parties to a suit, presumes contrary to law to take more than the just debt, shall be liable to make composition with his life or redeem himself [with his value].

LII

CONCERNING PROPERTY THAT HAS BEEN LENT [S.V. XXX]

1. If anyone lends any of his properties to another man and that one will not return them, he [who lent the property] should summon the other to court. He should go with witnesses to the house of the man to whom he lent the property and call upon him thus: "Since you do not wish to return the property that I lent to you, you may keep it to the next day as the Salic

law provides." And thus he should formally set a day for him [to return the property].

2. And then if he does not wish to return it, the lender should give him another seven days; and after seven days he should call upon him in the same way as he did before, that he might keep the property until the next day as the Salic law provides.

[2. And then if he does not wish to return it, the lender should give another seven days and if he then does not wish to return it, he should give him another seven days.]

3. If the borrower does not then wish to return the property, the lender should give him another seven days after which he should go to him again with witnesses to ask him to return that which is owed to him.

4. If he then will not make restitution, the lender should formally set a day for him [to return it]. If he sets a day for him three times, for each time or for each warning the debt shall be increased one hundred twenty denarii (i.e., three solidi).

5. If the borrower still will not return the property or will not give security to return the debt to him who lent it, over and above the nine solidi that were added for the three warnings (called *nectantheo antesalina* in the Malberg gloss), he shall be liable to pay six hundred denarii (i.e., fifteen solidi) as well as the debt.

LIII

ON REDEEMING ONE'S HAND FROM THE HOT WATER ORDEAL [S.V. XXXI]

1. If a man has been sentenced to the hot water ordeal and it is agreed that he who was sentenced may redeem his hand and offer oathhelpers, then he may redeem his hand for one hundred twenty denarii (i.e., three solidi) if it were a case such that he would be liable to pay six hundred denarii (i.e., fifteen solidi) in composition.[53]

2. If he gave more to redeem his hand, let the fine (*fredus*) to be exacted by the count be the amount he would have paid if he had been convicted for such a cause [involving the higher amount].

3. If it is such a case that if he were proved guilty he would be liable to pay thirty-five solidi, and if it is agreed that he may redeem his hand and offer

oathhelpers, he may redeem his hand for two hundred forty denarii (i.e., six solidi).

[3. If it is a more serious cause for which he should pay twelve hundred denarii (i.e., thirty solidi) in composition, and if it is agreed that he may redeem his hand and offer oathhelpers, he may redeem his hand for two hundred forty denarii (i.e., six solidi).]

4. But if he gave more, let the fine to be exacted by the count be the amount he would have paid if he had been convicted for such a cause [involving the higher amount].

5. If it is a more serious cause for which he can be judged liable to pay sixty-two and one-half solidi, and if it is agreed that he may redeem his hand, he may redeem his hand with fifteen solidi.

6. But if he gave more, let the fine to be exacted by the count be as much as if he had been convicted for such a more serious cause. This means of redeeming [one's hand from the ordeal] shall be in effect [in cases that involve compositions] up to the amount of a man's wergeld (*leodem*).

7. If someone charges another man with a crime involving the payment of wergeld and he has been sentenced to the ordeal, if it is agreed that he may offer oathhelpers and redeem his hand, he may redeem his hand with twelve hundred denarii (i.e., thirty solidi).

8. If he gave something more, the fine for the wergeld of that one shall be exacted by the count.

LIV

ON THE KILLING OF A COUNT [S.V. VII]

1. He who kills a count (called *leode saccemitem* in the Malberg gloss) shall be liable to pay twenty-four thousand denarii (i.e., six hundred solidi).

2. He who kills a sagibaron[54] (*sacebaronem*) or count (*obgrafionem*) who is a servant (*puer*) of the king and it is proved against him (called *leode saccemither* in the Malberg gloss) shall be liable to pay twelve thousand denarii (i.e., three hundred solidi).

3. If anyone kills a sagibaron who is a freeman and has established himself or another as sagibaron, he shall be liable to pay twenty-four thousand denarii (i.e., six hundred solidi).

4. There should not be more than three sagibarons in each court and if they have said something final about a case that has been submitted to

them, they shall make this secure and the case may not be removed to the count.

LV

ON DESPOILING DEAD BODIES [S.V. XX and XXI]

1. He who furtively despoils the body of a dead man before it is placed in the ground and it is proved against him (called *chreomosido* in the Malberg gloss) shall be liable to pay twenty-five hundred denarii (i.e., sixty-two and one-half solidi).

2. He who despoils or destroys the tomb covering a dead man (called *tornechale* in the Malberg gloss) shall be liable to pay fifteen solidi.

3. If a man destroys the enclosure (*charistatone*) over a dead man (called *manduale* in the Malberg gloss), or if he destroys the *lave* which is the burial mound over a dead man (called *chreoburgio* in the Malberg gloss), for each of these things he should be liable to pay six hundred denarii (i.e., fifteen solidi).

4. In an old law:[55] he who digs up and despoils a body already buried and it is proved against him (called *muther* in the Malberg gloss) shall be outlawed (*wargus*) until that day when it is agreeable to the relatives of the dead person and they ask on his behalf that he be permitted to come among men again. And that one who, before composition has been paid to the relatives, gives him [who was outlawed] bread or hospitality, whether it be his parents or his wife or other near relative who does it, shall be liable to pay six hundred denarii (i.e., fifteen solidi). The perpetrator of the crime who is proved to have committed it or dug it up (called *tornechale* in the Malberg gloss) shall be liable to pay eight thousand denarii (i.e., two hundred solidi).

5. He who in evil or stealth places a dead body on top of another one in a wooden (*nauco*) or stone sarcophagus and it is proved against him (called *chaminis* in the Malberg gloss) shall be liable to pay eighteen hundred denarii (i.e., forty-five solidi).

6. He who despoils the shrine (*basilicam*) over a dead body (called *chreotarsino* in the Malberg gloss) shall be liable to pay twelve hundred denarii (i.e., thirty solidi) in addition to payment of the value of the thing destroyed plus a payment for the time its use was lost.

7. He who burns down a shrine (*basilicam*) where relics are kept or a basil-

ica that has been blessed (called *chenechruda* in the Malberg gloss) shall be liable to pay two hundred solidi.[56]

LVI

CONCERNING THE MAN WHO REFUSES TO COME TO COURT [S.V. II]

1. If a man refuses to come to court or delays in carrying out what was judged against him by the rachimburgi, if he will not give security (*fidem*) for the composition or for the ordeal or for other penalty, he should be remanded to the presence of the king.

2. There should be twelve witnesses there who offer oath three at a time that they were present when the rachimburgi gave their judgment that he should go to the ordeal or give a pledge for the amount of the composition, and he neglected to do so.

3. Three others should then offer oath that they were present on that day when the rachimburgi gave their judgment that he should go to the ordeal or pay composition, that is, on that day forty days from the time that a day had formally been set again for him in court, and he was still unwilling to comply with the law.

4. Then let him be summoned to come before the king in fourteen days and three witnesses should offer oath that they had been there when he was summoned and had a day formally set for him. And if he has not come then, all nine witnesses, having been sworn, shall give their testimony as stated above.

5. Likewise on that day, if he has not come, another day should formally be set for him and there should be three witnesses there when the day is set. Then if he who calls the man to court fulfills all these things and he who was called to court still will not come to court or carry out the law, then the king before whom he was summoned shall place him outside his protection (*extra sermonem suum*).

6. The guilty man and all his property will then belong to the fisc or to him to whom the fisc gives it. And whoever feeds him or gives him hospitality, even though it be his own wife (called *lampicii* in the Malberg gloss), shall be liable to pay six hundred denarii (i.e., fifteen solidi) until he [the outlawed man] has paid composition according to law for all those things legally charged against him.

6a. If a man comes to an agreement (*coniunxerit*) with someone else by law and that one fails to sign a note or to pay a penalty, then the rachimburgi ought to hear him [the first man] according to law as is the quality of the case and that one who called him [the second man] to court should declare the amount of the penalty or debt to him at his house; and if then he [the second man] still will not pay, then he [the first man] should observe the law and afterwards invite the count to his [the second man's] house so that that one shall pay according to law from his properties what the penalty is for this case.

LVII

CONCERNING THE RACHIMBURGI [S.V. IV]

1. If there are rachimburgi sitting on a court while a case is being pled between two men, the one who is bringing the suit ought to say to them: "Speak the Salic law to us." If they are not willing to speak the law, he who is pursuing the case ought to say to them: "Here I summon (*tangono*) you to speak the law to me according to the Salic law." Then if they are still not willing to speak the law, seven of those rachimburgi (called *schodo* in the Malberg gloss) shall on a day formally set each be liable to pay one hundred twenty denarii (i.e., three solidi).
2. Then if they are not willing to speak the law nor to pay the composition nor to sign a note to pay, then on the day formally set again they shall each be liable to pay six hundred denarii (i.e., fifteen solidi).
[1. If those rachimburgi sitting on a court will not speak the law when a case is being pled between two parties, he who is bringing the suit should say to them: "Speak the Salic law to us." If then they will not speak, he who is bringing the suit should say again: "I summon (*tangono*) you to speak the law on this matter to me." He should do this two or three times. If indeed they still will not speak, he who is pursuing the suit should say: "I summon you to speak the Salic law to me." Then seven of those rachimburgi shall on the day formally set each be liable to pay nine solidi.]
3. If there are rachimburgi who do not give judgment according to the law, the man against whom they passed judgment should plead his case and if he can prove to them that they did not render justice according to the law, each one of them shall be liable to pay six hundred denarii (i.e., fifteen solidi).

[3. If the rachimburgi have not rendered justice according to Salic law, they shall pay fifteen solidi to those against whom they passed judgment.]

4. If the rachimburgi have spoken the law and he against whom they passed judgment challenges them that they have not rendered justice according to law [and he is unable to prove his charge], he shall be liable to pay fifteen solidi to each of them.

[4. If the rachimburgi have spoken the law and he against whom they passed judgment challenges them and does not want to accept their verdict and charges them with passing judgment contrary to law [and he is unable to prove his charge], he shall pay each of the seven rachimburgi six hundred denarii (i.e., fifteen solidi).]

LVIII

CONCERNING THE *CHRENECRUDA* (i.e., INVOLVING THE KIN IN THE PAYMENT OF COMPOSITION FOR HOMICIDE) [S.V. XVII]

1. If anyone kills a man and, having given up all his property, he still does not have enough to pay the total composition, let him offer twelve oath-helpers [who will support his oath] that neither above the earth nor below the earth does he have more property than he has already given.

2. Afterwards he should enter his house and in his hand collect dust from its four corners, and then he should stand on the *duropello*, that is, on the threshold, looking into the house, and then with his left hand he should throw the earth over his shoulders onto him who is his nearest relative.

3. If his mother and brother have already paid [and the composition is still not fully paid], then he should throw the earth over the sister of his mother or her children. If there are none of these, then he should throw the earth over three from the maternal kin and three of the paternal kin who are next most nearly related.

[3. If the father or mother or brother have already paid for him [and the composition is still not fully paid], then he should throw the earth over the sister of his mother or her children; but if there are none of these, [he should throw the earth] over those three from the paternal and maternal kin who are next most nearly related.]

4. And afterwards without a shirt and barefoot, with stick in hand, he should go jump over his fence [i.e., abandon his house?] and those three

from the maternal side shall pay half of whatever is the value of the composition or the judgment set; and those others who come from the paternal side should do the same [i.e., pay the other half].

5. If any of these does not have that with which to pay his full share, let him who is poor throw the *chrenecruda* over him who has more so that he pays the entire judgment.

6. If he does not have that with which to pay the entire judgment [if he does not have that with which to pay the judgment or make the full composition], then he who has the man who committed the homicide in his surety (*sub sua fide*) should present him in court, and after presenting him in four courts, he may remove (*tollant*) his surety. And if no one exercises the surety for him by paying the composition, that is, does not pay that which would redeem him, then he shall make composition with his life [i.e., become a slave to the party to whom the composition is owed].

[6a. At the present time, if a man does not have enough of his own property to pay or defend himself from the law, it is fitting that everything be done from the beginning as set out above.]

LIX

CONCERNING ALLODIAL LANDS (*de alodis*) [S.V. XXXIV]

1. If a man dies and leaves no children, and if his father or mother survives him, this person shall succeed to the inheritance.[57]

2. If there is no father or mother but he leaves a brother or sister, they shall succeed to the inheritance.

3. If none of these is living, then the sister of the mother shall succeed to the inheritance.[58]

4. If none of the mother's sisters live, then the sisters of the father will succeed to the inheritance.

5. If there is no father's sister, after these kindred whoever is closest who comes from the father's kin shall succeed to the inheritance.

6. But concerning Salic land (*terra Salica*), no portion or inheritance is for a woman but all the land belongs to members of the male sex who are brothers.

[6. Indeed concerning Salic land (*terra Salica*) no portion of the inheritance shall pass to a woman, but the male sex acquires it, that is, the sons succeed to the inheritance.]

[Where the allodial property comes to grandchildren after a long time, let them divide it not by branch of family but by individual person (*non per stirpem sed per capita*).]

[But where after a long time a contest over allodial property arises among grandchildren, let the property be divided not by branch of family but by individual person (*non per stirpem sed per capita*).]

LX

CONCERNING HIM WHO WISHES TO REMOVE HIMSELF FROM HIS KIN GROUP (*parentilla*)[59] [S.V. XXXV]

1. He who wishes to remove himself from his kin group (*parentilla*) should go to court and in the presence of the thunginus or hundredman break four sticks of alderwood over his head and throw them in four bundles into the four corners of the court and say there that he removes himself from their oathhelping (*iuramento*), from their inheritance, and from any relationship [with his kin].

2. If afterward one of his relatives dies or is killed, none of that one's inheritance or composition will belong to him.

3. If he [who removed himself from parentela] dies or is killed, the claim for his composition or inheritance will not belong to his relatives but to the fisc or to him to whom the fisc wishes to give it.

[3. Likewise if he [who removed himself from parentela] dies, no claim or inheritance of his will belong to his relatives but it will go thence with twelve oathhelpers.]

LXI

ON PILLAGING (*charoena*) [S.V. XXXVI]

1. He who seizes something by force from another man's hand shall return the full value of the object and in addition (called *alcham* in the Malberg gloss) he shall be liable to pay twelve hundred denarii (i.e., thirty solidi).

[1. He who seizes something by force from another man's hand or robs or despoils him shall be liable to pay twelve hundred denarii (i.e., thirty solidi) in addition to restoring the full value of the object taken.]

2. He who forcefully plunders a dead man shall be liable to pay twenty-five hundred denarii (i.e., sixty-two and one-half solidi) [to the relatives, in addition to returning that which he took]. Likewise if he forcefully seizes spoils from a man still living (called *mosido* in the Malberg gloss), he shall be liable to pay sixty-two and one-half solidi [in addition to returning the spoils].⁶⁰

3. He who takes by force from a man something which had been placed in the hand of a third person saying that he recognizes it as his own (called *charoena* in the Malberg gloss) shall be liable to pay twelve hundred denarii (i.e., thirty solidi) [in addition to returning the object taken].

LXII

CONCERNING THE COMPOSITION FOR HOMICIDE (i.e., BY WHAT MEANS THE RELATIVES OF A FATHER SHALL DIVIDE THE COMPOSITION AMONG THEMSELVES) [S.V. XIV]

1. If a man who is a father is killed, his children shall collect half of the composition and those relatives who are closest to his father and to his mother shall divide the other half among them.⁶¹

2. If there is no relative on one side, either the paternal or maternal, that portion of the composition will be collected by the fisc or by him to whom the fisc wishes to give it.

LXIII

CONCERNING THE FREEMAN KILLED WHILE IN THE ARMY [S.V. VIII]

1. If a man kills a freeman in the army while in the company of his companions (*in conpanio de conpaniones suos*) and that one is not an antrustion of the king (*in truste dominica*), and he is proved to have killed him (called *leude* in the Malberg gloss), he shall be liable to pay twenty-four thousand denarii (i.e., six hundred solidi).

[1. He who kills a freeman who lives by Salic law while he is in the army (called *leodardi trespellia* in the Malberg gloss) shall be liable to pay twenty-four thousand denarii (i.e., six hundred solidi).]

2. If it was an antrustion of the king who was killed, that one against whom it is proved (called *mother* in the Malberg gloss) shall be liable to pay seventy-two thousand denarii (i.e., eighteen hundred solidi).

LXIV

CONCERNING SORCERERS (*herburgium*) [S.V. XXXVII]

1. He who calls another man a sorcerer (*herburgium*)—that is, a *strioportio* or one who is said to carry a brass cauldron in which witches brew—if he is not able to prove it (called *humnisfith* in the Malberg gloss), he shall be liable to pay twenty-five hundred denarii (i.e., sixty-two and one-half solidi).

2. He who calls a free woman a witch (*striam* or *meretricem*) and is not able to prove it (called *faras* in the Malberg gloss) shall be liable to pay three times twenty-five hundred denarii (i.e., one hundred eighty-seven and one-half solidi).

3. If a witch eats a man and it is proved against him (called *granderba* in the Malberg gloss), he shall be liable to pay eight thousand denarii (i.e., two hundred solidi).[62]

LXV

ON SKINNING A DEAD HORSE WITHOUT THE CONSENT OF ITS OWNER [S.V. XLVI]

1. He who skins (*decorticaverit*) another man's horse without the consent of its owner and, having been interrogated, confesses, shall return the full value of the horse [plus composition and a payment for the time its use was lost].

[1. He who skins another man's horse without the consent of its owner (called *leudardi* in the Malberg gloss), if he confesses it, shall be liable to pay fifteen solidi and pay the full value of the animal in addition to a payment for the time its use was lost.]

2. But if he denies it and it is proved against him (called *secthis* in the Malberg gloss), he shall be liable to pay fourteen hundred denarii (i.e., thirty-

five solidi) in addition to payment of the value of the animal plus a payment for the time its use was lost.

LXVa

CONCERNING HIM WHO BETROTHS (*acquisierit*) ANOTHER MAN'S DAUGHTER AND THEN WITHDRAWS HIMSELF[63]

He who seeks another man's daughter in marriage in the presence of his own and of the girl's relatives and afterwards withdraws himself and is not willing to marry her (called *frifrasigena* in the Malberg gloss) shall be liable to pay twenty-five hundred denarii (i.e., sixty-two and one-half solidi).

LXVb

ON BURNING A BASILICA

He who voluntarily or through negligence sets fire to a basilica (called *alutrude theotidio* in the Malberg gloss) shall be liable to pay eight thousand denarii (i.e., two hundred solidi).

LXVc

CONCERNING THE DESTRUCTION OF PROPERTY (*terra condemnata*)

If anyone destroys the fruit of another's land and will not restore it, if he is summoned to court and is convicted, he shall be liable to pay six hundred denarii (i.e., fifteen solidi).

LXVd

CONCERNING CUTTING COULTERS (*cultello sexxandro*)

He who steals another man's coulter and it is proved against him must restore it to its owner and in addition be liable to pay six hundred denarii (i.e., fifteen solidi).

LXVe

ON KILLING PREGNANT WOMEN

1. He who kills a pregnant woman shall be liable to pay twenty-four thousand denarii (i.e, six hundred solidi). And if it is proved that the fetus was a boy, he shall also be liable to pay six hundred solidi for the child.[64]
2. He who kills a girl less than twelve years old or up to the end of her twelfth year shall be liable to pay two hundred solidi.[65]
3. He who kills a woman of mature age up to her sixtieth year, as long as she is able to bear children, shall be liable to pay twenty-four thousand denarii (i.e., six hundred solidi).[66]
4. But if she is killed afterwards when she is no longer able to bear children he shall be liable to pay two hundred solidi.

LXVf

CONCERNING THE PAYMENTS FOR THE TIME AN OBJECT'S USE WAS LOST (*delatura*)[67]

1. He who kills a man and pays for him what the law provides should pay in composition thirty solidi as an indemnity for the time lost [between the homicide and payment of compensation].
2. [For killing] a servant (*puero*) or freedman the indemnity shall be fifteen solidi.
3. For other crimes (*furtibus*) the indemnity shall be seven solidi.
4. In the king's causes the payment shall be tripled.

LXVg

THE HUNDREDS (*chunnas*)[68]

1. For one hundred twelve (*unum thoalasti*) [solidi composition], a man shall be liable to pay three solidi.
2. For six hundred (*sexan chunna*), he shall be liable to pay fifteen solidi.
3. For seven hundred (*septun chunna*), he shall be liable to pay seventeen and one-half solidi.

4. For twelve hundred (*thuwalt chunna*), he shall be liable to pay thirty solidi.

5. For twice seven hundred (*thue septun chunna*), he shall be liable to pay thirty-five solidi.

6. For twice nine hundred (*thu neune chunna*), he shall be liable to pay forty-five solidi.

7. For twenty-five hundred (*tho thosundi fitme chunna*), he shall be liable to pay sixty-two and one-half solidi.

8. For four thousand (*fitter thusunde*), he shall be liable to pay one hundred solidi.

9. For eight thousand (*actoe thusunde*), he shall be liable to pay two hundred solidi.

10. For thirty times eight hundred (*thrio thusunde therte chunna*), he shall be liable to pay six hundred solidi.

11. For forty times eight hundred (*fitter thusunde thue actoe chunna*), he shall be liable to pay eight hundred solidi.

Capitularies[69]

CAPITULARY I

LXVI

CONCERNING FAMILY PROPERTY HELD IN ALLODIAL TENURE (de rebus in alode patris)[70]

If anyone sequesters [i.e., has the land placed in the hand of a third party] another man's property held as allodial land from his father (*patris*), he against whom the case is brought [i.e., he whose land was sequestered] should offer three witnesses [to the fact that] he had it from the allodial property of his own father, and another three witnesses to the means whereby his father had this property. If he does this, he can liberate the property in dispute. If he does not do this, he should present three oathhelpers who will support his claim that he had it from the allodial property of his family. If he does this, he will free himself from penalty in this case. If he does not do this, then he who brought suit (*suo fel troctum* in the Malberg gloss) [shall have it]; and afterwards as the law states he [who was unable to secure witnesses or oathhelpers] shall be liable to pay thirty-five solidi to him who claimed the property.

LXVII

CONCERNING GIFTS (*chane crenodo*)

If a father or kin group (*parentilla*) gives a girl in marriage, whatever was given to her on that day, a like portion should be reserved for her brothers [and sisters]. Likewise when a son reaches manhood (cuts his beard—*ad capillaturias*), whatever is given to him, a similar portion should be kept [for the other sons and daughters] when the remaining property is divided among themselves.

LXVIII

ON KILLING A FREEMAN AND THE MANNER IN WHICH THE RELATIVES RECEIVE COMPOSITION FOR HIS LIFE

He who kills a freeman, and it is proved against him that he killed him, should make composition to the relatives according to law. His [the dead man's] children (*filius*) should get half the composition. Half of the rest should go to the mother [i.e., the children's mother], so that one-fourth of the wergeld comes to her.[71] The other one-fourth should go to the near relatives, that is, to the three nearest on his [i.e., the dead man's] father's side and three on his mother's side. If the mother [i.e., the wife] is not living, the relatives should divide her half of the half-wergeld among themselves, that is the three closest from the father's side and three from the mother's side; whoever is the closest relative of the aforementioned three shall take [two parts] and leave a third part to be divided among the other two; then he of the remaining two who is the closer relative shall take two parts of that third and leave a third part to the other relative.[72]

LXIX

CONCERNING THE NUMBER OF CASES IN WHICH TWELVE (*thoalapus* or *thalaptas*) MAY OFFER OATH

[On these occasions twelve may offer oath:] One is the case of the marriage gift, another concerns property lost in the army, and a third is the case of a man recalled into slavery. If they [the twelve] offer oath in other than these three cases, he [whose oath they support] must restore the full value of the property [in dispute] and be held liable for whatever fine there is in this case. Of those who have offered oath, the three eldest shall be liable to pay fifteen solidi, and the remaining oathhelpers shall pay five solidi.

LXX

ON CREMATION (*creobeba*)

1. He who kills a freeman either in a forest or in some other place and burns the body in order to conceal the crime, if it is proved against him, shall pay six hundred solidi composition.[73]

[1. He who kills a freeman either in a forest or in some other place and burns the body with fire in order to conceal the crime shall be liable to pay twenty-four thousand denarii (i.e., six hundred solidi).]

2. He who kills an antrustion or a woman of such rank and tries to despoil (*talare*) the body or burn it with fire, and it is proved against him, must pay eighteen hundred solidi composition.

[2. He who kills an antrustion or a woman in such a manner, and either hides [the body] or cremates it with fire shall be liable to pay seventy-two thousand denarii (i.e., eighteen hundred solidi).]

LXXI

1. If a Salic man forcefully castrates another Salic man and it is proved against him, he shall be liable to pay two hundred solidi, and in addition he must pay nine solidi composition for the medical treatment.[74]

2. He who castrates an antrustion and it is proved against him shall be liable to pay six hundred solidi, and in addition he must pay nine solidi composition for the medical treatment.

LXXII

If anyone from a band of followers (*contubernio*) presumes to attack a free woman or a girl on the road or in some other place, both one or more who have been proved to have committed this crime shall be liable to pay two hundred solidi. And from that band of followers, if some still remain who did not commit the crime but were known to have been there, if they were more or fewer than three in number, they shall be liable to pay forty-five solidi.

[If anyone with an assembled band of followers assaults and presumes to attack by force a free woman or girl either on the road or some other place, both one or more who are mixed up in this violent act shall each of them be liable to pay two hundred solidi. And if from that band of followers some still remain who are known not to have committed the crime but nevertheless were there, if they are more or fewer in number than three, each one of them shall be liable to pay forty-five solidi for this.]

LXXIII

CONCERNING THE ANTRUSTION SUMMONED TO APPEAR IN COURT (*ghalmalta*)

1. If an antrustion wishes to summon another antrustion to court (*admallare*) in some cause, wherever he can find him he ought with witnesses to summon him [to come] before a judge within seven days to respond or be present before the judge in that cause which is charged against him. And if he [the man summoned] does not come there or if he delays to come, he who summoned him to court should again set a day for him [to come to court] (*solsatire*); and after fourteen days he should summon him again (*iterata vice*) to respond to the court or be present in a place where antrustions owe their responsibilities (*mitthiu redebent*).

[1. If an antrustion wishes to summon another antrustion to court in some cause, wherever he can find him he ought with witnesses to summon him within seven days to come before the judge or respond in court concerning the case which is charged against him. If he does not come there or he delays in coming, he who summoned him to court should again set a day for him [to come to court] (*solsatire*). And afterwards he should summon him again to come to court in fourteen days to give a response.]

2. And if the man summoned comes to the place, then he who called him to court, if the case is such a minor one that the composition involved is less than thirty-five solidi, should offer oath (*videredum* or *wedredo*) with six oathhelpers. And afterwards he who had been summoned, if he believes it proper for him to do so in such a case, shall absolve himself with the oaths of twelve oathhelpers.

3. But if it is a more serious case, one where he who is found guilty will be liable to pay thirty-five solidi or more (but less than forty-five), he who summoned him to court shall offer oath (*videredum* or *wedredo*) with nine oathhelpers. And he who was summoned, if he recognizes it as proper for himself to do so, shall absolve himself with oaths given for him by eighteen oathhelpers.

4. If indeed it is such a case that the composition is forty-five solidi or more—up to the amount of the wergeld (*ad leudem*)—he who summoned him to court shall offer oath with twelve oathhelpers; and he who was summoned to court, if he knows that it is proper for him to do so, can absolve himself with oaths given by twenty-five oathhelpers.

[4. If indeed it is such a case that the composition is forty-five solidi or more—up to the amount of the wergeld (*ad leudem*)—he who summoned [the others] to court shall offer oath with twelve; and he who was summoned, if he knows that he is innocent, shall absolve himself with oaths given by twenty-five.]

5. But if a man has summoned someone to court in a suit involving a judgment that is the amount of the wergeld (*leudem*), he who summoned him should offer oath (*vidrido* or *wedredo iurare*) with twelve; and if he [who was summoned] neglects to come to court or does not want to place his hand in the cauldron, he [who summoned] should heat up the cauldron after fourteen days.

6. If it is an antrustion who is not able to absolve himself by oath in the case described above involving the payment of wergeld, or who refuses to put his hand in the cauldron or neglects to come to court, then he who summoned him shall on that day summon him again (*solem illi collocet*) to come to court in forty days. If he does not come there, then he who summoned him shall summon him again (*solem illi collocet*). And after fourteen days he should summon him into the presence of the king and have twelve there who in individual turn offer oath that they were there when he had summoned [the antrustion] to court (*ad mithio*) in fourteen days and [that one] gave neither oath nor his hand [in this case involving] the payment of wergeld.

And let there be three others who will say that he [the summoner] had set a day (*solem collocasset*) in forty days [i.e., had summoned him again to appear in forty days] and that one in no way conducted himself according to the laws about antrustions summoned to court.

Let him [the summoner] offer three witnesses who will say how he had summoned him [the antrustion] to come into the presence of the king. These nine witnesses should offer oath as we have said above that he did not come then. Likewise on that day when he still had not come, he set a day (*collocat ei solem*) for him [i.e., he summoned him again] and those three witnesses were there where he issued the summons. Then when he who summoned him [the antrustion] has done all these things and he who was summoned to court will not come or behave according to law, the king before whom he had been summoned shall put him outside his protection (*extra sermonem suum*). Then that one [summoned] and all his possessions will be liable; and whoever feeds or offers him hospitality, even if it is his own wife, shall be liable to pay fifteen solidi until he pays in composition everything charged against him by law.

[6. If it is an antrustion who is not able to absolve himself by oath in the case described above involving the payment of wergeld, or who refuses to put his hand in the cauldron or neglects to come to court, then he who summoned him shall on that day summon him again (*solem illi collocet*) to come to court in forty days. If he does not come there, then he who summoned him shall summon him again (*solem collocet*). And after fourteen days he should summon him [the antrustion] into the presence of the king and provide witnesses who will offer oath three times each that they were there when he [the summoner] admonished him and set a day for him (*solem collocasset*) [i.e., summoned him to court] in fourteen days and that one in this case involving the payment of wergeld did not absolve himself by oath or place his hand in the cauldron. And likewise let him [who summoned] have three other witnesses who will say that, a day having been set for forty days hence, the antrustion summoned in no way [performed] as provided by the laws.

And for a third time he [the summoner] shall likewise present three witnesses who will say how he had summoned him [the antrustion] to come into the presence of the king; and these nine witnesses, as said above, should offer oath that he [the antrustion] did not come there. Likewise when he did not come on that day, he summoned him (*collocet ei solem*) again and those three witnesses were there when he set the day for [i.e., summoned] him (*sol collocabatur*).

If he who summoned him [the antrustion] to court has done all these things, and he who was summoned still will not come to court, then the king before whom he was summoned shall put him outside his protection; and whoever feeds him or offers him hospitality, even if it is his own wife, shall be liable to pay fifteen solidi, until he makes composition for all those things charged against him by law.]

7. If an antrustion summons another antrustion to court for any cause or asks him to be an oathhelper, and if he has not summoned him according to law, he shall be liable to pay fifteen solidi in addition to what the law provides for cases not completed within a year.

8. If an antrustion bears witness against another antrustion, he shall be liable to pay fifteen solidi.

LXXIV

If anyone destroys a house by force, and if this house is proved to have had props (*ebrius*) for supporting the roof, and if it is proved against him that he presumed to do this, he shall be liable to pay forty-five solidi [in addition to paying the value of the house plus a payment for the time its use was lost].

[If anyone forcefully demolishes another's house, and the house is proved to have had props (*iberus*) for supporting the roof, he who has done this shall be liable to pay eighteen hundred denarii (i.e., thirty solidi). And if he presumes to take away something from that house in a cart, he shall be liable to pay twelve hundred denarii (i.e., thirty solidi) in addition to the above sum and in addition to a payment for the time its use was lost.]

LXXV

[CONCERNING HIM WHO TAKES A LIVING MAN DOWN FROM A GALLOWS (*furca*)]

1. If anyone presumes to take down a living man from a gallows (*furca*), he who carries him away and it is proved against him shall either lose his life for him or pay two hundred solidi.[75]
2. But if anyone takes down a man already dead from the gallows without the consent of the judge or the agreement of the man whose case it is, he who presumed to take him down will be liable to pay according to Salic law whatever amount the Salic law decrees for the crime for which the man was hung.[76]

LXXVI

CONCERNING LAWFUL DELAYS (*agsoniis*)

This should be observed: If anyone burns down a house and he does not have the property whereby he can replace that which was destroyed (*liberavit*), if illness detains him or by chance he has at his house a close relative who is dead, or he is delayed by a royal commission, he can be excused for one of these delays (*sunnis*) if it can be proved.

[This should be observed in the case where a man burns down another man's house and he does not have the property with which to replace that which he has destroyed. If he has been summoned into court and the one who has been summoned does not come, if illness or a royal commission detains him or by chance he has at his house a close relative who is dead, for one of these reasons for delay a man can be excused. Otherwise he must make composition with his life or be liable to pay two hundred solidi.]

LXXVII

[CONCERNING HIM WHO RESIDES IN ANOTHER MAN'S HOUSE]

1. If anyone resides in his house with another freeman and another freeman voluntarily and not by chance sends or throws a stone over his roof, and this is proved against him, for the contempt of him [who owns the house] and of other freemen [who reside therein], he and others, if they were with him, each one of them will be liable to pay fifteen solidi.

[1. If anyone resides in his house with a freeman, and another freeman deliberately throws a stone on his roof, then he [who threw the stone] and each other person found guilty will each pay nine solidi composition on account of the insult to him [who owns the house] and to the others residing in the house.]

2. But if it was a half-free man (*letus*) who presumed to do this, he shall be liable to pay seven and one-half solidi.

[2. If it is certain who threw or did this, he will be liable to pay seven solidi composition.]

LXXVIII

If a freeman throws another freeman into a well or pit and puts him there in order to kill him, if [the man thrown] has been found there where he cannot escape [before he dies], then he who commits this crime and it is proved against him shall be liable to pay two hundred solidi.

[If anyone throws a man into a well and he escapes living from that place, he [who threw him] shall be liable to pay four thousand denarii (i.e., one hundred solidi). But if the man dies in the well (called *musthest* in the

Malberg gloss), he [who threw him] shall be liable to pay twenty-four thousand denarii (i.e., six hundred solidi).]

Here Ends Book I. II Begins.

CAPITULARY II

The Pact Issued by Kings Childebert and Chlotar for Keeping the Peace[77]

THE DECREE OF KING CHILDEBERT

Because the madness of many increases and the frightfulness of evil grows, it is necessary [to issue this edict] so good order can be reestablished. Therefore, in the presence of ourselves and the greater persons (*maiores*) of the Frankish palace, it is decreed that whoever after this decree [is issued] is proved to be a thief shall lose his life.

LXXIX

IF A FREEMAN IS ACCUSED OF THEFT

If anyone accuses a freeman of theft and that one denies it, let the truth be proved through twelve oathhelpers (*iuratores*), half chosen by him who was charged with the theft; and [if the accusation is proved against him] let him make amends for the theft if he has the means. And if he does not have the means [to make amends for his crime], let him be presented to his relatives at three courts and if they will not redeem him, he shall pay with his life.

LXXX

CONCERNING A CONCEALED THEFT

If anyone tries to conceal a theft and secretly pays composition without [the judgment of] a judge, both he who made [the composition] and he who received it are thieves.

LXXXI

CONCERNING THE MAN WHOSE HAND IS BURNED IN THE ORDEAL (i.e., THE MAN PROVED GUILTY BY THE ORDEAL).

If a freeman is accused of theft and having been charged burns his hand at the ordeal [i.e., he is proved guilty by the ordeal], let him make composition for the theft for which he was charged.

LXXXII

LET SLAVES BE SENT TO THE ORDEAL BY LOT (*ad sortem*)[78]

1. If a slave is accused of theft, let his master be required to present him in court in twenty days, and if the matter is doubtful let him [the slave] be sent to the ordeal by lot. But if he delays presenting himself in court (*detricaverit*) with legitimate excuses (*sunnis*), let another court be held in twenty days and let the prosecutor of the cause offer three [witnesses] similar to himself and three other selected [witnesses] who will offer oath before the court that everything has been done that the Salic law prescribes. And if the slave's lord does not present his slave, he [the lord] shall make composition according to law for the crime of which he [the slave] was accused and thus make an end to this case concerning his slave (*de servo cessionem faciat*).
2. If the slave has stolen (*involaverit*) less than a triens and chooses the wrong lot (*mala sorte*) [i.e., fails the ordeal], the slave's lord shall pay three solidi and the slave receive three hundred lashes.

LXXXIII

CONCERNING HIM WHO HOLDS ANOTHER MAN'S BONDSMEN (*mancipia*) ILLEGALLY

1. If anyone illegally holds another man's bondsmen (*mancipia*) and does not return them within forty days, he shall be guilty of stealing the bondsmen.

2. If a half-free man (*ledus*) is charged with something for which he is sent to the ordeal by lot (*ad sortem ambulaverit*) and chooses the wrong lot [i.e., fails the ordeal], let him compound half the amount of a freeman and give six oathhelpers, half of whom were selected by himself.

Here Begins Book III.

THE DECREE OF KING CHLOTAR

LXXXIV

It is decreed that the hundreds (*centenas*) shall exercise watchfulness whenever the night watch does not seize thieves, their crimes neglected as a result of some collusion. Let him who has lost property receive its full value from his hundred; and let the thief be pursued and, if he appears in another hundred, let [that hundred] escort him [back] and be warned that if it [the second hundred] neglects to do so, it will be condemned to pay fifteen solidi. Indeed, he who lost [the property] shall without doubt receive [its value] from that hundred [to which the thief fled], which is the second or third. If the track of the thief is proved either at the present time or at a long time in the future, if he who pursues the thief catches him, he shall receive the whole composition for him. If he is found by someone in trust (*per truste*), that person shall have half the composition and exact the full value from the thief.

LXXXV

If anyone finds stolen goods (*furtum*) in another man's house that is under lock and key, the owner of the house shall make composition with his life.[79]

LXXXVI

If anyone is taken anywhere with stolen goods, he shall be subjected to the above law. If he is accused on suspicion, he shall be put to the ordeal by lot (*ad sortem veniat*). If he chooses the wrong lot (*malam sortem priserit*) [i.e., fails the ordeal], he shall be a thief. Nevertheless each party shall select three men each [to observe the ordeal] so that there can be no collusion.

LXXXVII

CONCERNING JUDICIAL PROOF FOR DIFFERENT KINDS OF SLAVES

If slaves of the church, of the fisc, or of anyone else are accused by anyone of some crime, let them go to the ordeal by lot (*ad sortem veniat*), or let them appeal (*promoveatur*) to the people, or let their value (price—*pretius*) be pledged (*reformetur*) by their lords. If it [the accusation] is proved, they shall be subjected to punishment.

LXXXVIII

CONCERNING THE PENALTY FOR ACCUSED SLAVES

If the slave of a powerful person (*de potentibus*) who possesses many things is suspected of having committed a crime, in each case let the slave's master agree in the presence of witnesses that he will present him [the slave] before the judge within twenty days. If the slave's lord has not presented him in the agreed time, some collusion intervening, he shall pay the fine and composition (*inter fredo et faido*) in accordance with the nature of the charge. If the slave flees before his lord is warned, his lord shall make restitution in full for the crime; and when the slave is found, his lord shall give up the slave to be punished.

LXXXIX

If anyone secretly accepts from a thief composition for stolen property, let them both be guilty of theft. Thieves must be presented before the judges; no one shall presume to conceal anyone guilty of theft. He who does this shall be guilty of the same offense.

LXL

CONCERNING THIEVES WHO FLEE TO A CHURCH

1. It has been agreed with the bishops that no one shall presume to drag a thief or other guilty person from the porch (*de atrio*) of a church; [if a man does this], he shall be punished according to the canons (*canonibus*).[80] If there are churches that do not have enclosed porches, then an arpennis[81] of ground on either side of the wall should be regarded as the porch; no one because of eagerness for his task may take a fugitive out of the aforesaid place. If he does this and is caught, he shall be condemned to a fitting punishment.

2. But if a slave abandoning his lord flees to a church where his lord has arrived first, let him remain there unpunished; and if a price can be agreed on thereafter, let it not be refused. But if he [the lord] has not been given the price demanded for his slave and he [the slave] flees [to someone else], let him who will not return him pay his price (*pretium*); afterwards if he is found and it is agreeable, let him make restitution for (*reformetur*) the price received by his lord. We decree this concerning fiscal slaves (*fiscalibus*) and [concerning the slaves] of all lords.

LXLI

THAT SELECTED HUNDREDMEN (*centenarii*) WILL BE PLACED IN TRUST

In order to keep the peace we order that selected hundredmen be placed in trust so that through their faith and care the abovesaid peace may be observed.[82]

LXLII

And because in appeasing God the affection of brotherhood guards an unbroken chain between us, the hundredmen or those said to be in trust shall have the right to pursue thieves between provincial communities and to follow marked tracks, and let the suit remain in trust where the violence was done, just as has been said, so that he [the thief] will hasten to make full restitution to him who lost his property, provided nevertheless that he pursued the thief. If he [the thief] has been found by someone in trust, let half the composition and the payment for the time the use of the property was lost be paid to him who lost it from the property of the thief. He who followed the thief shall receive a full composition and payment or whatever has been lost; nevertheless the fine (*fredus*) shall be reserved for the judge in whose province the thief is.

LXLIII

He who following tracks or pursuing a thief does not wish to come in [before the court], if he has been summoned and no legitimate excuse detains him, shall judicially be condemned to pay five solidi.

Indeed we have established this pact to keep the peace in the name of God and it is our wish that these prescribed things be observed perpetually; and let it be known that if any judge presumes to violate this decree, he will be subjected to the loss of his life; and we order all things said above to remain as before.

Book III of the Salic Law Ends.

In What Manner the Collection [of Laws] Within is Seen to Contain Four Books

The first king of the Franks determined and made provisions for those matters to be adjudicated in Titles I to LXV;[83] some time thereafter with his optimates he added Titles LXVI to LXXVIII. A long time later King Childebert[84] considered what should be added and thus provided the titles from LXXVIII to LXXXIII, which are recognized to have been worthily added there, and he further entrusted these writings to his brother Chlotar.[85] Chlotar willingly received these titles from his older brother and afterward, since he had taken over his realm, he determined that which he ought to add and arrange more fully, which became Titles LXXXIII to LXLIII. Later with his brother he issued these laws revised. And it was agreed between them that all things should remain as previously provided.

1. King Theuderic reigned seventeen years.[86]
2. King Chlodovec ruled three years.[87]
3. King Childebert ruled seventeen years.[88]

4. King Dagobert ruled five years.[89]
5. King Chilperic ruled five years.[90]
6. Likewise King Theodoric ruled seventeen years.[91]
7. For seven years no king ruled.[92]
8. King Childeric ruled eight years.[93]
In sum, there are 78 years.

CAPITULARY III

LXLIV

CONCERNING CONTEMPT FOR THE LAW (*mitio fristatito*).

If anyone presumes to detain or strike someone in trust (*trustem*) while he is following tracks, he [who does this] shall be liable to pay twenty-five hundred denarii (i.e., sixty-two and one-half solidi).

LXLV

IF ANYONE CUTS A MAN DOWN (*abaterit*) FROM THE GALLOWS (*furcas*) WITHOUT THE CONSENT OF HIS LORD OR OF THE JUDGE

If anyone without the consent of the judge cuts a [dead] man down (*abaterit*) from a gallows or presumes to take him down (*reponere*) from the branch where he was hanged, he shall be liable to pay twelve hundred denarii (i.e., thirty solidi).[94]

LXLVI

CONCERNING HIM WHO STEALS A LIVING MAN FROM THE GALLOWS

If anyone presumes to take down or carry away a man still alive from a gallows (*furca*) (called *morchamo* in the Malberg gloss), he shall be liable to pay four thousand denarii (i.e., one hundred solidi).[95]

LXLVII

CONCERNING HIM WHO PRESUMES TO CUT THE HAIR OF ANOTHER MAN'S CHILD

1. If anyone presumes to cut the hair of a boy without the consent of his relatives (called *vidridarchi* in the Malberg gloss), he shall be liable to pay eighteen hundred denarii (i.e., forty-five solidi).[96]
2. If a man cuts a girl's hair without the consent of her relatives, he shall be liable to pay four thousand denarii (i.e., one hundred solidi).[97]

LXLVIII

CONCERNING THE WOMAN WHO JOINS HERSELF TO HER SLAVE

1. If a woman joins herself in marriage with her own slave, the fisc shall acquire all her possessions and she herself will be outlawed (*aspellis*).
2. If one of her relatives kills her, nothing may be required from that relative or the fisc for her death. The slave shall be placed in the most severe torture, that is, he shall be placed on the wheel. And if one of the relatives of the woman gives her either food or shelter, he shall be liable to pay fifteen solidi.

LXLIX

CONCERNING PROCURERS (*conciliatoribus*)

1. If anyone procures another man's son or daughter for the purpose of marrying him or her off without the consent of the relatives, and if this is proved against him and the relatives suffer loss (*damnati fuerint*) from this, the procurers are indeed robbers or the companions of robbers and shall be condemned to death and the fisc shall acquire their property.
2. But robbers shall not suffer more than what was written in the law above.

C

CONCERNING THE WIDOW WHO WANTS TO GO TO ANOTHER HUSBAND[98]

1. If a widow after the death of her husband wants to go to another husband, first he who wishes to receive her must give a betrothal fine (*reipus*) for her according to law. And if the woman had children by her former husband, she ought to consult her children's relatives. If she had received twenty-five solidi as a dos [from her previous husband], she should give three solidi as a fee for release of her mundium (*achasium*) to the closest relatives of the dead husband; and if his [the husband's] father or mother is not alive, the *achasius* is owed to a brother of the dead man or to that nephew who is the son of his oldest brother. And if there are none of these, then the judge, that is the comes or count (*grafio*), should make inquiry concerning her and should place her in the king's protection (*verbum regis mittat*) and the fisc shall acquire the *achasius* which should have gone to the relatives of the dead husband.

2. If indeed she received sixty-two and one-half solidi as a dos, let six solidi be given as the *achasius*, that is, for each ten solidi, one shall be given as the *achasius*, and [the remainder of] the dos which the earlier husband had given her will be claimed and defended by his children, after the mother's death, without any share going to him [the second husband]. The mother may not presume to sell or to give away any of this dos. But if the woman does not have children by the former husband and wishes to enter another marriage with her dos, she must give the *achasius*, as said above. And afterwards let her cover a bench and prepare the bed with coverlet; and with nine witnesses let her summon the relatives of the dead husband and say: "You are my witnesses that I have given the *achasius* in order to have peace with his [my former husband's] relatives, and I leave here the covered bed and the worthy bedspread, the prepared bench and an armchair that I brought with me from my father's house." Then she may give herself to another husband with two parts of her dos.

3. But if she does not do this, she loses the two parts of her dos and in addition she shall be liable to pay sixty-two and one-half solidi to the fisc.

4. Concerning half-free women (*militunias vel litas*), this law should be observed by half.

CI

CONCERNING MEN WHO TAKE SECOND OR OTHER WIVES

1. If anyone has lost his wife and wishes to have another, he may not give to the second wife the dos which he had given to the first wife. But if her [the former wife's] children are still small, he may make decisions carefully concerning the property or dos of his former wife until they [the children] come of age; but even so, he must not presume to sell or to give away any of this property.

2. If indeed he has no children by the former wife, the closest relatives of the dead woman shall recover two parts of the dos and leave two beds, two covered benches and two armchairs. If they do not do this, they may recover only one-third of the dos; nevertheless [it shall be done thus] if they have not come to an agreement beforehand concerning the transfer (*per adfatimus*) [of the dos].

CII

CONCERNING A MAN KILLED BETWEEN TWO VILLAGES (*villas*)

1. If a man is killed near a village (*villa*) or between two close neighboring villages—in a place where the homicide was not observed—the judge, that is the *comes* or *grafio*, should go to the place and sound his horn there. If someone comes who identifies the body, let it be brought to the notice of the relatives. But if no-one comes who identifies the body, then those neighbors in whose field or on whose boundary the body was found should make a platform (*bargo*) five feet in height and raise the body on to it in the presence of the judge. And the judge should announce and declare: "This man was killed in your field or on your boundary line (*vestibulum*); I call you to witness that he should not be removed for seven days, and I summon you to court concerning this homicide—you should come to the next court and you will be told what you ought legally to do."

2. Then those neighbors to whom this announcement was made by the judge, if they are of the better class (*meliores*), shall clear (*exuent*) themselves with sixty-five oathhelpers within forty days [by offering oath] that neither had they killed him nor do they know who killed him. Neighbors

who are lesser people (*minoflidis*) should each present fifteen oathhelpers who shall offer oath as stated above. If they do not do this within forty days, they must make satisfaction for the dead person as the law requires.
3. If indeed they offer oath as stated above and clear themselves (*idonia-verint*) by means of such an oath, no composition should be required of them.

CIII

CONCERNING PLEDGES (*pignoribus*)

If anyone through ignorance takes a pledge (*pignoraverit*) from his debtor without a judgment before he has called him to court (*eum nestigan the thigio*), he shall lose his debt; and, in addition, if he has taken the pledge with evil intent, he shall make composition according to law, this is, he must return the full value [of the pledge] and in addition be liable to pay fifteen solidi.

CIV

CONCERNING THE WOMAN WHO HAS HER HAIR CUT OR PULLED

1. If anyone pulls a woman's hair so that her hood (*obbonis*) falls to the ground, he shall be liable to pay fifteen solidi.
2. But if he undoes her headband so that her hair falls to her shoulders, he shall be liable to pay thirty solidi.
3. If a slave strikes a free woman or pulls her hair, he shall lose his hand or pay five solidi.
4. He who strikes a pregnant free woman in the stomach or in the kidney with fist or foot, and she does not lose her fetus but she is weighed down almost to death on account of this, shall be liable to pay two hundred solidi.[99]
5. If the fetus emerges dead but she herself lives, he [who struck her] shall be liable to pay six hundred solidi.
6. But if the woman dies because of this, he shall be liable to pay nine hundred solidi.

7. If the woman who died had been placed under the protection of the king for any reason, he [who struck her] shall be liable to pay twelve hundred solidi.

8. If the child which was aborted was a girl, he shall pay twenty-four hundred solidi.

9. In the case of half-free women (*militunias vel letas*) or Roman women, half of these amounts should be observed.

10. If a man strikes a female slave and her fetus is killed, if it was a little girl, he must pay sixty-two and one-half solidi and one denarius as composition.

11. If the female slave kept her lord's storeroom or workroom (*cellarium aut genitium*), he must pay one hundred solidi and a denarius as composition for her.

CV

CONCERNING HIM WHO PRESUMES TO SPEAK IN ANOTHER'S CAUSE

1. If anyone [presumes to speak in another's cause] and it was not asked of him nor was he adopted by having a stick thrown in his lap (*laesverpita fuerit*) and he cannot justify himself, he shall be liable to pay fifteen solidi.

2. Afterwards the man whose cause it is may take his suit to court according to the laws.

CAPITULARY IV

Decree of King Chilperic For Keeping the Peace[100]

CVI

Deliberating in the name of God, it was agreed together with our highest-born optimates and antrustions and all of our people that our inheritance does not extend beyond the Garonne River; wherever in our region an inheritance is to be given, that inheritance ought to be given and received just as in the other places like Thérouanne (*Turrovaninsis*).[101]

CVII

It was likewise agreed that we would grant the betrothal fine (*reipus*) to all our men (*leodibus*) so that breach of the peace (*scandalum*) will not be created in our area for some minor matter.

CVIII

In like manner it was pleasing and agreed that if a man had neighbors but after his death sons and daughters remained, as long as there were sons, they should have the land, just as the Salic law provides. And if the sons are already dead, then a daughter may receive the land just as the sons would have done had they lived. But if she is dead and a brother survives, then the brother shall have the land, not the neighbors. And if the brother dies and no other brother survives, then a sister may succeed to possession of that land.[102]

CIX

Concerning ditches and individual lands, that those men who have inherited them shall keep the custom of our father which they had concerning that property.

CX

And likewise it was agreed that if a man takes a wife and they have no children, if the man dies and the wife survives, then the woman shall have half of her dos (*dotem*) and the relatives of the dead husband half; if the woman dies and there are no children, the husband likewise shall have half the dos and the relatives of the woman half.

CXI

In such wise it was pleasing and agreed that if a slave kills a freeman, then the slave's lord may take oath with six oathhelpers that his knowledge is clean—he did not advise the slave nor was the deed his wish—and then he may give up the slave to vengeance. And if he is not able to hand over the slave, he may offer oath and give a pledge that he [the slave] is not there where he can touch him nor does he know where he can get him so that he might surrender his slave to the relatives of the dead man so that they might do to him whatever they wished, and he [the slave's lord] will be absolved.

CXII

It is likewise decreed that whoever has been summoned to court and does not have witnesses to the truth that he may bring before the court and it is necessary that he give a pledge that he will go to the ordeal but he does not have that with which to give a pledge, he shall hold a stick (*fistu-cam*) in his left hand and remove it with his right.

CXIII

It is decreed in like manner that if a slave is accused of a theft that involves the ordeal by lot,[103] the slave's lord should send the slave to the ordeal within ten days. If he has not sent him there in ten days, then he should send him there in forty-two days, and then the slave should come there for the ordeal; and let him do justice to him who suffered the theft with six solidi. And if he has not come in forty-two days and no legitimate reason for delay is given, then the slave will be judged guilty and the case will not go further against his lord except that it is the law concerning the slave that either the slave himself be given up or his lord pay composition for the slave, that is twelve solidi in addition to return of the thing stolen [or its value] plus a payment for the time its use was lost. And if a legitimate excuse has delayed him for forty-two days, then let him be brought before the court in eighty-four days. And if he [the lord] has not brought him [the slave] there, then he [the slave] will be judged guilty, as said before; if he does not have a legitimate excuse for forty-two days, he shall pay forty solidi composition. And if he will not give a pledge or pay composition for this thing within forty-two days, then he may ask that one who is concerned to pay within fourteen days, as said before. And if he will not pay in fourteen days, then let him ask [again] in seven days. And if in that seven days he has not paid composition or given a pledge, then let him go to the next court in the presence of the sitting and speaking rachimburgi that they should hear him, and let the count be summoned there with the stick (*fistuco*) placed before him, and let him go and take as much from his property as the rachimburgi heard before. And let the count with the seven rachimburgi—either good believable antrustions or those who know the causes of action—go to the house of that one and set the amount that the count should take. And if the count has not been summoned before the sitting rachimburgi, let him not presume to go there. If he has been summoned and does not wish to go there, let him be liable [to pay] with his life. And if the count presumes to take more than the amount set or the law allows, let him know that he will suffer the loss of his life. And if he [the count] does not deny it, let him who brought the charge bring the seven summoned (*ferrebannitus*) rachimburgi who heard the case earlier to be present before us. And if the seven cannot come and legitimate excuses prevent them and all cannot come, then let three of them come and speak on oath and state the legitimate reasons for delay on behalf of their colleagues. If neither seven nor three rachimburgi have been able to give [legitimate excuses], let the count and he who accepted it return the property of that one from whom it was taken contrary to law and justice and let him who brought the charge with evil intent pay composition to him to whom the property belonged.

Whenever a freeman has been summoned to court in a cause or forceful action of any kind, let him in like manner do just as the law directs. If the evil man who committed the deed does not have the property with which to pay composition for his evil deed, the count should follow the law, as we have heard before, and [the perpetrator of the deed] should be summoned and heard in three courts in the presence of the rachimburgi so that his relatives may redeem him from their own property, if they wish, and let them know that if they do not wish to do so, he will come into our presence in a fourth court; and we order that he [the perpetrator] be handed over to him who bore the deed to do with as he wishes. He who summons the court should lead him to us and follow the antrustions according to law; let him do the law within eighty-four days of the summons, just as it is written above.[104]

CXIV

Among those things announced in churches, it should be announced to those living around where the court will meet.

CXV

If anyone has a case to bring before the courts, let him make his case known to his neighbors and let him make his oath (sworn declaration—*videredum*) before the rachimburgi; and if they have some doubt about this, let the case be called to court. But let him not presume to go to court before this; and if he does presume to go to court before this, let him lose his case. But if he is indeed an evil man who committed his evil deed in the district and does not have where he lives that with which to make composition, and he has fled to the forest, and neither agent (*agens*) nor relatives can lead him forth into our presence, then let the agent and him to whom the evil was done accuse him before us; and we will place that one outside of our protection (*nostro sermone*) so that whoever finds him can kill him in any way without fear.

CXVI

Concerning theft, it is agreed that it will be observed just as the custom was in the time of our mother's brother and of our father; let it be done thus and let evil men be restrained.[105]

CAPITULARY V

CXVII

1. He who kills a servant (*puerum*) of the king or freedman (*libertum*) shall be liable to pay one hundred solidi.
2. He who kills either a free or tributary (*tributarium*) Roman or one who is a soldier shall be liable to pay one hundred solidi.[106]

CXVIII

He who injures a hunting decoy-deer (*stadalem vaidaris*) or a doe assigned to a stag (*bovum cervi atribute*) shall be liable to pay eighteen hundred denarii (i.e., forty-five solidi).[107]

CXIX

1. He who steals a hobble (*pedicam*) or takes a net or a fish basket snare (*nassam*) from a boat shall be liable to pay twelve hundred denarii (i.e., thirty solidi).[108]
2. He who steals a fish from a boat or from a net shall be liable to pay six hundred denarii (i.e., fifteen solidi).
3. If a man finds a trap (*pedicam*) that holds a hunted animal or [an animal that has been shot by] a poisoned arrow (*sagitatum detoxirum*) or if he tries to hide an animal that the dogs have chased or steals a hunted animal from its hanging place (*bargo*) or from a house (*de mansionem*), he shall be liable to pay twelve hundred denarii (i.e., thirty solidi).[109]
4. He who steals a suckling piglet from an enclosure (*de rane*) shall be liable to pay four hundred denarii (i.e., ten solidi).[110]

CXX

He who challenges another man to trial by hot water (*ad calidam*), unless he has the permission of the king (*praeter evisionem dominicam*), shall be liable to pay six hundred denarii (i.e., fifteen solidi).

CXXI

If anyone's male slave is charged with killing another man's female slave, he [the slave's lord] shall be liable to pay six hundred denarii (i.e., fifteen solidi) plus the price at which the slave (*mancipius*) is valued. If it is charged [that he killed] a skilled female slave (i.e., one skilled in handwork—*ambahtonia*) or a pigherder or a slave craftsman (*artificiis*), similar provisions should be observed. If it is charged [that he killed] laborers (*operariis*) or lesser slaves (*minoribus mancipiis*), he [the slave's lord] shall be liable to pay six hundred denarii (i.e., fifteen solidi) [plus the value of the slave].

CXXII

If anyone knocks a swineherd from his way or steals wood from the woods or from the woodpile that another man has cut up, or carries it off in his wagon, for either case he shall be liable to pay six hundred denarii (i.e., fifteen solidi).[111]

CXXIII

If anyone takes a boat by force, he shall be liable to pay six hundred denarii (i.e., fifteen solidi).[112]

CXXIV

If a freeman does business with another man's slave without the knowledge of his lord, or if he does business with a freedman (*liberto*) in a village (*villa*) without the knowledge of that one's lord (called *theolasinia* in the Malberg gloss), he shall be liable to pay six hundred denarii (i.e., fifteen solidi).[113]

CXXV

He who ties up others without cause and it is proved against him shall be lible to pay two hundred denarii (i.e., five solidi).[114]

CXXVI

He who gleans (*glenaverit*) another man's harvest without his consent shall be liable to pay six hundred denarii (i.e., fifteen solidi).

CXXVII

1. He who robs a dwelling or eats anything from a dwelling shall be liable to pay six hundred denarii (i.e., fifteen solidi).
2. He who does something on this dwelling or plot of land (*sortem*) with a harrow or plow, and it is proved against him (called *acrebrasta* in the Malberg gloss), shall be liable to pay six hundred denarii (i.e., fifteen solidi).[115]

CXXVIII

If anyone steals another man's property saying that it is his own, and he is not able to prove it, he shall be liable to pay fifteen solidi to him from whom he has stolen it.

CXXIX

If anyone breaks into a garden or turnip field (*nabinam*), he shall be liable to pay six hundred denarii (i.e., fifteen solidi).[116]

CXXX

1. If a freedman rapes another man's freedwoman, he shall be liable to pay eight hundred denarii (i.e., twenty solidi).
2. In addition he shall pay ten solidi to the count (*graphione*), and the woman shall be returned to the custody of her lord.
3. If he [the freedman] rapes a free woman, he must make composition with his life.

CXXXI

1. If anyone accuses another of having committed perjury and he can prove it, he who committed perjury shall pay fifteen solidi as composition.
2. But if he [who made the accusation] cannot prove it, he who spoke such a blameworthy thing shall pay fifteen solidi and afterwards, if he dares, he may fight.[117]

CXXXII

If a man has witnesses who are proved to be false, [each of them] shall sustain a fine (*multa*) of fifteen solidi. He who accused them [the witnesses] of giving false testimony shall put his hand in the cauldron [i.e., submit to the ordeal of hot water], and if he takes his hand out clean (*sana*), they shall sustain that fine noted above. But if his hand sustains a dirty burn (*conburet*), he [who accused the witnesses of a false testimony] shall sustain a fine of fifteen solidi [to each of the witnesses].

CXXXIII

If anyone takes another man's wife while her husband is still living and is brought to court (*mallobergo*),[118] he shall be liable to pay eight thousand denarii (i.e., two hundred solidi).

CAPITULARY VI

Here Begins the Decree of Childebert,[119] King of the Franks

Illustrious men. In the name of God on every Kalends of March we together with our optimates from every condition have made inquiry [concerning conditions in our realm]; we wish this notice to come to the attention of each and all.

I

With the help of God at *Antonaco* on the Kalends of March in the twentieth year of our reign [we issue this decree]. (Andernach 594)
1. Let it be observed that grandchildren (*nepotes*) of a dead father or mother born from their son (*filio*) or daughter (*filia*) shall come to the property of the grandparents (*aviaticas*) together with their uncles (*avunculus*) and aunts (*amitas*) just as if their own mother or father lived. It is pleasing that

this should be observed concerning such grandchildren born of a son or daughter, however many have been born from brother or sister.[120]

2. Afterward together with our people (*leudis*) it was agreed as follows. We decree that no one be joined in an incestuous marriage, that is, [in marriage with] the wife of a brother or with the sister of a wife or with the wife of an uncle (*patruo*) or with consanguinous relatives (*parenti consanguineos*). If anyone marries his father's wife, let him lose his life. And concerning marriages already established that are now seen to be incestuous, we order that they be corrected by proclamation of the bishop. He who does not wish to listen to the bishop will be excommunicated; he shall sustain this condition perpetually before God and be a stranger in all things from our palace. And he who does not wish to accept relief (*medicamenta*) from his priest shall lose all his property to his legitimate relatives.

II

Likewise from Maestricht (*Treiectum* 595)[121]

1. It is decreed that when a man possesses for ten years in unbroken succession a slave or field or any other property belonging to [i.e., by tenure from] one duke or one judge, no one has the right of interference except that in the case of orphans we concede the right [to reclaim] up to twenty years. If anyone presumes to interfere [after these time limits], he shall be liable to pay fifteen solidi, and will lose the property which he [seized] and put in a third party's hand (*intertiavit*). In other cases a legal claim (*lex*) is excluded by a thirty-year period unless an interregnum causes delay.

2. In like manner it was decreed on the Kalends of March in the presence of all that whoever presumes to commit *raptus*, a most grievous crime, shall suffer the loss of his life; and none of our optimates may entreat on behalf of that one, but each one will pursue him as an enemy of God. Whoever presumes to disobey our edict shall first be sent to the judge in whose district (*pago*) it is; that judge having collected aid shall kill the ravisher (*raptor*) or outlaw him (*forbatuos*). If he has sought refuge in a church, let him be given up by the bishop without a prayer and be sent into exile.[122] If the woman consented to her seizure (*raptum*), they shall both be sent into exile [if they had sought refuge in a church]; and if they are captured outside a church they shall both be killed and their property shall be acquired by their legitimate relatives or by the fisc.

3. Concerning homicides, we order that whoever by rashly daring deed kills another man without cause shall lose his life. He may not redeem himself with a price nor make composition. It is decreed that no one of his relatives or friends may aid him who resorts (*discendat*) to such a solution, but he who presumes to aid him shall compound his full wergeld, because it is just that he who is known to kill deserves (*discat*) to die.[123]

4. Concerning assault (*farfalio*) it is decreed that whoever presumes to threaten an assault in court, without a doubt shall pay his wergeld in composition, the assault not being restrained. Perhaps it may happen that the judge consents and receives the assailant to guard; let him sustain the loss of his life in all things.

5. Concerning thieves and malfactors, we decree that this be observed: if five or seven men of good faith without enmity intervening have said on oath [that someone] is a criminal (*criminosum*), just as he acted without law let him die without law.[124] If a judge has been convicted of releasing a seized thief, let him lose his life so that discipline will be observed among the people in all things.

III

Likewise on the Kalends of March at Cologne (*Colonia*).

1. It is fitting and we decree that every judge who hears of a criminal brigand should go to his house and tie him up there so that if he is a free Frank he can be directed into our presence and if he is a lesser person (*de leviores personas*), he can be hanged in that place.

2. He who does not wish to aid the hundredman or any other judge pursuing a malfactor is condemned to pay sixty solidi in all matters.

3. Whoever has a criminal slave and, when the judge asks for him, will not present him, shall pay his full wergeld in composition.

4. Likewise it is decreed that if there is a theft, the hundred (*centena*) will immediately restore the value in full and the hundredman shall institute a charge when the need of the hundred demands it.[125]

5. In like manner it is decreed that if a hundred, following a track, sends our faithful men [pursuing] that track into another hundred and they are unable to remove [the thief] from that other hundred, [the other hundred] must either return that convicted thief or immediately restore the full value [of the objects stolen] and establish [their own] innocence through the oaths of twelve persons.[126]

6. If a church slave or a fiscal slave commits a theft, he shall sustain punishment just as the slaves of other Franks.

7. It is pleasing that this be observed with regard to the Lord's day. If any freeman presumes to do any servile work on the Lord's day, except for that pertaining to cooking and eating, if he is a Salic Frank, he shall be liable to pay fifteen solidi. If he is a Roman, he shall pay seven and one-half solidi as compensation. If he is a slave, he shall pay three solidi or pay composition by his back [i.e., be flogged].

Asclepiode recognizes this.[127]

Auspiciously given at Cologne on the Kalends of March in the XXII year of our reign.

The Seven Types of Cases

I

[THE FIFTEEN SOLIDI CAUSES]

1. He who is summoned to court in accordance with royal justice and does not come, if a lawful excuse (*sunnis*) does not detain him, shall be liable to pay fifteen solidi.[128]
2. He who summons another man to court and does not come himself, if a lawful excuse does not detain him, shall be liable to pay fifteen solidi.[129]
3. He who steals a castrated pig (*porcellum tartussum*), that is up to one year old, [shall be liable to pay] fifteen solidi.[130]
4. He who steals a hawk from its perch shall be liable to pay fifteen solidi.[131]
5. If any man bars the road (*facit via latina*) to another man, he shall be liable to pay fifteen solidi.[132]
6. He who cuts off [another man's] middle finger shall be liable to pay fifteen solidi.[133]
7. He who strikes off [another man's] little finger [shall be liable to pay] fifteen solidi.[134]

II

THE THIRTY-FIVE SOLIDI CAUSES

1. If anyone finds another man's animals without a herder in his harvest and shuts them up so that no one knows they are inside, and if one of these animals dies, then he [who shut them up] will be liable to pay thirty-five solidi.[135]

2. If anyone steals a boat that is under lock and key, he shall be liable to pay thirty-five solidi.[136]

3. He who strikes off [another man's] second finger—the one he uses to release an arrow—[shall be liable to pay] thirty-five solidi.[137]

4. . . .

5. He who steals an ox [shall be liable to pay] thirty-five solidi.[138]

6. If a Frank cuts off the ear of another Frank, [he shall be liable to pay] thirty-five solidi.[139]

7. If anyone steals or hides a tame deer that has a brand, [he shall be liable to pay] thirty-five solidi.[140]

III

THE FORTY-FIVE SOLIDI CAUSES

1. He who cuts a boy's hair without the consent of his relatives shall be liable to pay forty-five solidi.[141]

2. He who steals a hawk kept under lock and key shall be liable to pay forty-five solidi.[142]

3. He who steals a small boat (*ascum*) kept under lock and key shall be liable to pay forty-five solidi.[143]

4. He who cuts hay on another man's meadow and carries the hay in his wagon from that place to his house and unloads it [shall be liable to pay] forty-five solidi.[144]

5. He who cuts off [another man's] thumb [shall be liable to pay] forty-five solidi.[145]

6. He who cuts off [another man's] nose [shall be liable to pay] forty-five solidi.[146]

7. If a man receives another man's fleeing slave (*mancipia*), [he shall be liable to pay] forty-five solidi.

IV

THE SIXTY-TWO AND ONE-HALF SOLIDI CAUSES

1. If anyone shoots at a man with a poisoned arrow and it misses, he shall be liable to pay sixty-two and one-half solidi.[147]
2. He who attacks another man with his weapons and tries to kill him, but is prevented [from doing it], shall be liable to pay sixty-two and one-half solidi.
3. If anyone secretly robs the body of a man who has been killed before it is placed in the ground, [he shall be liable to pay] sixty-two and one-half solidi.[148]
4. If anyone invades another man's place (*villam*), [he shall be liable to pay] sixty-two and one-half solidi.[149]
5. If anyone cuts another man's hand and the hand hangs crippled, [he shall be liable to pay] sixty-two and one-half [solidi].[150]
6. He who is secretly hired and having received payment tries to kill a man, and it is proved against him, [shall be liable to pay] sixty-two and one-half solidi.[151]

V

THE ONE HUNDRED SOLIDI CAUSES

1. He who digs up and despoils a dead body [shall be liable to pay] one hundred solidi.[152]
2. He who in theft robs a sleeping man [shall be liable to pay] one hundred solidi.[153]
3. He who kills a child in its mother's womb [shall be liable to pay] one hundred solidi.[154]
4. If any freeman sets another man's half-free man (*lidum*) free with a denarius in the presence of the king without the consent of his lord, [he shall be liable to pay] one hundred solidi.[155]
5. If anyone strikes off another man's hand or cuts out his tongue or castrates him or cuts through [his penis] incapacitating him, he shall be liable to pay one hundred solidi.[156]
6. He who [finds] a freeman without hands and feet whom his enemies have left on the road and kills him [shall be liable to pay] one hundred solidi.[157]

7. Likewise, whoever throws another man into the sea and that one escapes from it alive shall be liable to pay one hundred solidi.[158]

VI

THE TWO HUNDRED SOLIDI CAUSES

1. If anyone contrary to the order of the king presumes to block a man who has arranged to move and has the king's approval, [he shall be liable to pay] two hundred solidi.[159]

2. If anyone gives another man herbs to drink so that he dies, he shall be liable to pay two hundred solidi.[160]

3. If anyone steals a Frank and sells him, he shall be liable to pay two hundred solidi.[161]

4. If anyone kills a free girl, [he shall be liable to pay] two hundred solidi.[162]

5. If anyone sets fire to a basilica, [he shall be liable to pay] two hundred solidi.[163]

6. If anyone asks a count to seize another man's property and he has not summoned his adversary (*iactivum*) legally to court so that [the count] seizes [the property] unjustly before [the accused] has been summoned to court and given a pledge (*fides*), he [shall be liable to pay] two hundred solidi.[164]

7. He who on the road attacks a girl betrothed to another being led to her husband with her bridal train (*ducte*), and forcefully has intercourse with her [shall be liable to pay] two hundred solidi.[165]

VII

THE SIX HUNDRED SOLIDI CAUSES

1. He who kills a long-haired boy [shall be liable to pay] six hundred solidi.[166]

2. He who beats up a woman so that she dies [shall be liable to pay] six hundred solidi.

3. He who kills a free woman after she begins to have children [shall be liable to pay] six hundred solidi.[167]

4. He who kills a count (*grafione*) [shall be liable to pay] six hundred solidi.[168]

5. He who kills a sagibaron [shall be liable to pay] six hundred solidi.[169]
6. If anyone kills a Frank within four walls (*solia*), [he shall be liable to pay] six hundred solidi.[170]
7. If a Frank kills another Frank, [he shall be liable to pay] six hundred solidi.[171]

VIII

THE EIGHTEEN HUNDRED SOLIDI CAUSES

1. If anyone kills and murders a freeman in the army, he shall be liable to pay eighteen hundred solidi.[172]
2. If anyone kills and murders a count (*grafionem*), [he shall be liable to pay] eighteen hundred solidi.[173]
3. If anyone kills and murders a free woman who is able to have children, [he shall be liable to pay] eighteen hundred solidi.[174]
4. If anyone kills a long-haired boy and it is declared murder (*in mordrem miserit*), [he shall be liable to pay] eighteen hundred solidi.[175]
5. If anyone kills a bishop (*episcopum*) and it is declared murder (*in mordrem miserit*), [he shall be liable to pay] eighteen hundred solidi.[176]
6. If anyone on the road attacks and kills a legate (*legadario*) of the king and it is declared murder (*in mordrem miserit*), he shall be liable to pay eighteen hundred solidi.
7. If anyone attacks and kills an antrustion who is negotiating (*pagaverit*) between two kings and it is declared murder (*in mordrem miserit*), he shall be liable to pay eighteen hundred solidi.[177]

CAPITULARY VII[178]

In the Name of the Lord the *Capitula* [Interpretations] of the *Lex Salica* Begin

I

Concerning Title I of *Lex Salica*, that is, concerning the summons.

Concerning this title it has been established that he who has been summoned to court has forty days to appear. But if the count does not hold a court within that period of time, then the time is extended until the next meeting of the count's court and from then he is given seven days' space of time; thus not the exact span of time but the closest court of the count is conceded to him.

II

Concerning Title XI[179] of *Lex Salica*: if anyone kills another man's slave or sells or sends away a freeman, he shall be liable to pay fourteen hundred denarii (i.e., thirty-five solidi) in addition to return of the value of the person plus a payment for the time his labor was lost.

Concerning this title it has been judged by all that if a slave appears to have been sold unjustly or a freeman unjustly sent away, another person may not be restored in place of that one. Although others have said that a slave set free (*ingenuus dimissus fuerat*) ought not to go back to his original servitude, they [the judges] have judged that he should be restored to his original master and servitude.

III

Concerning Title XIV[180] of *Lex Salica*: if a freeman takes another man's female slave in marriage, he shall be associated with her in servitude.

Concerning this title it has been adjudged by all that if a free woman marries a slave not only will she remain in servitude with that slave but also all of her property—if she holds property divided with her relatives—will belong to the master whose slave she married. And if she has not already shared with her relatives in the paternal or maternal property, she now cannot respond to anyone seeking her nor can she become a later sharer in the inheritance of paternal property with the other heirs. Likewise if it is a Frankish man who presumes to marry some one else's female slave, they have adjudged that the same provision will obtain.

IV

Likewise concerning this title[181]: if anyone takes another man's wife while her husband still lives, he shall be liable to pay eight thousand denarii (i.e, two hundred solidi).

Concerning this title it has been adjudged that the penalty provided above (i.e., two hundred solidi), should be paid by that one who took her illegally to the living husband whose wife was taken away contrary to law.

V

Concerning Title XXVI[182]: if a boy under twelve commits an offense, a fine (*fredus*) will not be required of him.

Concerning this title it has been adjudged that if a child (*invans*) under twelve years of age unjustly takes the property of another, he shall pay composition according to the law but he shall not pay the additional fine (*fredus*); and let him be summoned to court just as that one can be summoned who does something against the law and let him be led to court by the count just as he who has done something against the law can be led. If someone wishes to challenge (*interpellare*) him [the boy] concerning his paternal or maternal property, it has been adjudged that this should wait until the boy is twelve years old.

VI

It has been adjudged by all that if a Frankish man or a freeborn woman voluntarily places himself or herself in servitude, if he or she while free had legally transferred their property to the church of God or to someone else, he to whom it was transferred shall have it and hold it; and if he or she had sons or daughters while free, they [the children] shall remain free.

VII

Concerning Title XXXVII[183]: If a slave kills a freeman, he shall be handed over to the relatives of the dead man to count as half of the composition, and the lord of the slave must pay the other half; however, if he [the lord] knows the law, he can summon himself to court (*se obmalare*) [to establish his slave's innocence] so that he does not have to pay the wergeld (*leodem*).

Indeed the law makes no distinction between ecclesiastical slaves or slaves held by benefice holders (*beneficiario*) and the slaves of other persons, so thus ecclesiastical or beneficial slaves just like freedmen can be handed over or set free or held for the interrogation of the lord emperor.

VIII

Concerning Title XLVI,[184] that, is concerning him who wishes to marry a widow.

It has been adjudged by all that, just as it was written in the Salic law, a man can only accept her [the widow] in marriage if he has the consent and agreement of her relatives, just as our ancestors have observed.

IX

Concerning Title XLVII[185]: concerning him who occupies the dwelling (*villa*) of another.

Concerning this title it has been adjudged that no one may hold or possess the villa or property of another man by simply moving in for some years; but on whatever day the invader of that property has been challenged, he should return that property to him seeking it or, if he can, defend and vindicate himself according to law.

X

What the laws provide about affatomie (*acfatmire*), which is a handing over [transfer of property or adoption of an heir].[186]

They have adjudged concerning this title that just as one's ancestors had this custom for a long time, so all who live by Salic law shall have it and do it in the future.

XI

They have further judged that if a slave carries a charter of freedom but he does not have a legitimate author of the charter, the slave's lord can declare the charter false.

XII

And they have judged that all men who seek something from another man shall have the right first to produce witnesses against him; and if that man from whom it is sought says that he holds it [the thing in dispute] legally and if he can produce witnesses who affirm the truth of this, they have judged that the truth of this matter shall be proved according to those laws (*capitula*) of our lord emperor which first set out how something is to be legally held.

Lex Salica Karolina

Systematic Version

The Salic Law[1]

The Frankish People[2]

1. The whole Frankish people, established by the power of God, are strong in arms, weighty in council, firm in the compact of peace, pure in body, distinguished in form, brave, swift, and austere. Recently converted to the Catholic faith, they are free from heresy, rejecting barbarian rites with the help of God, keeping the faith; and according to their customs they seek the key to wisdom and desire justice.

2. Those who at that time were rulers spoke the Salic law in the presence of the notables (*proceres*) of their own people, i.e., Wisogaste, Salegaste, and Widogaste, Arogaste, Bedogaste, and Virovade, who were from the places called Salechamne, Bodecamne and Widocamne.

3. At a time pleasing to God, Clovis, king of the Franks, fiery and handsome and renowned, first received Catholic baptism, [and] the noble kings Clovis, Childebert, and Chlotar clearly emended that which seemed less suitable in the pact.

4. Let him who esteems the Franks live by the present decree. May Christ protect their kingdom, give them rulers, fill them with the light of his grace, protect their army, and give them the protection of the faith. May Jesus Christ, lord of lords, bestow with his gracious love the joys of peace and times of happiness. For this is the people who while small in number are great in strength. In battle [that nation] shook off the powerful and very harsh yoke of the Romans from its neck. And, after the knowledge of baptism, the Franks decorated with gold and precious stones the bodies of the blessed martyrs whom the Romans had mutilated with fire or sword or else had thrown to the beasts to be torn. And after the knowledge of baptism, the Franks, having found the bodies of the blessed martyrs whom the Romans had mutilated with fire or sword, decorated them with gold and precious stones.

5. It was pleasing and agreed to between the Franks and their notables that to preserve peace among themselves they should with care prevent all growth of quarrels. And just as their nation was preeminent among other peoples located next to it on account of the strength of its arms, so also it should undertake to make an end to criminal acts with its legal authority.

6. And so, these four men were elected from among many, Wisogastes, Arogastes, Salegastes, and Vindogastes, who, in three assembled courts (*mallos*), carefully discussing the origin of all cases [in order to determine how] to settle them, declared in what way justice should be done.

The Titles of the Salic Law

The Book of the Salic Law

I [I][3]

CONCERNING A SUMMONS TO COURT [*Pactus I*]

1. If anyone summoned to court in accordance with the king's laws does not come, if a lawful excuse (*sunnis*) does not detain him, he shall be liable to pay six hundred denarii (i.e., fifteen solidi).

2. If that man who summoned the other person does not come himself, and a lawful excuse does not detain him, he must also pay six hundred denarii (i.e., fifteen solidi) to the man whom he summoned.

3. Moreover, he who summons the other man should go with witnesses to his house and summon him in this way or denounce him to his wife [or to anyone else in his family] so that he has made it known to the other in what manner he has been summoned.

4. If a man is occupied with a commission from the king, he cannot be summoned to court.

5. But if he should be in the district on his own business, he can be summoned, as was said above.

II [LIX]

CONCERNING HIM WHO REFUSES TO COME TO COURT
[*Pactus* LVI]

If a man fails to come to court and refuses to carry out what has been declared against him by the rachimburgi, if he will not offer a pledge to guarantee either the composition or other legal penalty (*de ulla lege*), then he must be summoned to the presence of the king.

There should be twelve witnesses who individually offer their statements under oath that they were present at the time the rachimburgi rendered judgment.

Three others likewise should offer oath that they were present on that day when the rachimburgi offered their judgment that he [the accused] should clear himself either by the ordeal of hot water (*aeneum*) or by composition, that forty days had passed since the day had been set for a second time in court, and he still would not carry out the law.

Then within fourteen days the accused should be summoned into the presence of the king, and the three should give their testimony under oath that they had summoned him. And then if he will not come, nine witnesses under oath shall say that all these things are true that we have said above. So let a court day be formally set again for him and let him have witnesses there when the day was set. And if he who called him to court carries out all these things but that one who was summoned will neither come to the court nor do justice to him, then the king, to whom he was summoned, shall decree that he is outside of his protection (*extra sermonem suum*) and so the guilty man and all of his property shall go to the fisc or to anyone to whom the fisc wishes to give them. And whoever gives him bread or offers him hospitality, even if it is his own wife, shall be adjudged to pay a fine of six hundred denarii (i.e., fifteen solidi) until he has made composition for all of those things imposed on him according to law.

III [LIII]

CONCERNING HIM WHO UNJUSTLY REQUESTS A COUNT (*grafio*) TO TAKE THE PROPERTY OF ANOTHER [*Pactus* LI]

1. If anyone unjustly requests a count to take the property of another before that one has been called to court as an adversary according to law, he shall be judged liable to pay a fine of eight thousand denarii (i.e., two hundred solidi).
2. If the count, having been asked, presumes contrary to law to take more than the debt itself, he must redeem himself or make composition with his life.

IV [LX]

CONCERNING THOSE RACHIMBURGI WHO DO NOT RENDER JUSTICE ACCORDING TO LAW [*Pactus* LVII]

1. If there are rachimburgi sitting on the court when a case is pleaded between two litigants, let them be reminded by the man who is bringing his suit that they should speak the Salic law. And if they are not willing to administer such law, then they should be reminded a second and a third time by the man who is bringing his suit.

But if they are not willing to speak it, then he who is bringing his suit should say, "I summon you to judge between me and my opponent." And if even then they delay in administering the law, on the day set each of the seven of them shall be fined one hundred twenty denarii (i.e., three solidi).
2. And if then the rachimburgi hesitate still longer and will not either speak

the law or pay the composition of three solidi, then each of those seven on the day designated shall be fined six hundred denarii (i.e., fifteen solidi).

3. Likewise, if they shall be proved to have rendered justice contrary to law, each of the seven will be fined six hundred denarii (i.e., fifteen solidi).

4. But if the rachimburgi do render justice, and he against whom they judged does not wish to accept the decision saying that he was judged contrary to law and he does not wish to approve it, he shall be fined six hundred denarii (i.e., fifteen solidi) for each of the seven rachimburg.

V [XX]

CONCERNING HIM WHO UNJUSTLY DENOUNCES TO THE KING A MAN WHO IS INNOCENT OR ABSENT [*Pactus* XVIII]

1. If anyone unjustly accuses of lesser crimes before the king a man who is innocent or absent, he shall be fined twenty-five hundred denarii (i.e., sixty-two and one-half solidi).

2. But if he should unjustly charge the other with such a crime that he should be put to death if it were true, that one who made the accusation shall be fined eight thousand denarii (i.e., two hundred solidi).[4]

VI [LVIII]

CONCERNING THE BURNING OR PILLAGING OF CHURCHES AND THE MURDER OF CLERICS [cf. *Pactus* LXVb and LV, 7]

1. If anyone sets fire to a consecrated church or to a place where the relics of saints are found, or takes anything pillaged from the altar of that church or anything else from inside that church, he shall be liable to pay eight thousand denarii (i.e., two hundred solidi).[5]

2. If anyone sets fire to a holy shrine (*basilicam sanctificatam*) where relics are kept, he who did these things shall be liable to pay eight thousand denarii (i.e., two hundred solidi).

[alternative version: he shall make composition with his life or become a monk.]

3. If anyone kills a deacon, he shall be judged liable to pay twelve thousand denarii (i.e., three hundred solidi).

4. If anyone kills a presbyter, he shall be judged liable to pay twenty-four thousand denarii (i.e., six hundred solidi).

VII [LVI]

CONCERNING HIM WHO KILLS A COUNT (*grafio*) [*Pactus* LIV]

1. If anyone kills a count he shall be judged liable to pay twenty-four thousand denarii (i.e., six hundred solidi).

2. If anyone kills a sagibaron who is a servant of the king (*puer regis*), he shall be judged liable to pay twelve thousand denarii (i.e., three hundred solidi).[6]

3. If anyone kills a sagibaron who is a freeman who had put himself in the position of a sagibaron, he shall be judged liable to pay twenty-four thousand denarii (i.e., six hundred solidi).

4. There should not be more than three sagibarons in each court where the people are accustomed to come together. And if a case has been concluded before them according to law, it cannot be removed to the count.

VIII [LXVI]

CONCERNING THE MAN KILLED IN THE ARMY [*Pactus* LXIII]

1. If anyone kills a man while he is in the army, he shall pay three times the compensation that he would have paid while at home (*in patria*), so long as that man was not among the antrustions of the king (*ex truste regali*).

2. But if he [the man killed] is one of the antrustions of the king, he [who killed him] shall be judged liable to pay [three times] what he would have paid at home, that is, seventy-two thousand denarii (i.e., eighteen hundred solidi).

IX [XVI]

CONCERNING HIM WHO ATTACKS THE DWELLING (*villam*) OF ANOTHER [*Pactus* XLII]

1. If anyone attacks another's dwelling (*villam*), he and all those who are convicted of being in his band of men (*contubernio*) shall be judged liable to pay twenty-five hundred denarii (i.e., sixty-two and one-half solidi).
2. If anyone attacks another dwelling (*villam*) and breaks doors, kills dogs, strikes men, or carries away anything in a wagon, he shall be judged liable to pay eight thousand denarii (i.e., two hundred solidi). And whatever he has taken away from there, he must restore.
3. And as many as are convicted of being in his band of men (*contubernio*) each of them shall be judged liable to pay twenty-five hundred denarii (i.e., sixty-two and one-half solidi).

X [XVIII]

CONCERNING ARSON [*Pactus* XVI⁷]

1. If anyone sets fire to another person's house while people are sleeping inside, he shall be judged liable to pay twenty-five hundred denarii (i.e., sixty-two and one-half solidi) to him whose house it was, in addition to a payment for the damage done plus a payment for the time its use was lost.

And whoever was inside and escaped should bring him [the arsonist] to court, and he [the arsonist] shall pay each one of them a composition of twenty-five hundred denarii (i.e., sixty-two and one-half solidi). And whatever they have lost there, he [the arsonist] should restore to its place. And if anyone was burned inside, he who set the fire shall be liable to pay eight thousand denarii (i.e., two hundred solidi) to the relatives of the dead.
2. If anyone burns a barn (*spicarium*) or granary (*maholum*) with the grain (*annona*) in it, he shall be liable to pay twenty-five hundred denarii (i.e., sixty-two and one-half solidi).

3. If anyone burns a sty (*sudem*) with pigs in it, or a stable (*scuriam*) with animals or hay in it, he shall be liable to pay twenty-five hundred denarii (i.e., sixty-two and one-half solidi), in addition to a payment for the damage done plus a payment for the time their use was lost.

4. If anyone cuts down (*capulaverit*) or burns the hedge (*concisam*) or fence (*sepem*) belonging to someone else, he shall be liable to pay six hundred denarii (i.e., fifteen solidi) in addition to a payment for the damage done plus a payment for the time their use was lost.

XI [XLIII]

CONCERNING THE KILLING OF FREEMEN [*Pactus* XLI]

1. If any freeman kills a Frank or other barbarian who lives by Salic law, he shall be judged liable to pay eight thousand denarii (i.e., two hundred solidi).

2. But if he throws him into a well or holds him under water [and kills him], he shall be liable to pay twenty-four thousand denarii (i.e., six hundred solidi).

3. But if he beats him [to death] with branches or stones (*allis*) or anything else, or burns him, he [who did this] shall be liable to pay twenty-four thousand denarii (i.e., six hundred solidi).

4. If anyone kills a man who is among the king's antrustions (*in truste dominica est*), he shall be liable to pay twenty-four thousand denarii (i.e., six hundred solidi).

5. But if he throws him [the antrustion] into a well or holds him under water, or beats him to death with stones (*allis*) or branches, or burns him, he shall be liable to pay seventy-two thousand denarii (i.e., eighteen hundred solidi).

6. If anyone kills a Roman man who is a tablemate of the king (*convivam regis*), he shall be liable to pay twelve thousand denarii (i.e., three hundred solidi).

7. If a Roman man who is a landowner, that is, he is one who owns private property in the district where he lives, shall be killed, he who is convicted of killing him is liable to pay four thousand denarii (i.e., one hundred solidi).

8. If anyone kills a Roman who pays tribute, he shall be liable to pay eighteen hundred denarii (i.e., forty-five solidi).[8]

9. If anyone finds a man at a crossroads without hands and feet whom his enemies have left mutilated [and he kills him], he shall be liable to pay four thousand denarii (i.e., one hundred solidi).

10. If anyone throws a freeman into a well or into the sea or over a precipice where he is in danger of death, and he who was thrown in some manner escapes alive from that danger, he who threw him shall be liable to pay four thousand denarii (i.e., one hundred solidi).

11. Moreover, if the man who was thrown dies, his full wergeld (*leode*) must be paid in composition.

12. And so for each person he must make composition by a greater or lesser amount.

13. If he escapes death from the precipice, he [who threw him] must pay as composition one-half of the wergeld (*leodis*) which he should have paid if he had killed him. But if he dies, each one must be compounded for according to the size of his wergeld.[9]

14. If anyone accuses a freeman of [doing] something to some comrade of his, and because of his warning or lie the one who was accused is killed, if the charge is proved against him, he [who made the accusation] shall pay one-half of the man's wergeld. And the one who killed him must make full composition according to law.[10]

XII [XLIV]

CONCERNING HOMICIDES COMMITTED BY A BAND OF MEN (*contubernio*) [*Pactus* XLII]

1. If anyone, having gathered together his band of men, attacks a freeman in his home and kills him there, he shall be liable to pay twenty-four thousand denarii (i.e., six hundred solidi).

2. But if the man who was killed was an antrustion of the king's (*in truste dominica*), he [who killed him] shall be liable to pay seventy-two thousand denarii (i.e., eighteen hundred solidi).

3. But if the corpse of the man killed has three or more wounds, the three who are charged and, because they were in that group of men, are convicted, will be compelled individually to pay the above amount in full.

And three others from that same band of men shall each be liable to pay thirty-six hundred denarii (i.e., ninety solidi). And in the third place, three more from that same band of men will each be liable to pay eighteen hundred denarii (i.e., forty-five solidi).

4. If indeed a Roman or a half-free man (*lidus*) has been killed by such a band of men, half the above amounts shall be paid as composition.[11]

XIII [XLV]

CONCERNING THE COMPOSITION TO BE PAID FOR HOMICIDE COMMITTED AT A BANQUET [*Pactus* XLIII]

1. If at a banquet where there are four or five men one of these is killed, those who remain either must give up one to be convicted or else they all must pay the compensation for the dead man. This law should be observed in cases where up to seven men come together at a banquet.

2. If there are more than seven at that banquet, not all will be held liable to punishment, but those against whom the crime is credited must pay composition according to law.

3. If anyone outside of his house, either making a journey or standing in a field, has been killed by a band of men (*contubernium*) and he has received three or more wounds: three men from that band who have been convicted will each pay the composition for the death of that man, and three others from that same group will each be liable to pay twelve hundred denarii (i.e., thirty solidi) composition. And still another three from that same band will each be liable to pay six hundred denarii (i.e., fifteen solidi).

XIV [LXV]

CONCERNING THE COMPOSITION FOR HOMICIDE [*Pactus* LXII]

1. If the father of someone is killed, let his children collect half of the composition for him and the nearest relatives from his father's kin as well as from his mother's kin shall divide the other half.

2. But if there is no near kin on either the paternal or on the maternal side,

that portion [of the composition] shall go to the fisc or him to whom the fisc grants it shall have it.

XV [XIX]

CONCERNING WOUNDS [*Pactus* XVII]

1. If anyone attempts to kill someone else [with any kind of weapon] and the blow misses him, or if he attempts to strike him with a poisoned arrow and the blow misses him, he shall be liable to pay twenty-five hundred denarii (i.e., sixty-two and one-half solidi).
2. If anyone strikes a man on the head so that his blood falls on the ground, he shall be liable to pay six hundred denarii (i.e., fifteen solidi).
3. If anyone strikes a man on the head so that three bones protrude, he shall be liable to pay twelve hundred denarii (i.e., thirty solidi).
4. If anyone strikes a man on the head so that the brain shows and the three bones over the brain protrude, he shall be liable to pay eighteen hundred denarii (i.e., forty-five solidi).[12]
5. If indeed the wound penetrates between the ribs to the internal organs (*interanea*), he [who gave the blow] shall be liable to pay twelve hundred denarii (i.e., thirty solidi).
6. If indeed the wound is always running and [the victim] does not come back to health, he [who gave the blow] is liable to pay twenty-five hundred denarii (i.e., sixty-two and one-half solidi) in addition to the cost of medical attention (*medicatura*) which is three hundred sixty denarii (i.e., nine solidi).
7. If any freeman strikes another freeman with his fist but his blood does not flow, he shall be liable to pay one hundred twenty denarii (i.e., three solidi) for each blow up to three blows.
8. But if blood does appear, let him be liable to make composition in the amount he would pay if he had wounded the other with an iron weapon, that is, six hundred denarii (i.e., fifteen solidi).
9. If anyone strikes another [three times] with his closed hand, that is with his fist, he shall be liable to pay three hundred sixty denarii (i.e., nine solidi); indeed he is liable to pay three solidi for each blow by his fist.
10. If anyone accosts another man on the road and tries to rob him, but that one escapes in flight, [the attacker] shall be liable to pay twelve hundred denarii (i.e., thirty solidi).[13]

11. But if he seizes him and robs him, he shall be liable to pay twenty-five hundred denarii (i.e., sixty-two and one-half solidi).

XVI [XXXI]

CONCERNING DISABLING INJURIES [*Pactus* XXIX]

1. If anyone cuts off another's hand or foot, or gouges out his eye, or cuts off his ear or nose, he shall be liable to pay four thousand denarii (i.e., one hundred solidi).

2. But if the maimed hand remains hanging, [he who did it] will be liable to pay eighteen hundred denarii (i.e., forty-five solidi).[14]

3. If the hand itself is struck through, [he who struck the blow] will be liable to pay twenty-five hundred denarii (i.e., sixty-two and one-half solidi).

4. If anyone cuts off a thumb from the hand, or a big toe from the foot, he shall be liable to pay eighteen hundred denarii (i.e., forty-five solidi).[15]

5. But if the maimed thumb or big toe remains hanging, [he who struck the blow] will be liable to pay twelve hundred denarii (i.e., thirty solidi).[16]

6. If he cuts off the second finger [the index finger], which is used to release an arrow from the bow, he shall be liable to pay fourteen hundred denarii (i.e., thirty-five solidi).

7. If anyone cuts off the next three fingers altogether with one blow, he shall be liable to pay eighteen hundred denarii (i.e., forty-five solidi).

8. If anyone cuts off the middle finger, he shall be liable to pay six hundred denarii (i.e., fifteen solidi).

9. If anyone cuts off the fourth finger, he shall be liable to pay six hundred denarii (i.e., fifteen solidi).

10. If he cuts off the little finger, he shall also be liable to pay six hundred denarii (i.e., fifteen solidi).[17]

11. If anyone cuts away the foot of another and it remains hanging there, he shall be liable to pay eighteen hundred denarii (i.e., forty-five solidi).

12. But if the foot is completely cut off, [he who did it] shall be liable to pay twenty-five hundred denarii (i.e., sixty-two and one-half solidi).

13. If anyone pulls out another's eye, he shall be liable to pay twenty-five hundred denarii (i.e., sixty-two and one-half solidi).

14. If he cuts off someone's nose, he shall be liable to pay eighteen hundred denarii (i.e., forty-five solidi).

15. If he cuts off someone's ear, he shall be liable to pay six hundred denarii (i.e., fifteen solidi).

16. If anyone cuts out another man's tongue so that that man is unable to speak, he shall be liable to pay four thousand denarii (i.e., one hundred solidi).

17. If he knocks out a tooth, he shall be liable to pay six hundred denarii (i.e., fifteen solidi).

18. If any freeman castrates another freeman or cuts into his penis so that he is incapacitated, he shall be liable to pay four thousand denarii (i.e., one hundred solidi).

19. But if he takes it [the penis] away completely, he shall be liable to pay eight thousand denarii (i.e., two hundred solidi).[18]

XVII [LXI]

CONCERNING THE *CHRENECRUDA* (i.e., INVOLVING THE KIN IN THE PAYMENT OF COMPOSITION FOR HOMICIDE) [*Pactus* LVIII]

1. If anyone has killed a man and does not have in his whole property enough to pay the entire judgment (*legem totam*), let him offer twelve oathhelpers who will support his oath that he does not have more property either above the earth or below the earth than that which he has already given.

2. Afterwards he should enter his house and in his fist collect earth from its four corners and stand on the threshhold (*durpilo*), that is in the doorway, and, facing into the house (*intus captare*), with his left hand he should throw the earth over his shoulder onto him who is his closest relative.

If his father or mother or brother has paid [part of the fine], then he should throw the earth onto the sister of his mother and over her children, that is, over those three from the maternal kin who are most closely related.

And afterwards, without a shirt and barefoot with a stick in his hand, he should jump over his fence (*supra sepem*) so that those three [from the maternal side] shall pay half of the amount of the composition or the amount of the judgment [and the other half shall be paid] by those other [three] who come from the father's side.

But if anyone of these is poor and does not have that with which to pay his full share, whoever of these has more should have the *chrenechruda* thrown over him again. The one who was poor shall throw [the earth] and that one [who receives it] shall pay the entire judgment.

And if that one does not have that with which to pay the entire judgment (*totam legem*), then he who has him in trust (*in fide*) [i.e., his surety] should cause that one who committed the homicide to be present in four courts (*mallos*). And if he [his surety] does not wish to redeem him [the homicide] by offering composition, he [the homicide] must make composition with his life.

XVIII [XV]

CONCERNING HIM WHO ROBS A FREEMAN [*Pactus* XIV]

1. If anyone falling upon him robs a freeman, he shall be liable to pay twenty-five hundred denarii (i.e., sixty-two and one-half solidi).
2. If a Roman man robs a Frank, he shall be liable to pay twenty-five hundred denarii (i.e., sixty-two and one-half solidi).
3. But if a Frank robs a Roman, he shall be liable to pay twelve hundred denarii (i.e., thirty solidi).
4. If anyone without the approval of the king presumes to attack a man bearing the orders of the king, or if he presumes to bar the road to him, he shall be liable to pay eight thousand denarii (i.e., two hundred solidi).
5. If anyone stealthily robs a sleeping freeman, he is liable to pay four thousand denarii (i.e., one hundred solidi) in addition to return of the objects stolen [or their value] plus a payment for the time their use was lost.

XIX [XXXIV]

CONCERNING HIM WHO TIES UP A FREEMAN WITHOUT CAUSE [*Pactus* XXXII]

1. If anyone ties up a freeman without cause, he shall be liable to pay twelve hundred denarii (i.e., thirty solidi).
2. If indeed he takes the bound man to another place, he shall be liable to pay eighteen hundred denarii (i.e., forty-five solidi).

3. If indeed a Roman binds a Frank without cause, he shall be liable to pay six hundred denarii (i.e., fifteen solidi).[19]

4. If a Frank binds a Roman without cause, he shall be liable to pay six hundred denarii (i.e., fifteen solidi).

5. If anyone takes by force from the count (*grafioni*) a man heavily bound, let him redeem his life [by composition].

XX [XVII]

CONCERNING HIM WHO ROBS A DEAD BODY [*Pactus* LV]

1. If anyone stealthily robs a dead body before it is placed in the ground, he shall be liable to pay four thousand denarii (i.e., one hundred solidi).[20]

2. If anyone digs up a dead body and robs it, he shall be liable to pay eight thousand denarii (i.e., two hundred solidi). And afterwards, the relatives of the dead ought to request of a judge that the perpetrator of the crime not be allowed to live among men; and anyone who gives him hospitality before he satisfies the relatives shall be liable to pay six hundred denarii (i.e., fifteen solidi).

3. If anyone puts a dead body on top of another in either a wooden (*noffo*) or stone container, which are ordinarily called sarcophagi, he shall be liable to pay twenty-five hundred denarii (i.e., sixty-two and one-half solidi).[21]

4. If anyone destroys the wooden enclosure (*aristatonem*) over a dead body, for each one of his acts he shall be liable to pay six hundred denarii (i.e., fifteen solidi).[22]

XXI [LVII]

CONCERNING THE DESPOILING OF CORPSES [*Pactus* LV][23]

1. If anyone in stealth robs the body of a dead man before it is placed in the ground, he shall be liable to pay twenty-five hundred denarii (i.e., sixty-two and one-half solidi).

2. If anyone despoils the tomb that holds a dead man or destroys it, he shall be liable to pay six hundred denarii (i.e., fifteen solidi).[24]

3. If anyone destroys (*capulaverit*) the enclosure (*aristatonem*) which has been erected (*stapplus*) over the dead or the mound or cairn that has been

erected for the dead (*aut mundualem, quod est ea structura, sive selave, qui est ponticulus*), which have been made according to the custom of our ancestors: whoever destroys this or despoils the dead body within shall be liable to pay six hundred denarii (i.e., fifteen solidi) for each one of these things.

4. If anyone puts a dead body on top of another in a wooden (*naufo*) or stone sarcophagus, he will be liable to pay thirteen hundred [sic] denarii (i.e., thirty-five solidi).

5. If anyone has dug up or despoiled a body already in the sepulchre, let him be an outlaw (*wargus*)—that is, let him be expelled from that district until it is agreeable to the relatives of the dead and those relatives themselves have sought on his behalf that he be allowed to live within the district. And whoever gives him bread or hospitality before that time, even if it is his wife who does this, that one shall be liable to pay six hundred denarii (i.e., fifteen solidi).

6. But the perpetrator of the crime, if he himself did it or if it is proved that he has hired a for-hire person to do this, he shall be liable to pay eight thousand denarii (i.e, two hundred solidi).[25]

7. If anyone despoils the structure erected in the form of a shrine (*basilica*) over a dead body, he shall be liable to pay twelve hundred denarii (i.e., thirty solidi) in addition to a payment for the damage caused plus a payment for the time its use was lost.

XXII [XXII]

CONCERNING THE MAN WHO TOUCHES THE HAND OR ARM OF A FREE WOMAN [*Pactus* XX]

1. If any freeman touches the hand or finger of a free woman, he shall be liable to pay six hundred denarii (i.e., fifteen solidi).

2. If he touches her arm, he shall be liable to pay twelve hundred denarii (i.e., thirty solidi).

3. If he puts his hand above her elbow, he shall be liable to pay fourteen hundred denarii (i.e., thirty-five solidi).

4. If indeed he touches her breast, he shall be liable to pay eighteen hundred denarii (i.e., forty-five solidi).

XXIII [XIV]

CONCERNING FREEMEN WHO ABDUCT WOMEN [*Pactus* XIII]

1. If three men seize a free girl from her house or work-room (*screuna*), each one of them shall be liable to pay twelve hundred denarii (i.e., thirty solidi).
2. Moreover, any over three shall each be liable to pay two hundred denarii (i.e., five solidi).
3. Each of those who came with arrows [i.e., armed] shall be liable to pay [an additional] one hundred twenty denarii (i.e., three solidi).
4. But the abductor himself is liable to pay twenty-five hundred denarii (i.e., sixty-two and one-half solidi).
5. But if the girl who was dragged out was in the protection of the king, he [who abducted her] shall be compelled to pay as a fine (*fredum*) twenty-five hundred denarii (i.e., sixty-two and one-half solidi).
6. But if a servant (*puer*) of the king or half-free man (*lidus*) drags a free woman away, he shall pay with his life.
7. If indeed a free woman has followed any of these men voluntarily, she shall lose her freedom.
8. Anyone who takes the woman betrothed to another and joins her to himself in marriage shall be liable to pay twenty-five hundred denarii (i.e., sixty-two and one-half solidi).
9. Moreover, he shall be liable to pay six hundred denarii (i.e., fifteen solidi) to her betrothed.
10. He who assails in the street a girl with her bridal party (*ducte*) who is being led to her husband and forcefully commits adultery with her shall be liable to pay eight thousand denarii (i.e., two hundred solidi).
11. If a freeman takes another's female slave in marriage, he himself shall be joined with her in slavery.
12. If anyone takes another's wife while the husband still lives, he shall be liable to pay eight thousand denarii (i.e., two hundred solidi).
13. If anyone rapes (*moechatus fuerit*) a free girl by force, he shall be liable to pay twenty-five hundred denarii (i.e., sixty-two and one-half solidi).
14. If anyone has intercourse in secret with her consent with a free girl who is betrothed, he shall be liable to pay eighteen hundred denarii (i.e., forty-five solidi).
15. He who joins another's half-free woman (*lidam*) to himself in marriage shall be liable to pay twelve hundred denarii (i.e., thirty solidi).

16. He who enters into a profane marriage with his sister or with the daughter of his brother or with the cousin of another degree, or with the wife of his brother or of his mother's brother, shall be subject to the following punishment: he shall be separated from such a union and even if the couple have had children, the children may not be legitimate heirs, but shall be marked by disgrace.

XXIV [XLVI]

CONCERNING THE WIDOW'S BETROTHAL FINE (*reippus*)
[*Pactus* XLIV]

1. If a man dies and leaves a widow and another man wishes to marry her, before the latter may marry her a thunginus or hundredman (*centenarius*) should convene a court, and a shield should be held up and three men should plead the case.

And then the man who wishes to marry the widow, accompanied by three witnesses to appraise [the coins], should have three solidi of equal weight and a denarius; and when this is done, if it is agreeable to them, he may marry the widow.

2. But if he does not do these things and marries her anyway, he shall be liable to pay twenty-five hundred denarii (i.e., sixty-two and one-half solidi) to him to whom the betrothal fine (*reippus*) is due.

3. But if he carries out all those things according to law which we provided above, and the one to whom the betrothal fine is owed accepted the three solidi and a denarius, then he may legally marry her.

4. It appears that it must be discerned to whom the betrothal fine is owed.

5. If there is a nephew, the oldest son of a sister [of the dead husband], he shall receive the betrothal fine.

6. But if there is no nephew, the oldest son of a niece shall receive it.

7. If moreover there is no son of a niece, the son of a cousin who comes from the maternal side shall receive it.

8. If moreover there is also no son of a cousin, then an uncle, the brother of the mother [i.e., of the dead husband's mother] shall receive the betrothal fine.

9. If there is no uncle, then the brother of him who had been married to the woman, if he has not come into the inheritance of his dead brother

who was the husband of this woman, shall receive the betrothal fine.

10. But if this man is not available, then he who is closest in kinship after those named above, up to the sixth degree, if he has not come into the inheritance of the dead husband, shall receive the betrothal fine.

11. If moreover there is no relative within the six degrees, the betrothal fine or [the proceeds of] any suit that has arisen from it shall be collected by the fisc.

XXV [LXX]

CONCERNING THE MAN WHO HAS BETROTHED HIMSELF TO ANOTHER MAN'S DAUGHTER AND THEN DOES NOT WISH TO MARRY HER [*Pactus* LXVa]

If anyone has sought another man's daughter in marriage in the presence of his own and of the girl's relatives and afterwards he withdraws himself and does not wish to marry her, he shall be liable to pay twenty-five hundred denarii (i.e., sixty-two and one-half solidi).

XXVI [XLVII]

CONCERNING THE MAN WHO MOVES INTO A STRANGE VILLAGE (*villam*) AND STAYS THERE FOR TWELVE MONTHS [*Pactus* XLV]

1. If anyone wishes to move into a village (*villam*) in place of another and some of those who live in the village take the position that they wish to receive him but there is one of them who opposes, he may not have the right to move there.

2. But if against the opposition of one or two he presumes to take up residence in that village, then the one who objects should go to him with witnesses and state that he should go forth from there within ten days; and if he is not willing, he [who objects] should come again to him with witnesses and demand that he depart within another ten days. And if he still is not willing, he [who objects] should demand for a third time that he leave within ten days. If thirty days pass and he still has not departed, he

[who objects] should at once summon him to court, and he should bring his witnesses to court with him. If moreover that one who has been summoned will not appear and no lawful excuse delays him and he has been summoned according to law as stated above, then he who was summoned shall make composition with his property (*fortuna*).

And let him [the accuser] ask the count (*grafio*) to go to that place and expel the man thence; and, because he was not willing to obey the law, he shall lose whatever he acquired there and in addition he shall be liable to pay twelve hundred denarii (i.e., thirty solidi).

3. He who invited another man to move into a strange village (*villam*) before it had been agreed upon [by the residents] shall be liable to pay eighteen hundred denarii (i.e., forty-five solidi).

4. But if anyone has moved into a strange village and no protest has been made according to law for twelve months, he may reside there secure just as the other neighbors do.

XXVII [XLVIII]

CONCERNING *AFATOMIAE* (i.e., THE TRANSFERENCE OF PROPERTY BY DONATION OR THE ADOPTION OF AN HEIR) [*Pactus* XLVI]

1. Let it be done thus. Let the thunginus or hundredman (*centenarius*) convene a court and have a shield in that court and three men should plead the case three times in that court, as is required. Afterwards, the man [who wishes to transfer his property] should throw a stick (*festucam*) into the lap (*laisum*) of a man who is not related to him, and to that one in whose lap he threw the stick let him say how much of his fortune he wishes to transfer.

Afterwards, that one in whose lap he threw the stick should remain in his house and receive three guests, and he should have in his control as much of the property as was transferred to him. Moreover, that one to whom it was entrusted should do all these things in the presence of assembled witnesses.

2. Afterwards, he should hand over his fortune to that one to whom he granted it in the presence of the king or in a lawful court; and afterwards let that one designated as heir receive the stick thrown into his lap in court

within twelve months. And it [the amount] should be neither less nor more but just as much as was granted to him.

And if anyone wants to contest this, the three witnesses should say under oath that they were in the court convened by the thunginus or hundredman and they had seen the man who was giving his property throw the stick into the lap of the one whom he had already chosen; and they should name the one who threw his property into the lap of the man selected. Also [they should name] him into whose lap he threw the stick and called him heir. Likewise three other witnesses should be named; and they should say under oath that the man into whose lap the stick had been thrown remained there in the house of that man who had given his property and he had assembled three or more guests there and had fed them, and that they had offered thanks to him there and had eaten porridge (*pultes*) at his table (*beudo*) and had assembled as witnesses.

Three other witnesses should say all these things under oath: that he who received the property in his lap [received it] in open court (*in malle publico*) which was a lawful court (*in mallo legitimo*) or in the presence of the king—that is, it was in the presence of a *theada* or thunginus—[and] that he who [made the gift] threw the stick into the lap of him whom he called heir publicly in the presence of all. And the nine witnesses should affirm all these things.

XXVIII [L]

CONCERNING FALSE TESTIMONY [*Pactus* XLVIII]

1. If anyone offers false testimony, he shall be liable to pay six hundred denarii (i.e., fifteen solidi).
2. If anyone accuses another of committing perjury and he cannot prove it, he shall be liable to pay six hundred denarii (i.e., fifteen solidi).
3. If anyone has been accused of perjury and the one who brought the charge can prove it, each one of his three oathhelpers who commit perjury with him shall be liable to pay six hundred denarii (i.e., fifteen solidi).
4. If there were more than three, they shall be liable to pay five solidi.[26]
5. Indeed he who was accused shall pay six hundred denarii (i.e., fifteen solidi) in addition to return of the objects in dispute [or their value] plus payment for the time their use was lost.

XXIX [LII]

CONCERNING THE MAN WHO DOES NOT REPAY A PROMISSORY NOTE OR PLEDGE (*fidem*) GIVEN TO ANOTHER [*Pactus* L]

1. If any freeman or half-free man (*lidus*) has given a promissory note or pledge (*fidem*) to someone else, then he to whom the note or pledge was given should in forty days, or at whatever other time it was agreed when the promise was made to him, go to the other's house with witnesses or with those who should evaluate the amount.

And if he [who gave the note or pledge] will not fulfill the promise he made, he shall be liable to pay six hundred denarii (i.e., fifteen solidi).

2. But if he [the debtor] is not willing to pay the abovementioned debt, he [who received the promise] ought to summon him to court thus: "I ask you, judge, that you summon for me, according to Salic law, that man called my adversary (*gasachionem*) who gave me a promise (*fidem*) for such and such a debt." Then the judge should say: "I [summon] him as your adversary (*gasachium*) in this court according to Salic Law." Then he to whom the promise was given ought to place on oath his oathhelpers (*fideiussori*) that he [his adversary] has neither paid the debt nor has he given security (*pignus*) for its payment to the other man before paying the one to whom he gave the note (*fidem*). And let him go quickly with witnesses to the house of the man who gave the promise (*fidem*) and ask him to pay his debt. And if he will not do it, let him [the creditor] set a day for him [to come to court]; if he has set a day for him, he may add three solidi to that which is owed. And thus up to three times he should make three summonses. If all these things are done, and he [the debtor] is still not willing to pay the debt, the debt shall increase nine solidi. That is, for each warning given or court day set, three solidi are to be added.

If he [the debtor] is still not willing to redeem the promise (*fidem*) that he made in lawful court (*placito*), then he to whom the promise (*fidem*) was given should go to the count of the place in whose district (*pago*) he lives and he should take a stick and make this statement: "Judge, I ask you, that since that man I have named who gave a promissory note (*fidem*) to me and whom I legally cited (*adiachtivum*) and called to court according to Salic law [has not paid his debt to me], I place myself and my fortune [in your hands] as security that I may put my hand on the fortune of that one"; and he [the creditor] should say for how much of a cause the promissory note was given to him. Then the count should assemble with himself seven suitable rachimburgi and go with these to the house of the promiser (*fideiussoris*) and demand of him, if he is present: "voluntarily pay this man the amount for which you gave him an agreement (*fidem*) and quickly pay that which you owe according to its lawfully estimated (*pretiatum*) value."

But if he will not do it then, whether he is present or absent, let the rachimburgi immediately take from his property the estimated value of that which he owes. And if the fine (*fredus*) has not been given previously in this case, the one whose case it is should keep two parts [of the payment] for himself and the count should receive a third part.

3. But if the count summoned there does not come and no legitimate delay or royal concern detains him, and if he delays to go there or to send a substitute so that the debt might be exacted with justice, he shall redeem himself by composition or pay with his life.

XXX [LIV]

CONCERNING SOMETHING THAT HAS BEEN LENT [*Pactus* LII]

If anyone has lent anything from his property to another man and that one will not return it to him, he [the lender] should summon him thus. He should go with witnesses to the house of the man to whom he lent the thing and call upon him thus:

"Since you will not return to me those properties that I lent to you, you may keep them until the next day, as the Salic law provides"; and thus he [the lender] should formally set a day for him [to return the properties]. If then he [the borrower] is still not willing to return the property, he [the lender] should likewise call upon him after seven more days, just as he had done before, that he [the borrower] might keep the property until the next day, as the Salic law provides.

And if he still is not willing to return the property, after another seven days he [the lender] should again go to him in the same way with witnesses and demand that he pay his debt.

And if he [the borrower] is still not willing to return that which is owed to him [the lender] nor to offer security for returning it as if it were a debt, in addition to the nine solidi that were added for the three warnings, let him be liable to pay six hundred denarii (i.e., fifteen solidi) composition.

XXXI [LV]

CONCERNING REDEEMING ONE'S HAND FROM THE ORDEAL BY HOT WATER [*Pactus* LIII]

1. If a man has been sentenced to the ordeal by hot water (*aeneum*) and it is agreed that he who was sentenced may redeem his hand and offer oathhelpers (*iuratores*), if it were such a case that if he were convicted he would have to pay a composition of six hundred denarii (i.e., fifteen solidi), he may redeem his hand for one hundred twenty denarii (i.e., three solidi).

2. If indeed he has given more to redeem his hand, let the fine (*fredus*) be paid to the count just as if he had been convicted for such a cause [i.e., a cause involving the higher payment].

3. If indeed it is such a case that if he were convicted he would have to pay fourteen hundred denarii (i.e., thirty-five solidi) and if it is agreed that he may redeem his hand and offer oathhelpers (*iuratores*), he may redeem his hand for nine solidi.[27]

4. But if he has given more, let it be paid to the count as a fine (*fredus*) as if he had been convicted of such a [higher] cause.

5. But if it is a more serious crime for which if convicted he would pay a fine of sixty-two and one-half solidi, and if it is agreed that he can redeem his hand, he may redeem his hand with fifteen solidi.

6. And if he has given more, let the fine (*fredus*) be paid to the count as if he had been convicted of such a [higher] cause; let this payment remain in effect up to the amount of his wergeld (*leudem*).

7. If someone is charged [with a crime] that would involve payment of the wergeld (*leudem*) and he is sentenced to the ordeal, if it is agreeable he may redeem his hand [with the payment of thirty solidi].[28]

8. And if he has given more, let it be paid as a fine (*fredus*) to the count as if he had been convicted for such a [higher] cause.

XXXII [XXI]

CONCERNING MAGIC PHILTERS OR POISONED POTIONS
[*Pactus* XIX]

1. If anyone has given an herbal potion to another to drink and that one dies, he [who did it] shall be liable to pay eight thousand denarii (i.e., two hundred solidi).[29]
2. But if he [the victim] drinks and does not die, he who gave the drug shall be liable to pay twenty-five hundred denarii (i.e., sixty-two and one-half solidi) for such a magic potion.
3. If anyone has administered a magic potion to another or has put him tied up in some place, he shall be liable to pay twenty-five hundred denarii (i.e., sixty-two and one-half solidi).
4. If anyone gives an herbal potion (*herbas*) to a woman that makes it impossible for her to have children, he shall be liable to pay twenty-five hundred denarii (i.e., sixty-two and one-half solidi).

XXXIII [XXVI]

CONCERNING THOSE WHO KILL BOYS OR GIRLS OR CUT THEIR HAIR [*Pactus* XXIV]

1. If anyone kills a boy up to twelve years of age, whether he is long- or short-haired, he shall be liable to pay twenty-four thousand denarii (i.e., six hundred solidi).
2. If anyone cuts the hair of a long-haired boy without the consent of his relatives, he shall be liable to pay eighteen hundred denarii (i.e., forty-five solidi).
3. If indeed he cuts a girl's hair he shall be liable to pay twenty-five hundred denarii (i.e., sixty-two and one-half solidi).
4. If anyone kills a pregnant woman, he shall be liable to pay twenty-eight thousand denarii (i.e., seven hundred solidi).
5. If anyone kills a child in its mother's womb or a child within nine days of birth before it has a name, he shall be liable to pay four thousand denarii (i.e., one hundred solidi).

6. If anyone kills a free girl before she reaches the age to have children, he shall be liable to pay eight thousand denarii (i.e., two hundred solidi).

7. If anyone kills a free woman after she begins to bear children, he shall be liable to pay twenty-four thousand denarii (i.e., six hundred solidi).

8. If anyone kills a woman after she is no longer able to have children, he shall be liable to pay eight thousand denarii (i.e., two hundred solidi).

9. If a boy less than twelve years old commits a crime, a fine (*fredum*) will not be required of him.

XXXIV [LXIV]

CONCERNING LAND HELD BY ALLODIAL TENURE (*de alode*) [*Pactus* LIX]

1. If a man dies and leaves no children, if his father or mother survive, they shall succeed to his inheritance.

2. If the father or mother are not living and he leaves brothers or sisters, they shall secure the inheritance.

3. But if none of these is living, the sisters of the father will succeed to the inheritance.[30]

4. If indeed none of the father's sisters lives, his mother's sisters shall claim the inheritance for themselves.

5. If moreover none of these is living, whoever is nearest from the father's kin shall succeed to the inheritance.

6. Indeed concerning Salic land (*terra Salica*), no part of the inheritance may pass to a woman but all the inheritance of land goes to the male sex.

XXXV [LXIII]

CONCERNING HIM WHO WISHES TO REMOVE HIMSELF FROM HIS KIN GROUP (*parentela*) [*Pactus* LX]

1. If anyone wishes to remove himself from his kin group (*parentela*), let him go to court and in the presence of a thunginus or hundredman (*centenarius*) break four sticks of alder wood over his head and throw these four pieces into the court and say there that he removes himself from its

[his *parentela*'s] oathhelping (*iuramento*), from its inheritance, and from any relationship (*ratione*) with it.

2. And if afterwards one of his relatives either dies or is killed, nothing from that one's inheritance or from the composition [due him] shall belong to him [who removed himself from the *parentela*].

3. And if he himself is killed or dies, composition for him or his inheritance will not belong to [his relatives] as heirs but to the fisc or to him to whom the fisc wishes to give it.

XXXVI [LXIV]

CONCERNING *CHAROENA* (PILLAGING OR PLUNDERING) [*Pactus* LXI]

1. If anyone takes or seizes something by force from another's hand, let him restore the thing in full and in addition pay twelve hundred denarii (i.e., thirty solidi) composition.

2. If anyone is convicted of taking by force from a man something which had been placed in the hand of a third person, he shall be liable to pay twelve hundred denarii (i.e., thirty solidi).

XXXVII [LXVII]

CONCERNING HIM WHO CALLS ANOTHER A SORCERER (*herinburgium*) [*Pactus* LXIV]

1. If anyone calls another a sorcerer (*herinburgium*) or a *strioportium*, one who is said to carry a bronze cauldron where witches (*striae*) brew, and he cannot prove it, he shall be judged liable to pay twenty-five hundred denarii (i.e., sixty-two and one-half solidi).

2. If anyone calls a free woman a witch (*striam*) or a harlot (*meretricem*) and cannot prove it, he shall be liable to pay seven thousand denarii (i.e., eighty-two and one-half solidi).[31]

3. If a witch eats a man and is convicted, he or she shall be liable to pay eight thousand denarii (i.e., two hundred solidi).

XXXVIII [XXXIII]

ON BLOCKING A ROAD [*Pactus* XXXI]

1. If anyone blocks the road to a freeman (*baroni*) or strikes him, he shall be liable to pay six hundred denarii (i.e., fifteen solidi).
2. If anyone blocks the road to a free woman or strikes her, he shall be liable to pay eighteen hundred denarii (i.e., forty-five solidi).
3. If anyone closes the road that leads to a mill, he shall be liable to pay six hundred denarii (i.e., fifteen solidi).

XXXIX [XII]

CONCERNING THEFTS COMMITTED BY FREEMEN [*Pactus* XI]

1. If a freeman outside someone's house steals something worth two denarii, he shall be liable to pay six hundred denarii (i.e., fifteen solidi) in addition to return of the object stolen [or its value] plus a payment for the time its use was lost.
2. But if outside someone's house he steals something that is worth forty denarii, he shall be liable to pay fourteen hundred denarii (i.e., thirty-five solidi) in addition to return of the object stolen [or its value] plus a payment for the time its use was lost.
3. If a freeman breaks into a house and steals something worth two denarii, he shall be liable to pay twelve hundred denarii (i.e., thirty solidi), in addition to return of the object stolen [or its value] plus a payment for the time its use was lost.
4. If indeed he steals something worth more than five denarii, he shall be liable to pay fourteen hundred denarii (i.e., thirty-five solidi), in addition to return of the object stolen [or its value] plus a payment for the time its use was lost.
5. If any freeman cuts a key or duplicates it and thus has entered a house and taken something from it by theft, he shall be liable to pay eighteen hundred denarii (i.e., forty-five solidi) in addition to return of the object stolen [or its value] plus a payment for the time its use was lost.
6. If indeed he takes nothing, but fleeing escapes, he shall be liable to pay twelve hundred denarii (i.e., thirty solidi) on account of the break-in.

XL [XIII]

CONCERNING THEFTS COMMITTED BY SLAVES [*Pactus* XII]

1. If a slave steals something worth two denarii outside someone's house, and is proved to have done so, let him receive one hundred twenty lashes of the whip or else in place of this let him pay one hundred twenty denarii (i.e., three solidi) in addition to return of the object [or its value] plus a payment for the time its use was lost.

2. But if he steals something worth forty denarii, let him be castrated or redeem himself by paying two hundred denarii[32] (i.e., six solidi); moreover, the lord of the slave who committed the theft shall restore the full value of the object stolen to its place.

XLI [XLII]

CONCERNING THE SLAVE WHO IS ACCUSED OF THEFT [*Pactus* XL]

1. If a man's slave is charged with such a theft that if a freeman did it he would have been liable to pay six hundred denarii (i.e., fifteen solidi), the slave shall be stretched over a rack (*scamnum*) and receive one hundred twenty lashes.

2. If indeed he [the slave] confesses before being tortured and his lord agrees, let him redeem his back [i.e., avoid the punishment] by a payment of one hundred twenty denarii (i.e., three solidi) and let the slave's lord restore the full value of the object stolen to its proper place.

3. If moreover it is such a crime that if a freeman did it he would have to pay fourteen hundred denarii (i.e., thirty-five solidi) for it, the slave likewise stretched out shall receive one hundred twenty lashes.

4. And if he has confessed during this torture (*supplicio*), he shall either be castrated or shall pay two hundred forty denarii (i.e., six solidi). Indeed the slave's lord must return the full value of the object stolen to its proper place.

5. And if the slave has not confessed and the one who tortures him wishes to continue to torture that slave but the slave's lord does not want him to, that one [who tortures] ought to give a pledge for the slave's value [to the slave's lord] so that he may keep the slave for greater torture.

And if after the slave has been subjected to greater torture he still has not confessed, let [the man] who was torturing him keep him. Indeed the slave's lord, who had already received a pledge for him, should keep the value (*praecium*) of his slave.

6. If a slave confesses against his lord, let him never be believed.

7. But if the slave is charged with a major crime, one for which a freeman would be liable to pay eighteen hundred denarii (i.e., forty-five solidi), and he has confessed under torture, he shall receive capital punishment.

8. If a slave is charged with a crime and the slave's lord is present, he [the lord] should be warned by him who seeks redress that he should not delay in handing his slave over to legal torture; and the one who seeks redress should have branches prepared which have the thickness of a little finger and he should have a rack prepared where he is able to stretch that slave.

9. But if the slave's lord delays the torture and the slave is present, let him who seeks redress from the slave's lord set a court day where after seven days he should hand over his slave for torture.

10. If after seven days he [the lord of the slave] still delays in handing over his slave for torture, he who seeks redress for these things should again set a day for him. And thus again he should set a court day after seven days, that is, fourteen days after the first warning.

11. But if after fourteen days have passed, he [the slave's lord] is still not willing to hand over his slave for torture, the lord must accept responsibility for the whole case and composition. That is, if it were such a case that a freeman would have to pay six hundred denarii for it (i.e., fifteen solidi), the lord of the slave must pay this amount.

12. But if it is a more serious crime, one for which a freeman would have to pay eighteen hundred denarii (i.e., forty-five solidi), and the lord has not handed over his slave, he [the lord] must pay this number of solidi and restore the full value of the object stolen to its proper place.

13. And if it is a still more serious crime than this for which the slave is demanded [for torture], the slave's lord shall receive the full weight of the law to absolve himself as a freeman, not as a slave.

14. If moreover the slave is absent, then he who seeks redress for these things should warn the lord of the slave separately that he should present his slave within seven days. And if he does not do this, then he who seeks redress should with witnesses set a court day for him. And yet a third time he should set a court day for him within seven days so that the total number of days comes to twenty-one.

But if after the third court he [the slave's lord] is still not willing to hand over his slave bound for torture, and each court day has been set, then the lord of the slave shall, as we have said above, pay composition to him seeking redress as if a freeman had committed the crime, not a slave.

15. But if a female slave is charged with such a crime that a male slave would have been castrated for it, her lord must pay two hundred forty denarii (i.e., six solidi), if he is willing, or else she must receive two hundred forty lashes of the whip.

XLII [XI]

CONCERNING THE THEFT OF SLAVES OR OTHER *MANCIPII* [*Pactus* X]

1. If anyone steals another man's male or female slave, he shall be liable to pay fourteen hundred denarii (i.e., thirty-five solidi) in addition to return of the stolen slave [or his value] plus a payment for the time his labor was lost.

2. If the male or female slave taken by that freeman carried anything from his or her lord's property, he [who committed the theft] will be liable to pay six hundred denarii (i.e., fifteen solidi) in addition to return of the value of the property involved plus a payment for the time its use was lost. And he is also liable to pay as we have said in the previous case (i.e., thirty-five solidi for the slave).

3. If anyone kills or sells another's slave or sets him free, he shall be liable to pay fourteen hundred denarii (i.e., thirty-five solidi) in addition to return of the value of the slave involved plus a payment for the time his labor was lost.

4. If any freeman takes another man's slave along with him during a theft (*in texaca*) or conducts any business with him, he shall be liable to pay six hundred denarii (i.e., fifteen solidi) in addition to return of the value involved plus a payment for the time his labor was lost.

5. If anyone steals or sells a male or female slave valued at (six or) fifteen or twenty-five solidi—whether he or she is a swineherd or blacksmith (*fabrum*) or vinedresser or miller (*mulinarium*) or carpenter or any other craftsman—he shall be liable to pay eighteen hundred denarii (i.e., forty-five solidi) in addition to return of the value of the slave involved plus a payment for the time his or her labor was lost.

6. If anyone steals a male or female slave from the household service of his or her lord, he must pay one thousand denarii (i.e., twenty-five solidi) for the full value of the slave plus fourteen hundred denarii (i.e., thirty-five solidi); in addition he must return the stolen slave [or his or her value] plus a payment for the time his or her labor was lost.

XLIII [XLI]

CONCERNING THOSE WHO ENTICE AWAY OTHER MEN'S SLAVES (*mancipia*) [*Pactus* XXXIX]

1. If anyone entices away another man's slave (*mancipium*) and he is convicted of this, he shall be liable to pay six hundred denarii (i.e., fifteen solidi).

2. If anyone kidnaps another's slave, that is, if he fraudulently takes him away from servitude to his lord, and leads him across the sea or into another region, and there he [the slave] is found by his lord, let him name in a public court (*in mallo publico*) the man by whom he was kidnapped from his native land, and let his lord have three witnesses there.

And again when the slave has been recalled from across the sea or from whatever region, he should in another court name the man who had kidnapped him, and again there should be three witnesses there. And let it be done in the same manner in a third court so that there are nine witnesses who can swear that they had heard this slave speaking in the same way about his kidnapper. Afterwards he who kidnapped him shall be liable to pay fourteen hundred denarii (i.e., thirty-five solidi) in addition to return of the slave in dispute plus a payment for the time his labor was lost.

Nevertheless, with this stipulation he should state the names of the men and of their villages (*villarum*) in the same way in all three courts.

3. If anyone kidnaps or sells a freeman and afterwards he is returned to his native land, he [who kidnapped him] shall be liable to pay four thousand denarii (i.e., one hundred solidi).

4. If anyone sells a freeman and afterwards he is not returned to his own property in his native land, he [who sold him] shall be liable to pay eight thousand denarii (i.e., two hundred solidi).

XLIV [XL]

CONCERNING STOLEN HORSES [*Pactus* XXXVIII]

1. If anyone steals a horse that pulls a cart (*carruam*), he shall be liable to pay eighteen hundred denarii (i.e., forty-five solidi) in addition to return of the stolen animal [or its value] plus a payment for the time its use was lost.

2. If anyone steals a Frank's stallion (*warannionem*), he shall be liable to pay eighteen hundred denarii (i.e., forty-five solidi) in addition to return of the stolen animal [or its value] plus a payment for the time its use was lost.

3. If anyone steals a gelded horse, he shall be liable to pay fourteen hundred denarii (i.e., thirty-five solidi) in addition to return of the stolen animal [or its value] plus a payment for the time its use was lost.

4. If anyone steals one of the king's stallions (*warannionem*), he shall be liable to pay thirty-six hundred denarii (i.e., ninety solidi) in addition to return of the stolen animal [or its value] plus a payment for the time its use was lost.

5. If anyone steals a stallion (*amissarium*) with a herd that contains between seven and twelve mares, he shall be liable to pay twenty-five hundred denarii (i.e., sixty-two and one-half solidi) in addition to return of the stolen animals [or their value] plus a payment for the time their use was lost.

6. If it came from a herd in which there were fewer (no more than six head), it is fitting that the amount be observed as set forth in the case above.

7. If anyone steals a one- or two-year-old colt (*pulledrum*), he shall be liable to pay six hundred denarii (i.e., fifteen solidi) in addition to return of the stolen animal [or its value] plus a payment for the time its use was lost.

8. But if he steals a following foal [i.e., one not yet weaned], he shall be liable to pay one hundred twenty denarii (i.e., three solidi) in addition to return of the stolen animal [or its value] plus a payment for the time its use was lost.

9. If anyone strikes another's mare and she survives, he shall be liable to pay six hundred denarii (i.e., fifteen solidi) in addition to payment of the value of the animal plus a payment for the time its use was lost.

10. If she dies from this, however, he [who mistreated it] shall be liable to pay twelve hundred denarii (i.e., thirty solidi).

11. If anyone steals a pregnant mare, he shall be liable to pay eighteen hundred denarii (i.e., forty-five solidi).

12. If anyone steals a mare or riding horse (*caballum*), he shall be liable to pay fourteen hundred denarii (i.e., thirty-five solidi).

13. If anyone gelds another's stallion without the consent of its owner, he shall be liable to pay six hundred denarii (i.e., fifteen solidi). And for each one of those mares that the stallion was accustomed to service, let him pay a *triens*, which is a third of a solidus (i.e., thirteen and one-third denarii).

14. If anyone out of arrogance or enmity mistreats or injures another's riding horses or mares, he shall be liable to pay twelve hundred denarii (i.e., thirty solidi).

15. If anyone cuts off the tail (*excurtaverit*) of another's horse without the consent of its owner, he shall be liable to pay one hundred twenty denarii (i.e., three solidi).

16. If anyone flays (*excoriaverit*) another's horse, he shall be liable to pay one hundred twenty denarii (i.e., three solidi).

XLV [XXV]

CONCERNING MOUNTING A HORSE WITHOUT THE PERMISSION OF ITS OWNER [*Pactus* XXIII]

If anyone mounts and rides another's horse without the permission of its owner, he shall be liable to pay six hundred denarii (i.e., fifteen solidi). And when he dismounts from it, he shall be liable to pay another six hundred denarii (i.e., fifteen solidi).

XLVI [LXVIII]

CONCERNING SKINNING A HORSE [*Pactus* LXV]

1. If anyone skins (*decorticaverit*) another's horse without the permission of its owner, and having been questioned confesses, he must restore the full value (*in capitala*) of the horse.

2. But if he denies it and is convicted of doing it, he shall be liable to pay six hundred denarii (i.e., fifteen solidi)[33] in addition to paying the value of the animal plus a payment for the time its use was lost.

XLVII [VI]

CONCERNING THE THEFT OF DOGS [*Pactus* VI]

1. If anyone steals or kills a hunting (*seusium*) dog which is trained (*magister sit*), he shall be liable to pay eighteen hundred denarii (i.e., forty-five solidi) in addition to a payment for the value of the animal plus a payment for the time its use was lost.
2. If anyone steals or kills one of the other hunting dogs, either a pig dog (*veltrem porcario*) or a rabbit dog (*veltrem leporarium*)—which are called tracking dogs (*argutarius*)—, he shall be liable to pay six hundred denarii (i.e., fifteen solidi) in addition to a payment for the value of the animal plus a payment for the time its use was lost.
3. But if anyone steals or kills a dog that watches a house or courtyard, one which is usually bound by day lest he cause damage and released after the sun has set, he shall be liable to pay six hundred denarii (i.e., fifteen solidi) in addition to a payment for the value of the animal plus a payment for the time its use was lost.
4. If anyone steals or kills a herd dog, he shall be liable to pay one hundred twenty denarii (i.e., three solidi) in addition to a payment for the value of the animal plus a payment for the time its use was lost.

XLVIII [XXXV]

CONCERNING THE HUNT [*Pactus* XXXIII]

1. If anyone either steals or hides anything from the various hunts,[34] he shall be liable to pay eighteen hundred denarii (i.e., forty-five solidi). It is fitting to observe the same law for both hunting and fishing.
2. If anyone either kills or steals a domesticated deer bearing a brand, one which has been tamed for hunting and its owner can prove with witnesses that he had it with him on the hunt and with it had killed two or three beasts, he [who kills or steals it] shall be liable to pay eighteen hundred denarii (i.e., forty-five solidi).
3. But if anyone either kills or steals a domesticated deer which is yet to be

placed in the hunt, he shall be liable to pay fourteen hundred denarii (i.e., thirty-five solidi).[35]

4. If anyone kills and hides a deer which the dogs of another man have chased and tired, he shall be liable to pay six hundred denarii (i.e., fifteen solidi).

5. If anyone kills or steals a tired boar which the dogs of another man have chased, he shall be liable to pay six hundred denarii (i.e., fifteen solidi).

XLIX [VII]

CONCERNING THE THEFT OF BIRDS [*Pactus* VII]

1. If anyone steals a hawk from a tree, he shall be liable to pay one hundred twenty denarii (i.e., three solidi) in addition to return of the object stolen [or its value] plus a payment for the time its use was lost.

2. If anyone steals a hawk from a perch, he shall be liable to pay six hundred denarii (i.e., fifteen solidi) in addition to return of the object stolen [or its value] plus a payment for the time its use was lost.

3. If anyone steals a hawk kept under key, he shall be liable to pay eighteen hundred denarii (i.e., forty-five solidi) in addition to return of the object stolen [or its value] plus a payment for the time its use was lost.

4. If anyone steals a sparrow hawk (*sparvarium*), he shall be liable to pay one hundred twenty denarii (i.e., three solidi) in addition to return of the object stolen [or its value] plus a payment for the time its use was lost.

5. If anyone steals a domesticated goose or duck, he shall be liable to pay one hundred twenty denarii (i.e., three solidi) in addition to return of the object stolen [or its value] plus a payment for the time its use was lost.

6. If anyone steals a rooster or hen or a swan or a domesticated crane, he shall be liable to pay one hundred twenty denarii (i.e., three solidi) in addition to return of the object stolen [or its value] plus a payment for the time its use was lost.

7. If anyone steals a turtle dove from another's nest or some other little bird from a snare or trap, he shall be liable to pay one hundred twenty denarii (i.e., three solidi) in addition to return of the object stolen [or its value] plus a payment for the time its use was lost.

L [III]

CONCERNING THE THEFT OF CATTLE (*animalium*) [*Pactus* III]

1. If anyone steals a nursing calf, he shall be liable to pay one hundred twenty denarii (i.e., three solidi) in addition to return of the animal stolen [or its value] plus a payment for the time its use was lost.
2. If anyone steals a yearling calf or a two-year-old heifer, he shall be liable to pay six hundred denarii (i.e., fifteen solidi) in addition to return of the animal [or its value] plus a payment for the time its use was lost.
3. If anyone steals a cow with a calf, he shall be liable to pay fourteen hundred denarii (i.e., thirty-five solidi) in addition to return of the animals [or their value] plus a payment for the time their use was lost.
4. If anyone steals a cow without a calf, he shall be liable to pay twelve hundred denarii (i.e., thirty solidi) in addition to return of the animal stolen [or its value] plus a payment for the time its use was lost.
5. If anyone steals a cow broken to the yoke he shall be liable to pay fourteen hundred denarii (i.e., thirty-five solidi) in addition to return of the animal stolen [or its value] plus a payment for the time its use was lost.
6. If anyone steals an ox, he shall be liable to pay fourteen hundred denarii (i.e., thirty-five solidi) in addition to return of the animal stolen [or its value] plus a payment for the time its use was lost.
7. If anyone steals a bull which rules a herd on a three-village common, i.e., a *trespellius*, he shall be liable to pay eighteen hundred denarii (i.e., forty-five solidi) in addition to return of the animal stolen [or its value] plus a payment for the time its use was lost.
8. If anyone steals a bull which rules one herd and has never been yoked, he shall be liable to pay eighteen hundred denarii (i.e., forty-five solidi) in addition to return of the animal stolen [or its value] plus a payment for the time its use was lost.
9. If anyone steals a two-year-old bull, he shall be liable to pay fourteen hundred denarii (i.e., thirty-five solidi) in addition to return of the animal stolen [or its value] plus a payment for the time its use was lost.
10. If anyone steals one of the king's bulls, he shall be liable to pay thirty-five hundred [sic] denarii (i.e., ninety solidi) in addition to return of the animal stolen [or its value] plus a payment for the time its use was lost.
11. If anyone steals twelve head of cattle so that not even one of them remains, he shall be liable to pay twenty-five hundred denarii (i.e., sixty-two

and one-half solidi) in addition to return of the animals stolen [or their value] plus a payment for the time their use was lost.

12. But if he steals twelve and others remain, he shall be liable to pay fourteen hundred denarii (i.e., thirty-five solidi) in addition to return of the animals stolen [or their value] plus a payment for the time their use was lost. And thefts up to twenty-five animals shall be concluded by this judgment.

13. If anyone steals twenty-five head of cattle and others remain, he shall be liable to pay twenty-five hundred denarii (i.e., sixty-two and one-half solidi) in addition to return of the animals stolen [or their value] plus a payment for the time their use was lost.

LI [II]

CONCERNING THE THEFT OF PIGS [*Pactus* II]

1. If anyone steals a suckling piglet from the first or middle enclosure (*chranne*) and is convicted for it, he shall be liable to pay one hundred twenty denarii (i.e., three solidi) in addition to return of the animal stolen [or its value] plus a payment for the time its use was lost.

2. But if he steals from the third enclosure, he shall be liable to pay six hundred denarii (i.e., fifteen solidi) in addition to return of the animal stolen [or its value] plus a payment for the time its use was lost.

3. If anyone steals a piglet from a sty (*supe*) which has been locked, he shall be liable to pay eighteen hundred denarii (i.e., forty-five solidi) in addition to return of the animal stolen [or its value] plus a payment for the time its use was lost.

4. If anyone steals a piglet from the pigs in a field guarded by a swineherd, he shall be liable to pay six hundred denarii (i.e., fifteen solidi) in addition to return of the animal stolen [or its value] plus a payment for the time its use was lost.

5. If anyone steals a piglet that can live without its mother, he shall be liable to pay forty denarii (i.e., one solidus) in addition to return of the animal stolen [or its value] plus a payment for the time its use was lost.

6. If anyone strikes a breeding sow so that she loses her piglets, he shall be liable to pay two hundred seventy [sic] denarii (i.e., seven solidi) in addition to paying the value of the animals plus a payment for the time their use was lost.

7. If anyone steals a sow with piglets, he shall be liable to pay eight hundred denarii (i.e., seventeen and one-half solidi) in addition to return of the animals stolen [or their value] plus a payment for the time their use was lost.

8. If anyone steals a one-year-old piglet, he shall be liable to pay one hundred twenty denarii (i.e., three solidi) in addition to return of the animal stolen [or its value] plus a payment for the time its use was lost.

9. If anyone steals a two-year-old piglet, he shall be liable to pay six hundred denarii (i.e., fifteen solidi) in addition to return of the animal stolen [or its value] plus a payment for the time its use was lost.

10. If anyone steals a piglet from the time it can eat up until it is one year old, he shall be liable to pay one hundred twenty denarii (i.e., three solidi) in addition to return of the animal stolen [or its value] plus a payment for the time its use was lost.

11. But if anyone steals a pig more than one year old, he shall be liable to pay six hundred denarii (i.e., fifteen solidi) in addition to return of the animal stolen [or its value] plus a payment for the time its use was lost.

12. If anyone steals a boar, he shall be liable to pay seven hundred denarii (i.e., seventeen and one-half solidi) in addition to return of the animal stolen [or its value] plus a payment for the time its use was lost.

13. If anyone steals a leader sow (*scrovam ducariam*), he shall be liable to pay seven hundred denarii (i.e., seventeen and one-half solidi) in addition to return of the animal stolen [or its value] plus a payment for the time its use was lost.

14. If anyone steals a dedicated gelded boar (*maialem*) which is said to have been consecrated, and he who lost it can prove with witnesses that it had been dedicated, then he [who stole the boar] shall be liable to pay seven hundred denarii (i.e., seventeen and one-half solidi) in addition to return of the animal stolen [or its value] plus a payment for the time its use was lost.

15. If anyone steals a gelded boar that has not been dedicated, he shall be liable to pay six hundred denarii (i.e., fifteen solidi) in addition to return of the animal stolen [or its value] plus a payment for the time its use was lost.

16. If anyone steals three or more pigs—up to six head—he shall be liable to pay fourteen hundred denarii (i.e., thirty-five solidi) in addition to return of the animals stolen [or their value] plus a payment for the time their use was lost.

17. If anyone steals fifteen pigs from a herd and the rest remain there, he shall be liable to pay fourteen hundred denarii (i.e., thirty-five solidi) in addition to return of the animals stolen [or their value] plus a payment for the time their use was lost.

18. If anyone steals twenty-five pigs from a herd where there are no more, he shall be liable to pay twenty-five hundred denarii (i.e., sixty-two and one-half solidi) in addition to return of the animals stolen [or their value] plus a payment for the time their use was lost.

19. But if others from this same herd remain over and beyond the twenty-five pigs taken, and these are not stolen, he [who took the twenty-five] shall be liable to pay fourteen hundred denarii (i.e., thirty-five solidi) in addition to return of the animals stolen [or their value] plus a payment for the time their use was lost.

20. But if he steals fifty pigs and others still remain, he shall be liable to pay twenty-five hundred denarii (i.e., sixty-two and one-half solidi) in addition to return of the animals stolen [or their value] plus a payment for the time their use was lost.

LII [IV]

CONCERNING THE THEFT OF SHEEP [*Pactus* IV]

1. If anyone steals a nursing lamb, he shall be liable to pay seven denarii (i.e., ____solidi),[36] in addition to return of the animal stolen [or its value] plus a payment for the time its use was lost.

2. If anyone steals a one- or two-year-old wether, he shall be liable to pay one hundred twenty denarii (i.e., three solidi) in addition to return of the animal stolen [or its value] plus a payment for the time its use was lost.

3. But if he steals two or three, he shall be liable to pay fourteen hundred denarii (i.e., thirty-five solidi) in addition to return of the animals stolen [or their value] plus a payment for the time their use was lost. This composition is observed in cases involving up to forty wethers.

4. If anyone steals [40 or] 50 wethers or 60 or more, he shall be liable to pay twenty-five hundred denarii (i.e., sixty-two and one half solidi) in addition to return of the animals stolen [or their value] plus a payment for the time their use was lost.

LIII [V]

CONCERNING THE THEFT OF GOATS [*Pactus* V]

1. If anyone steals a male or female goat, or two or three, he shall be liable to pay one hundred twenty denarii (i.e., three solidi) in addition to return of the animals stolen [or their value] plus a payment for the time their use was lost.
2. But if he steals more than three goats, he shall be liable to pay six hundred denarii (i.e., fifteen solidi) in addition to return of the animals stolen [or their value] plus a payment for the time their use was lost.

LIV [IX]

CONCERNING THE THEFT OF BEES [*Pactus* VIII]

1. If anyone steals one hive (*vas*) of bees that is kept under lock or under a roof, he shall be liable to pay eighteen hundred denarii (i.e., forty-five solidi) in addition to return of the objects stolen [or their value] plus a payment for the time their use was lost.
2. If anyone steals one beehive with bees where there are no more, he shall be liable to pay eighteen hundred denarii (i.e., forty-five solidi) in addition to return of the objects stolen [or their value] plus a payment for the time their use was lost.
3. If anyone steals one beehive with bees from among other hives kept under a roof or under lock and key, it is fitting to observe the provisions of the previous case.[37]
4. But if the beehive with bees is outside the building and where there are no more, let composition be made as contained in the earlier case [cf. LIV, 2].
5. If anyone steals up to six beehives from among many outside a building, he shall be liable to pay six hundred denarii (i.e., fifteen solidi) in addition to return of the objects stolen [or their value] plus a payment for the time their use was lost.
6. But if he steals seven or more and still others remain, he shall be liable to pay eighteen hundred denarii (i.e., forty-five solidi) in addition to return

of the objects stolen [or their value] plus a payment for the time their use was lost.

7. If anyone steals seven or more, where no others remain, he shall be liable to pay eighteen hundred denarii (i.e., forty-five solidi)[38] in addition to return of the objects stolen [or their value] plus a payment for the time their use was lost.

LV [VIII]

CONCERNING THE THEFT OF TREES [not in *Pactus*]

1. If anyone cuts down or steals an orchard tree (fruit tree—*pomarium*) or any other cultivated tree outside someone's enclosure, he shall be liable to pay one hundred twenty denarii (i.e., three solidi) in addition to return of the value of the tree plus a payment for the time its use was lost.

2. But if anyone cuts down or steals an orchard tree (fruit tree) or any other kind of cultivated tree inside someone's enclosure, he shall be liable to pay six hundred denarii (i.e., fifteen solidi) in addition to return of the value of the tree plus a payment for the time its use was lost.

3. We order this law also to be observed in the case of stolen vines.

4. If anyone steals timber from another's forest, or burns or cuts down or steals another's wood, he shall be liable to pay six hundred denarii (i.e., fifteen solidi) in addition to return of the material involved [or its value] plus a payment for the time its use was lost.

LVI [XXIV]

CONCERNING THEFTS COMMITTED IN A MILL [*Pactus* XXII]

1. If a freeman steals the grain (*annonam*) from another man's mill, he shall be liable to pay to him to whom the mill belongs six hundred denarii (i.e., fifteen solidi). And he shall be liable to pay him to whom the grain belongs likewise six hundred denarii (i.e., fifteen solidi) in addition to return of the stolen grain [or its value] plus a payment for the time its use was lost.

2. If anyone steals an iron tool from [another's] mill, he shall be liable to pay eighteen hundred denarii (i.e., forty-five solidi) in addition to return

of the object stolen [or its value] plus a payment for the time its use was lost.

3. If anyone breaks into the enclosure (*clusam*) of another's mill (*defarinario*) he shall be liable to pay six hundred denarii (i.e., fifteen solidi) in addition to return of anything stolen [or its value] plus a payment for the time its use was lost.

LVII [XXIX]

CONCERNING VARIOUS KINDS OF THEFTS [*Pactus* XXVII]

1. If anyone steals the bell (*tintinnum*) from another man's herd of pigs, he shall be liable to pay six hundred denarii (i.e., fifteen solidi).

2. But if he steals a bell from a cow, he shall be liable to pay one hundred twenty denarii (i.e., three solidi).

3. If anyone steals the bell (*schellam*) from a horse, he shall be liable to pay six hundred denarii (i.e., fifteen solidi).

4. If anyone steals the hobble (*pedicam*) from a horse, he shall be liable to pay one hundred twenty denarii (i.e., three solidi).

5. If the horses are lost, he must restore horses of equal value (*capitale*) in their place.

6. If anyone attempts to mow (*metere*) or reap (*refare*) another's harvest in theft, he shall be liable to pay six hundred denarii (i.e., fifteen solidi).

7. If anyone enters another's garden to commit a theft, he shall be liable to pay six hundred denarii (i.e., fifteen solidi).

8. If anyone takes away the grafted twigs (*inpotos*) from an apple (*malario*) or from a pear tree (*pirario*), he shall be liable to pay one hundred twenty denarii (i.e., three solidi).

9. If it was in a garden, he shall be liable to pay six hundred denarii (i.e., fifteen solidi).

10. If anyone strips the bark from an apple or a pear tree, he shall be liable to pay one hundred twenty denarii (i.e., three solidi).

11. If it was in a garden, he shall be liable to pay six hundred denarii (i.e., fifteen solidi).

12. If anyone steals another man's coulter (*cultellum*), he shall be liable to pay six hundred denarii (i.e., fifteen solidi).

13. If anyone enters with intent to steal into a turnip field, a bean patch, a

pea patch, a lentil patch, or any similar place, he shall be liable to pay one hundred twenty denarii (i.e., three solidi).

14. If anyone steals flax from another's field and carries it off on a horse or in a cart, he shall be liable to pay six hundred denarii (i.e., fifteen solidi).

15. But if he carries away only so much as he can carry on his back, he shall be liable to pay one hundred twenty denarii (i.e., three solidi).

16. If anyone cuts down a tree planted in another's field, he shall be liable to pay twelve hundred denarii (i.e., thirty solidi).

17. If anyone plows and sows another's land, he shall be liable to pay eighteen hundred denarii (i.e., forty-five solidi).

18. But if he plows only and does not sow, he shall be liable to pay six hundred denarii (i.e., fifteen solidi).

19. If anyone prevents a plow from entering another's field or throws the man plowing off the property or raises an objection (*testaverit*) against him, he shall be liable to pay six hundred denarii (i.e., fifteen solidi).

20. If anyone cuts another's meadow, let him lose his work and in addition be liable to pay six hundred denarii (i.e., fifteen solidi).

21. And if from there he carries hay in a cart to his house and unloads it, he shall be liable to pay eighteen hundred denarii (i.e., forty-five solidi) in addition to return of the material stolen [or its value] plus a payment for the time its use was lost.

22. But if he takes only so much as he can carry on his back, he shall be liable to pay one hundred twenty denarii (i.e., three solidi) in addition to return of the material stolen [or its value] plus a payment for the time its use was lost.

23. If anyone reaps the harvest of another's vineyard in theft, he shall be liable to pay six hundred denarii (i.e., fifteen solidi).

24. And if from there he carries off the wine to his house in a cart and there unloads it, he shall be liable to pay eighteen hundred denarii (i.e., forty-five solidi) in addition to return of the material stolen [or its value] plus a payment for the time its use was lost.

25. And it is fitting to observe this same law similarly in connection with the grain harvests.

26. If anyone breaks into another's enclosure, he shall be liable to pay six hundred denarii (i.e., fifteen solidi).

27. If anyone either sets fire to wood in another's forest or cuts another's lumber, he shall be liable to pay six hundred denarii (i.e., fifteen solidi).

28. If anyone steals from some place lumber hewn by an ax, he shall be liable to pay one hundred twenty denarii (i.e., three solidi).

29. If anyone presumes to cut down a tree after the year that it was marked for cutting, let him bear no blame for this.

30. If anyone cuts it down within the year, he shall be liable to pay one hundred twenty denarii (i.e., three solidi).

31. If anyone steals the net used for catching eels from a river, he shall be liable to pay eighteen hundred denarii (i.e., forty-five solidi).

32. If anyone steals a fishing net (*statuam*) or a trammel net (*tremachlum*) or a fish wier (*vertivolum*) from the river, he shall be liable to pay six hundred denarii (i.e., fifteen solidi).

33. If anyone breaks into a work room (*screonam*) which has a key [i.e., which is locked] and steals something, he shall be liable to pay eighteen hundred denarii (i.e., forty-five solidi).

34. And if he takes nothing from that place, let him be liable to pay six hundred denarii (i.e., fifteen solidi) for breach of the room (*sola*).

35. But if he breaks into a work room (*screonam*) which is without a key [i.e., which is not locked], he shall be liable to pay six hundred denarii (i.e., fifteen solidi).

36. If anyone carries on any business with another man's slave without the consent of his lord, he shall be liable to pay six hundred denarii (i.e., fifteen solidi).

37. If anyone steals a woman's girdle-belt (*brachile*), he shall be liable to pay one hundred twenty denarii (i.e., three solidi).

38. If anyone passes through another man's house without the permission of its owner, he shall be liable to pay twelve hundred denarii (i.e., thirty solidi).

LVIII [XXXIX]

CONCERNING FOLLOWING TRACKS (*de vestigio minando*) [*Pactus* XXXVII]

If anyone loses a cow or a mare or any other animal that has been stolen from himself, and he pursues it for up to three days by following its tracks, and he who led it away says or declares that he had bought or traded for it, he who was following the tracks ought to take possession of (*adhramire*) his property through a third party.

But if he who sought his property found it after more than three days, he with whom it was found, if he claims that he paid or traded something for it, may retain possession (*adhramire*) of it.

But if he who was following the tracks says that he recognizes it [his property] and does not wish to take possession through a third party, even though the other man denies his claim, nor does he go to court according to law (*solem secundum legem calcaverit*), and he is convicted of taking by force that which he said he recognized, he shall be liable to pay twelve hundred denarii (i.e., thirty solidi) in addition to return of the object in dispute plus a payment for the time its use was lost.

LIX [XLIX]

CONCERNING PROPERTY PLACED IN A THIRD PARTY'S HAND (*intertiatis*) [*Pactus* XLVII]

If anyone living by Salic law recognizes his male or female slave, horse or cow or mare or any other property of his in the possession of another, he should place it in the hands of a third party. And he with whom it is recognized should hand it over (*adhrammire*) [to a third party].

And if both men live between the Loire River and the Carbonaria Forest,[39] both he who recognizes [his property] and he with whom [the property] was recognized should appear before a court (*placitum*) within forty days. And at this court there should be present as many as are involved, he who sold or traded or perhaps gave in payment the property placed in a third party's hand [i.e., the property in dispute]; all these persons should be involved in the hearing, and let each one along with his associates remind the rest.

But if he who was summoned delays to come to the court (*placitum*) and no legitimate excuse (*sunnis*) detains him, then that one who did business with him should have three witnesses to the fact that he had sent word to him that he should come to court (*placitum*). And he should have three other [witnesses] likewise [to the fact] that he did business with him publicly. And if does this, then he escapes from the charge of theft. If moreover the man warned does not come and the witnesses testify against him, he will be known as the robber of him who recognized his property and he must pay composition to him according to law. And in addition he must restore the price paid to the man who did business with him. All these things should be done there where his party (*amallus*) is with whom the property was originally recognized or was transferred into a third hand (*intertiata*).

But if the man with whom the property is recognized lives beyond the Loire River or Carbonaria Forest, the meeting must be set for eighty days.

LX [LI]

CONCERNING THE SUMMONING OF WITNESSES [*Pactus* XLIX]

1. If anyone has suitable witnesses and perhaps they do not wish to come to court (*ad placitum*), he who has such suitable ones ought to summon them with other witnesses to court so that they may say under oath what they know.
2. If indeed they do not wish to come and no legitimate excuse detains them, each of them will be liable to pay six hundred denarii (i.e., fifteen solidi).
3. If indeed those called to give witness are present and do not wish to say under oath what they know when they are ordered (*ferbanniti fuerint*) to do so, let each one of them be liable to pay six hundred denarii (i.e., fifteen solidi).

LXI [X]

CONCERNING DAMAGE TO A CULTIVATED FIELD OR SOME OTHER ENCLOSURE [*Pactus* IX]

1. If anyone finds a cow or horse or any other sort of beast in his field, he ought not to injure it seriously.
2. But if he does so and confesses, let him make restitution of the full value of the animal; and he should keep for himself the weakened animal that he struck.
3. But if he has not confessed and is convicted of it, he will be liable to pay six hundred denarii (i.e., fifteen solidi) in addition to return of the full value of the animal plus a payment for the time its use was lost.
4. If anyone brands a cow or horse or mare that he has stolen, he shall be liable to pay six hundred denarii (i.e., fifteen solidi) in addition to return of the value of the animal plus a payment for the time its use was lost.
5. If anyone finds another man's animals in his field and they do not have a herder, and if he shuts them in and makes it known to no one and some of

these animals die, he shall be liable to pay fourteen hundred denarii (i.e., thirty-five solidi) in addition to return of the value of the animals plus a payment for the time their use was lost.

6. If anyone harms a cow or any other animal through his own neglect and he confesses this to its owner, let him restore an animal of the same value to its owner and keep the weakened one for himself.

7. But if he denies it but nevertheless is convicted, he shall be liable to pay six hundred denarii (i.e., fifteen solidi) in addition to return of the value of the animal involved plus a payment for the time its use was lost.

8. If a man's pigs or other animals in the care of the herder run into somone else's cultivated field and the owner [of the pigs] although denying it is convicted, he shall be liable to pay six hundred denarii (i.e., fifteen solidi) in addition to payment of the value of the damage involved plus a payment for the time lost.

9. If some animals have been shut up or led away (*minantur*) because of damage caused to another man's field, he who attempts to drive them out or release them shall be liable to pay six hundred denarii (i.e., fifteen solidi) in addition to payment of the value of the damages involved plus a payment for the time lost.

10. If anyone's animals are shut in because of causing damage, he must pay for the estimated damage and pay ten denarii in addition.

11. If anyone, on account of enmity or arrogance, opens another man's fenced enclosure or sends animals into a field or meadow or vineyard or any other worked area and he is proved to have done so by witnesses, to him to whom the worked area belongs he must pay the estimated damage, and in addition he shall be liable to pay twelve hundred denarii (i.e., thirty solidi).

LXII [XXXVI]

CONCERNING FENCES [*Pactus* XXXIV]

1. If anyone cuts off three branches with which a fence is bound together or twigs (*retortas*) by which the fence is held together or destroys three fence poles (*cambortos*), he shall be liable to pay six hundred denarii (i.e., fifteen solidi).

2. If anyone draws a harrow (*herpicem*) through another man's field after it

begins to sprout or crosses it with a cart outside the tracks, he shall be liable to pay one hundred twenty denarii (i.e., three solidi).

3. If anyone outside the tracks crosses another man's field with his cart after the stalks have grown, he shall be liable to pay six hundred denarii (i.e., fifteen solidi).

4. If anyone with evil intent has put something that has been stolen anywhere in another man's enclosed yard or house, the master [of the house] not knowing whose possession it is, and it is found there, that one who put it there with evil intent shall be liable to pay twenty-five hundred denarii (i.e., sixty-two and one-half solidi).

LXIII [XXIII]

CONCERNING HIM WHO MOVES OR STEALS ANOTHER MAN'S BOAT [*Pactus* XXI]

1. If anyone presumes to move another man's boat without its owner's permission, he shall be liable to pay one hundred twenty denarii (i.e., three solidi).

2. If he actually steals the boat, he shall be liable to pay six hundred denarii (i.e., fifteen solidi) in addition to return of the object stolen [or its value] plus a payment for the time its use was lost.

3. If anyone steals a boat or skiff (*ascum*) kept under lock and key, he shall be liable to pay fourteen hundred denarii (i.e., thirty-five solidi) in addition to return of the object stolen [or its value] plus a payment for the time its use was lost.

4. If anyone steals a skiff (*ascum*) kept under lock and key and hung carefully suspended, he shall be liable to pay eighteen hundred denarii (i.e., forty-five solidi) in addition to return of the object stolen [or its value] plus a payment for the time its use was lost.

LXIV [XXX]

CONCERNING HIRING (*locationibus*) [*Pactus* XXVIII]

1. If anyone secretly hires someone to kill a man and receive pay for this but the man does not do it, he [who hired him] shall be liable to pay twenty-five hundred denarii (i.e., sixty-two and one-half solidi).

2. And likewise he who accepts the money to kill the man [and does not kill him] shall be liable to pay twenty-five hundred denarii (i.e., sixty-two and one-half solidi).

3. If it [the commission to kill] was passed on to a third party, he [the third party] shall be liable to pay twenty-five hundred denarii (i.e., sixty-two and one-half solidi). So the giver, the receiver, and the transferer, each one of them, is liable to pay [the same amount].

LXV [XXXVIII]

CONCERNING FOUR-FOOTED ANIMALS THAT KILL A MAN
[*Pactus* XXXVI]

If a man is killed by some domesticated animal and his relatives can prove that the owner of the animal had not fulfilled the law [in taking care of the beast], let the owner of the four-footed animal pay half the composition [i.e., half the wergeld of the dead man]. And let him turn over to him seeking redress the animal itself which was the author of the crime to count for the other one-half of the composition; [it shall be done] in this way if the owner of the animal does not know how to defend himself legally.

LXVI [XXXVII]

CONCERNING THE KILLING OF MALE OR FEMALE SLAVES
[*Pactus* XXXV]

1. If a slave kills a male or female slave like himself, the lords may divide the killer between themselves.

2. If any freeman attacks (*adsallierit*) and robs another man's slave and is convicted of it, if the value of what he took is more than forty denarii (i.e., one solidus), he shall be liable to pay twelve hundred denarii (i.e., thirty solidi).

3. If what he took is valued at less than forty denarii, he shall be liable to pay six hundred denarii (i.e., fifteen solidi).

4. If anyone whips another man's slave so that he is not able to work for forty days, he shall be liable to pay forty denarii (i.e., one solidus) and a *triens* (that is, one-third of a solidus).

5. If a freeman robs another man's half-free man (*lidum*), he shall be liable to pay fourteen hundred denarii (i.e., thirty-five solidi).

6. If anyone stealthily robs the body of another man's dead slave and the spoils are worth more than forty denarii, he shall be liable to pay fourteen hundred denarii (i.e., thirty-five solidi).

7. If the spoils are worth less than forty denarii, he shall be liable to pay six hundred denarii (i.e., fifteen solidi).

8. If a slave kills a freeman, let the killer be handed over to the relatives of the dead man to count as half his composition; and the lord of the slave knows that he himself must pay the other half or, if he knows the law, he can summon himself to court (*se obmallare*) so that he does not have to pay the wergeld (*leudem*) [if it is proved that the slave is not at fault].

LXVII [XXVII]

CONCERNING HAVING INTERCOURSE WITH A FEMALE SLAVE [*Pactus* XXV]

1. If a freeman has intercourse with another man's female slave, he shall be liable to pay six hundred denarii (i.e., fifteen solidi).

2. If anyone has intercourse with the female slave of the king, he shall be liable to pay twelve hundred denarii (i.e., thirty solidi).

3. If any Frank joins another man's female slave with himself publicly, let him remain in servitude with her.

4. If a slave has intercourse with another man's female slave and she dies as a result of this crime, the slave shall be castrated or liable to pay two hundred forty denarii (i.e., six solidi). And the lord of the slave must pay the full value [of the dead female slave] to her lord (*in locum*).

5. If moreover the female slave does not die from this, the slave shall receive one hundred twenty lashes or pay one hundred twenty denarii (i.e., three solidi) to the lord of the female slave.

6. If a slave joins another man's female slave to himself in marriage without the consent of her lord, he shall be liable to pay one hundred twenty denarii (i.e., three solidi) or receive one hundred twenty lashes.

LXVIII [XXVIII]

CONCERNING SETTING BONDSMEN FREE [*Pactus* XXVI]

1. If anyone sets free with a denarius before the king another man's half-free man (*lidum*) who was in the army with his lord, without the consent of his lord, he shall be liable to pay four thousand denarii (i.e., one hundred solidi) [in addition to the value of the half-free man]. The property of the half-free man shall be returned to his lawful lord.

2. If anyone sets free with a denarius before the king another man's slave, he shall be liable to pay fourteen hundred denarii (i.e., thirty-five solidi) in addition to restoring the full value of the slave to his lord; and let his own lord receive the property of the slave.

LXIX [LXIX]

CONCERNING HIM WHO TAKES A MAN FROM THE GIBBET (*barco*) OR GALLOWS (*furcas*) [not in *Pactus*; cf. Cap. III, LXLV and LXLVI]

1. If anyone takes down a man from the gibbet or gallows without the consent of the judge, he shall be liable to pay eighteen hundred denarii (i.e., forty-five solidi).

2. If anyone without the consent of the judge presumes to take a man down from the gibbet (*ramo*) where he has been hung (*incrocatur*) he shall be liable to pay twelve hundred denarii (i.e., thirty solidi).

3. If anyone without the permission of the judge or of him who put it there, presumes to take the head of a man which his enemy had put on a stick (*in pallo*), he shall be liable to pay six hundred denarii (i.e., fifteen solidi).

4. If anyone takes a living man down from the gallows (*furca*), he shall be liable to pay four thousand denarii (i.e., one hundred solidi).

LXX [XXXII]

CONCERNING TERMS OF ABUSE (*convitiis*) [*Pactus* XXX]

1. If anyone calls another a pederast (*cenitum*), he shall be liable to pay six hundred denarii (i.e., fifteen solidi).

2. If anyone calls another *conchagatun* (covered in dung), he shall be liable to pay one hundred twenty denarii (i.e., three solidi).

3. If anyone calls another a little fox (*vulpiculam*), he shall be liable to pay one hundred twenty denarii (i.e., three solidi).

4. If anyone calls another a rabbit (*leporem*), he shall be liable to pay two hundred forty denarii (i.e., six solidi).

5. If anyone charges another with throwing down his shield while in the army or with fleeing because of fear, he shall be liable to pay one hundred twenty denarii (i.e., three solidi).

6. If anyone calls another an informer (*delatorem*) and cannot prove it, he shall be liable to pay six hundred denarii (i.e., fifteen solidi).

7. If anyone calls another a liar (*falsatorem*) and cannot prove it, he shall be liable to pay six hundred denarii (i.e., fifteen solidi).

Here Ends the Salic Law

Notes

Introduction

1. For a recent review of the literature on hospitality (though overly critical), see Walter Goffart, *Barbarians and Romans A.D. 418–585: The Techniques of Accommodation* (Princeton, 1980). For more information about the *laeti*, see Bernard S. Bachrach, *Merovingian Military Organization 481–751* (Minneapolis, 1972), pp. 10, 12, and 14; Peter Lasko, *The Kingdom of the Franks* (New York, 1971), pp. 14–16; Lucien Musset, *The Germanic Invasions* (London, 1975), pp. 75, 121–122; and J. M. Wallace-Hadrill, *The Long-Haired Kings* (New York, 1962, repr. Toronto, 1982), p. 151.

2. Row-grave cemeteries (so-called because the graves are in rows) are found along the frontiers from Britain to the Black Sea. Peter Lasko, *The Kingdom of the Franks*, pp. 16–24. Much of the material in these graves, including the Frankish ones, is Roman in origin of design and/or production.

3. Childeric I was buried at Tournai; his grave was discovered by some workmen in 1653.

> The Tournai treasure was scattered to the four winds at the moment of its discovery; and even such part of it as eventually reached the Cabinet des Medailles in Paris suffered further from pilfering in 1831. No scholar knows now, and no scholar ever knew, the nature and extent of King Childeric's grave-treasure. . . . But this much at least we can tell, either from what survives or from early descriptions: King Childeric was laid to rest, two centuries before Sutton Hoo, with magnificent war-gear, a cloak embroidered with some three hundred golden 'bees', a fine gold bracelet and buckles, a crystal globe and a miniature bull's head in gold (perhaps talismans), the severed head of his war-horse caparisoned in precious metals, a signet-ring bearing his name, a purse containing one hundred gold coins and a box containing two hundred silver coins. Nor is this a complete inventory. . . . Childeric was no savage; he had his contacts with the authorities of Roman Gaul and had played his part in its military history; and his seal-ring was engraved in Latin characters.

J. M. Wallace-Hadrill, "The Graves of Kings: An Historical Note on Some Archaeological Evidence," in *Early Medieval History* (New York, 1976), p. 43. See also E. Salin, *La Civilisation mérovingienne* (Paris, 1949–59), references scattered throughout all four volumes; and Peter Lasko, *The Kingdom of the Franks*, pp. 25–32.

4. Lucien Musset, *The Germanic Invasions*, pp. 229–230.

5. Gregory of Tours, in speaking of Clovis's victory over the Visigoths, adds:

37. . . . Then he drove the Goths out and brought the city under his own dominion. Thereupon after completing his victory he returned to Tours, bringing many gifts to the holy church of the blessed Martin.   38. Clovis received an appointment to the consulship from the emperor Anastasius, and in the church of the blessed Martin he clad himself in purple tunic and chlamys, and placed a diadem on his head. Then he mounted his horse, and in the most generous manner he gave gold and silver as he passed along the way which is between the gate of the entrance [of the church of St. Martin] and the church of the city, scattering it among the people who were there with his own hand, and from that day he was called consul or Augustus. Leaving Tours he went to Paris and there he established the seat of his kingdom.

Gregory of Tours, *History of the Franks* (selections translated with notes by Ernest Brehaut) (New York, 1969), p. 47. This is the only reference to Clovis's "consulship" and, in spite of much speculation by various scholars, it is not known whether Clovis ever actually received a consulship from the Emperor Anastasius, and if he did, what it signified. See Lucien Musset, *The Germanic Invasions*, pp. 230–231.

6. See B. Bachrach, *Merovingian Military Organization*, pp. 10, 14–17.

7. See the discussion of the Visigothic and Burgundian legislation in the section on "Roman Law and the Germanic Barbarians" below.

8. Patrick Wormald, "*Lex Scripta* and *Verbum Regis*: Legislation and Germanic Kingship, from Euric to Cnut," in *Early Medieval Kingship*, ed. P. H. Sawyer and I. N. Wood (Leeds, 1977), pp. 105–138. This argument is based on the fact that the Frankish code (unlike, e.g., the Visigothic and Lombard) was an unreasonable compilation: it is poorly organized and very incomplete. Therefore, Wormald argues, the Frankish code was never really intended to be consulted as a written code; it was the fact that the king caused it to be issued which was important. Clovis was acting as a king should act in issuing laws written in Latin.

9. Ian Wood, "Kings, Kingdoms, and Consent," in Sawyer and Wood, *Early Medieval Kingship*, pp. 6–29, especially pp. 23–26.

10. A fuller description of Frankish inheritance on the basis of the laws will be found in the section below on "The Franks as Seen Through Their Law Code."

11. Easy introductions to Roman law can be found in Hans Julius Wolff, *Roman Law: An Historical Introduction* (Norman, Okla., 1951); Wolfgang Kunkel, *An Introduction to Roman Legal and Constitutional History*, 2nd ed. (Oxford, 1973); and Barry Nicholas, *An Introduction to Roman Law* (Oxford, 1962).

12. For a brief introduction to the early Germanic law-making activities, see K. F. Drew, "The Early Germanic Law Codes," *Dictionary of the Middle Ages*, Vol. 7 (New York, 1987) and Paul Vinogradoff, *Roman Law in Medieval Europe*, 2nd ed. (Oxford, 1929). For a general overview stressing the Roman element in the barbarian laws, see Alan Watson, *The Evolution of Law* (Baltimore, 1985), pp. 77–93, and Ernst Levy, *West Roman Vulgar Law: The Law of Property* (Philadelphia, 1951), pp. 1–18.

13. See Giulio Vismara, "Edictum Theodorici," *Ius Romanum Medii Aevi*, Pars I, 2 b aa α (Milan, 1967).

14. Cf. Maria Teresa Guerra Medici, *I Diritti delle Donne nella Società altomedievale* (Naples, 1986), pp. 65–137.

15. See Jean Gaudemet, "Le Bréviare d'Alaric et les épitomes," *Ius Romanum Medii Aevi*, Pars I, 2 b aa β (Milan, 1965).

16. Pierre Riché, "Enseignement du droit en Gaule du VIe au XIe siècle," *Ius Romanum Medii Aevi*, Pars I, 5b bb (Milan, 1965), pp. 3–10, and *Education and Culture in the Barbarian West* (Columbia, SC, 1976), pp. 52–79.

17. See J. M. Pardessus, *Loi Salique* (Paris, 1843).

18. B. Bachrach, *Merovingian Military Organization*, pp. 15–17.

19. The "short" prologue to the *Pactus Legis Salicae* is thought to have been added to the code in the middle of the sixth century; the "long" prologue was added in the Carolingian period.

20. See J. M. Wallace-Hadrill, *The Long-Haired Kings*, pp. 2–9.

21. B. Bachrach, *Merovingian Military Organization*, pp. 10 and 14; Lucien Musset, *The Germanic Invasions*, pp. 121–122.

22. The later capitularies added by Clovis's sons and grandson contain a few references to church buildings and bishops. Cf. the 1,800 Solidi Cases, VI, 5 and VIII, 5; and Cap. VI, I, 2.

23. J. M. Wallace-Hadrill, *The Long-Haired Kings*, pp. 1–8; L. Halphen, *Les Barbares des grandes invasions aux conquêtes turques du XIe siècle* (Paris, 1926), pp. 53–57.

24. Henri Pirenne, *Mohammed and Charlemagne* (New York, 1957), pp. 79–107, and *Cambridge Medieval History*, Vol. II (New York, 1913), pp. 139–140.

25. This is not the view that prevails. Cf. B. Bachrach, *Merovingian Military Organization*, p. 17, who believes that the Merovingian army was made up entirely of professionals—either the king's retinue, the retinues of the other magnates of the kingdom, or the remnants of Roman imperial troops or colonial *laeti*. References in the Frankish laws, however, make it clear that the ordinary freeman spent time in the army. Note the following laws: LXIII, 1 and Capitulary I, LXIX. Also see the discussion of wergelds in the section below on social classes and note 41.

26. This discussion avoids naming the chief territorial divisions in the Merovingian kingdom, about which there is great controversy. I am inclined to think that the chief division was the hundred and that the most frequently utilized court was the hundred court, which was ordinarily presided over by the hundredman (*centenarius* or *thunginus*), although it could also be presided over by the hundredman's superior, the count. The picture is complicated by references in the laws to an official called a "sagibaron" who played some judicial role which seems to have been somewhat comparable to that of the rachimburgi (LIV). On the other hand, the wergeld of the sagibaron was the same as that of a count (600 solidi if a freeman, 300 solidi if a servile dependent [LIV, 2]), so he was a royal official, not a local representative.

My acceptance of the hundred as one of the chief territorial divisions of the Merovingian kingdom is at odds with the view of many Frankish specialists who regard the hundred as a very special type of unit and not the general one. This latter interpretation is characterized by J. M. Wallace-Hadrill:

By *centena*, I understand a Frankish settlement, part military and part colonizing in function, living under a royal official (of imperial origin) called the *centenarius*, upon land of the Merovingian fisc. How widespread these *centenae* were in the sixth century cannot be determined; but, so far as the territories of these two kings [the reference is to the pact between Childebert I and Chlotar I] were concerned, they were clearly not new at the date of the *pactus*.

The Long-Haired Kings, p. 193. See also *Cambridge Medieval History*, Vol. II, pp. 137–138; and Heike Grahn-Hoek, *Die fränkische Oberschicht im 6. Jahrhundert* (Sigmaringen, 1976), pp. 283–295.

27. Numbers in parentheses (except when preceded by S.V. indicating the Systematic Version) refer to the first version of the code translated below (*Pactus Legis Salicae*).

28. See Rebecca V. Colman, "Reason and Unreason in Early Medieval Law," *Journal of Interdisciplinary History* IV, 4 (Spring, 1974), pp. 571–591; Robert Bartlett, *Trial by Fire and Water: The Medieval Judicial Ordeal* (Oxford, 1986); and Wendy Davies and Paul Fouracre, eds., *The Settlement of Disputes in Early Medieval Europe* (Cambridge, 1986), pp. 221–222.

29. Davies and Fouracre, *Disputes in Early Medieval Europe*, pp. 18–19, 176, and 182–187.

30. For a more extended analysis of the Frankish feud, see J. M. Wallace-Hadrill, "The Bloodfeud of the Franks," in *The Long-Haired Kings*, pp. 121–147. Also note somewhat comparable material on the Anglo-Saxons in Dorothy Whitelock, *The Beginnings of English Society*, 2nd ed. rev. (Harmondsworth, 1972), pp. 36–37 and 42–47.

31. See note 6 to the first translation explaining the curious Frankish monetary system. Note that the operation of the judicial system provided the king with a significant income.

32. An interesting discussion of Frankish outlawry is to be found in Julius Goebel, Jr., *Felony and Misdemeanor* (New York, 1937, reprinted Philadelphia, 1976), pp. 44–61. It is hard to see how the judgment could ever be paid off if the man outlawed had had his property confiscated.

33. A later law (The Pact Between Childebert and Chlotar for Keeping the Peace, Cap. II, LXXIX) indicates that if a man is charged with theft, he will choose one-half of the oathhelpers, the plaintiff the other one-half. This practice may have been the usual one rather than that described in the text.

34. A varying amount. See the discussion on social classes below.

35. The plaintiff himself "heated the cauldron" for the ordeal (cf. LXXIII, 5).

36. But note that this is modified by a later law (Cap. I, LXVIII) where the wife gets one-fourth of the composition, the kin sharing another one-fourth.

37. A later law (Cap. IV, CX) provides that if there were no children and the husband died, his widow received one-half of the dos, the relatives of the husband one-half; if the wife died (and there were no children), the husband received one-half of the dos, the relatives of the wife the other one-half.

38. There are no provisions for divorce in the Frankish laws but, considering the strong legal position of the woman, dissolution with mutual consent may have

been in effect. Although no law can be cited to support this contention, there is a story related by Gregory of Tours that suggests dissolution even without the consent of one of the spouses. This is the story of the Merovingian queen Radegund, a daughter of King Berthar of Thuringia, who was married to the Frankish king Chlotar I. After Chlotar killed her brother, Radegund left her husband (over his protests), took the veil, and founded a monastery (the Holy Cross) at Poitiers. Radegund's life is interesting because her husband was unable to prevent her from deserting the marriage and, since she was thereafter able to found and endow a monastery, she undoubtedly was able to take her property with her. The story is even more interesting when we note that Chlotar had other wives. O. M. Dalton, translator, *History of the Franks by Gregory of Tours*, 2 vols. (Oxford, 1927), I, pp. 67–68. However, since there is nothing contrary in the Salic law, perhaps we must assume that plural marriages were not illegal. Certainly the Lombards accepted subordinate marriages the offspring of which had an accepted place in the inheritance. Suzanne Fonay Wemple, *Women in Frankish Society* (Philadelphia, 1981) does not give the woman such a strong legal position as indicated here but her argument, nonetheless, does accord the Merovingian woman greater privileges than would be enjoyed by her successors.

39. Niermeyer's *Lexicon* indicates an inheritance distinction between movable and real property as a meaning for *alodis*, but since the only example given for this meaning is *Lex Salica* itself, Niermeyer's definition is not very convincing. J. F. Niermeyer, *Mediae Latinitatis Lexicon Minus* (Leiden, 1976), p. 38.

40. The ambiguous statements in the laws have not prevented their use to support various theories about Frankish nobles. See Heike Grahn-Hoek, *Die fränkische Oberschicht im 6. Jahrhundert*, esp. pp. 55–78. See also R. Sprandel, "Struktur und Geschichte des merovingischen Adels," *Historische Zeitschrift* 193 (1961), pp. 33–71; Joseph Balon, *Études franques, I: Aux origines de la noblesse* (Namur, 1963), pp. 13–34; and F. Iresigler, "On the Aristocratic Character of Early Frankish Society," in *The Medieval Nobility*, ed. T. Reuter (Amsterdam, 1979), pp. 105–136.

41. These amounts vary somewhat in Cap. III, CIV, 1–11.

42. The actual phrase here is *in truste dominica* (XLI, 5).

43. That the wergeld of the Roman landholder (100 solidi) is the same as that of the Roman soldier (100 solidi) is strong indication that the ordinary Roman freeman who possessed land was liable for military service. See note 25 above.

44. See the discussion above on methods of proof.

45. This brief summary of the manuscript tradition is based on the work of the editors cited hereafter in the text. It is a tradition denied by Simon Stein, "Lex Salica I," *Speculum* (April, 1947), and "Lex Salica II," *Speculum* (July, 1947). Stein's argument is that *Lex Salica* was a mid-ninth century forgery, ecclesiastical in origin, and possibly associated with Archbishop Hincmar of Rheims. Although Stein's argument has not been widely accepted (see J. M. Wallace-Hadrill, "Archbishop Hincmar and the Authorship of Lex Salica," in *The Long-Haired Kings*, pp. 95–120), his articles are of interest for a number of reasons. Stein points out the very real difficulties encountered by the scholars commissioned to prepare a critical edition of *Lex Salica* for the *Monumenta Germaniae Historica* (one may ignore his petty personal criticisms of their work). Stein also points out a number of problems

about *Lex Salica* that are still not adequately solved: for example, the chronological relationship among the various main versions of the laws, the absolutely baffling nature of the Malberg glosses, and the really impossible numismatic references in the laws where forty denarii are the equivalent of one solidus. There is something obviously strange about *Lex Salica*, but treating it as a forgery (all the various versions done contemporaneously to create a false manuscript tradition—surely that is asking a bit much of even the ninth-century forgers!) is not the explanation. A somewhat earlier assessment of the problem is offered by O. M. Dalton in the Introduction to his translation of Gregory of Tours' *History of the Franks*, I, p. 207, n. 2. The more recent editorial work of K. A. Eckhardt has not gone without criticism. This matter will be taken up in the notes to the translation.

Pactus Legis Salicae

1. This translation is based on the edition of the laws by Karl August Eckhardt, *Monumenta Germaniae Historica, Leges Nationum Germanicarum*, Vol. IV, Part I (Hanover, 1962). Eckhardt's editions (some with German translation) in the *Germanenrechte* series published by the Historisches Institut des Werralandes (Göttingen, 1953–57) have also been used. Material enclosed in parentheses comes from the text. Material enclosed in brackets has been added to fill in what has obviously been left out or to explain the text.

It has been impossible for Eckhardt, as for earlier editors, to produce a truly critical edition of the laws (see section in Introduction on "Transmission of *Lex Salica*"). He sometimes gives preference to one family of manuscripts, sometimes to another, and he assumes the existence of a family of manuscripts, copies of which have not survived. Eckhardt's critics do not always agree with his choices. See Ruth Schmidt-Wiegand, "Die kritische Ausgabe der *Lex Salica*—noch immer ein Problem?" *Zeitschrift der Savigny-Stiftung für Rechtsgeschichte*, Germanistische Abteilung (1959), 301–319, and Alexander C. Murray, *Germanic Kinship Structure* (Toronto, 1983), pp. 119–133. For Eckhardt's own discussion of the redaction problem see K. A. Eckhardt, *Pactus Legis Salicae, I, Einführung und 80 Titel-Text, Germanenrechte Neue Folge* (Göttingen, 1954), pp. 58–129.

2. This prologue is thought not to be contemporaneous with the body of the law but added later in the sixth century.

3. All attempts to identify these men and places have failed, and it is thought that they have no special significance for the way the laws were actually collected together and issued.

4. Numbers in brackets refer to corresponding law in the Systematic Version of the *Lex Salica Karolina*—a translation of which follows the *Pactus Legis Salicae*.

5. The Malberg glosses (contained in some of the manuscripts) are thought to be Frankish words or the remnants of Frankish words for which no exact equivalent in Latin was found. But the problem of the glosses has not been adequately solved. For the most useful approach to determining the meaning of these presumably Germanic words, see the glossary prepared by H. Kern in J. H. Hessels, *Lex Salica* (London, 1880); Knut Jungbohn Clement, *Forschungen über das Recht der Salischen Franken vor und in der Königszeit* (Foreword and Register of Malberg and other Frankish words by Heinrich Zoepfl) (Berlin, 1878); and K. A. Eckhardt, glossaries

to the two volumes of the *Monumenta Germaniae Historica* containing his editions of the *Pactus Legis Salicae* and *Lex Salica*. I have made no attempt to translate the glosses but have retained the words as a matter of curiosity.

6. The Merovingian versions of the Salic law follow the rather unusual practice of citing almost all sums in both denarii and solidi (so many denarii equals so many solidi). Not only is this repetition unusual, but the relationship between the two coins is distinctive, for in the Salic law forty denarii equal one solidus. This does not seem to be based on the Roman imperial coinage system, nor is it the same as the Carolingian system where twelve denarii equalled one solidus. In the late empire, the bronze denarius had become very low in value, so that it required many more than forty to equal one gold solidus. Whether the Frankish denarius was a circulating coin is not certain (gold solidi were certainly minted by the Merovingians). Several laws specifically mention "one denarius," however, so presumably it was coined. For example, one freed a slave "with a denarius before the king" (XXVI, 2), and "the man who would marry a widow should have three solidi of equal weight and a denarius" (XLIV, 2).

7. The way that the Frankish laws cite compositions and fines is a little puzzling. Occasionally, composition (a payment in compensation to the injured party) and fine (a payment to the court or presiding judge) are identified separately and so the matter is clear. But most often only one payment is indicated, and this is composition (the fine presumably being understood to be some fraction of the composition or as set out in a section of the *Pactus* numbered LXVg in this translation and labeled "The Hundreds").

But not only is there the problem of distinguishing between fine and composition, some of the laws include another payment which I have translated as "return of the object or its value plus a payment for the time its use was lost (*excepto capitale et dilatura*)." Thus the man who is proved to have stolen a horse, for example, must pay the composition indicated in the law for such a theft, must return the horse (or its value) plus a payment to recompense the owner for the time he did not have his horse available for use, plus a fine to the court. When the law omits return of the object or payment for time lost, I have added these phrases in brackets.

8. A theft becomes more serious the deeper the thief penetrates into the property of the owner. To penetrate into an enclosure that is locked is the most serious of all. Cf. VII, 3; XI, 6; XXVI, 30.

9. The relationship of these coins is 14 denarii = 1 triens (*tremissis*); 40 denarii = 1 solidus; 3 triens = 1 solidus. This provides another instance of the difficulty with the money equivalents in *Lex Salica* for if 14 denarii = 1 triens and 3 triens = 1 solidus, then one would expect 42 denarii = 1 solidus rather than 40.

10. Again note how very high the penalty is when an object is stolen from a locked place.

11. It is very difficult to translate the Latin word *curtis*—the enclosed space of an agricultural unit (farm, manor, villa). I often use the word "courtyard," but occasionally have found that "inner courtyard" or "enclosed yard" or "stockyard" or "building enclosure" is better in specific instances.

12. The editor of these laws, although providing a single text, nonetheless follows this text with the alternative readings given in the eight most important manu-

scripts (or families of manuscripts). Occasionally he regards one or more of the alternatives as important enough to include in the main text. These alternative versions are included (enclosed in brackets) when they offer supplementary material or differ significantly from the main version.

13. The explanatory material is taken from one of the alternative readings.

14. The Systematic Version has 1,800 denarii or 45 solidi; these latter sums seem more reasonable.

15. Again it should be noted how serious breaking into a locked enclosure was.

16. Although the language of these and other laws about slaves speaks as if the slave were to pay for his misdeeds, his lord was ultimately responsible and presumably the lord usually paid. Certainly in the event that the money payment alternative to physical punishment of the slave were chosen, it was the lord who paid in order to avoid damage to his property, the slave. Nonetheless, it is quite possible that a slave was able to accumulate something for himself, but the laws do not refer to this.

17. The title of this law (in both the *Pactus* and Karolingian versions) is misleading. It is actually about men (of any status) who abduct women (of any status).

18. The Latin term *"puer"* appears a number of times in the laws (cf. XLII, 4; LIV, 2; LXVf, 2; and CXVII). The reference is clearly to someone of lowly status, perhaps even a slave. I have translated the word as "servant"—a weak term that could refer to either free or unfree.

19. The band of men could be as formal as the retinue of king or other powerful person, or a temporary group of men associated for the purpose of committing a violent act. The bands might thus be "faithful followers" or simply groups of armed men who constituted a threat to the peace. Cf. XLII below.

20. Cf. Cap. VI, II, 2 where the penalty has become much more severe.

21. Eckhardt adds the phrase "or be handed over to the flames," which he derives from one of the manuscript traditions. It doesn't really seem to fit here. The 200 solidi composition, however, seems low. One would expect the sum to be three times this, since death by a herbal potion is essentially a secret form of homicide.

22. This seems to mean that boys wore their hair long until they reached the age of twelve; the ceremony of cutting it admitted them to the privileges of majority. Evidently the same ceremony took place with girls although instead of cutting their hair, they fastened it up. References to cutting the hair of members of the royal family to make them ineligible for the throne probably meant having them tonsured (i.e., admitted to the monastic life) rather than simply having their long locks shorn. Cf. Cap. III (LXLVII, 1).

23. The *Lex Salica Karolina* provides 62 1/2 solidi in this case. Cf. S.V. XXXIII, 3. In Cap. III (LXLVII, 2) of the *Pactus* the sum is 100 solidi.

24. Cf. XXIV, 1 and XLI, 18.

25. Cf. XLI, 19; LXVe, 1.

26. Cf. Cap. VII, V.

27. Cf. XLI, 16. The value attached to an individual (his "man value") is known as his wergeld. See the section in the Introduction on "Social Classes" for a fuller discussion of this Germanic concept.

28. Cf. LXLVIII, 1.

29. See note 16 above.

30. The higher penalty imposed here indicates that the tree involved was inside an enclosure—and entry into an enclosure was a more serious offense than theft outside.

31. This law evidently differs from XXVII, 7 above in that the guilty party intended to steal something but did not actually take anything.

32. Such long lists of detailed injuries with the "price" of each injury noted are characteristic of the Germanic laws.

33. Cf. Rothair 26–29 in K. F. Drew, *The Lombard Laws* (Philadelphia, 1973), pp. 57–58.

34. This large composition indicates that the "bound man" taken from the count was one who had been apprehended in some offense and was being held for trial.

35. It is not clear just what procedure is referred to here. Cf. XXXVI below.

36. This item does not appear in the Systematic Version (S.V. XLIII).

37. This law appears in quite different forms in the various versions, none of which make much sense. It should probably read the reverse of the way it appears in the text: "If the slave is guilty of a crime for which a freeman or Frank would be liable to pay eighteen hundred denarii (i.e., forty-five solidi), he should compound fifteen solidi (i.e., six hundred denarii). If he is guilty of a more serious offense—one for which a freeman would be liable to pay eight thousand denarii (i.e., two hundred solidi)—and the slave has confessed between tortures, he shall be subjected to capital punishment."

38. Not all versions of the laws (including the *Lex Salica Karolina* that follows—XI, 4 in the Systematic Version) contain the phrase "or a free woman," which does not seem to belong here.

39. Presumably this refers to a person of Roman birth who was also in the king's household.

40. Since the "Roman who pays tribute" is valued at 62 1/2 solidi, and since Romans were valued at one-half the value of Franks, therefore a Frank "who owed tribute" would be valued at 125 solidi. This may well be the value of the half-free man (*lidus*) and the freedman whose status was between that of the slave and free.

41. These alternative versions are not in keeping with the other laws in the 65-title original issue attributed to Clovis. They imply something like "private justice," references to which appear in the Capitularies. Cf. Cap. III, LXLV and LXLVI. They appear only in Herold's edition of *Lex Salica*.

42. Cf. LXVe, 2.

43. Cf. XXIV, 8; LXVe, 3.

44. Cf. XXIV, 9.

45. Cf. XXIV, 1 and 4.

46. Cf. XXIV, 5; LXVe, 1.

47. Cf. XXIV, 5 and 6; LXVe, 1.

48. See note 20 above.

49. Cf. Cap. III, C.

50. Cap. III (C, 1–2) provides for a quite different line of preference.

51. Note *Theodosian Code* 3, 7, 1 and Interpretation where it is provided that in the case of widows wishing to remarry, where the consent of kinsmen is necessary,

in the case of dispute between the widow and her kinsmen, the decision will rest with those who do not expect to inherit from the woman.

52. This reference is one of those that have influenced scholars to date the Salic Law to the period following defeat of the Visigoths at Vouillé in 507: "beyond the Loire" would indicate land that had been part of Visigothic territory before the Frankish victory. The Carbonaria Forest would seem to indicate the area bounding the southern part of that portion of northeast Gaul originally settled by the Franks. See Auguste Longnon, "Carte de la Gaule," *Géographie de la Gaule au VIᵉ siècle* (Paris, 1878). For a comparable law, see K. F. Drew, *The Burgundian Code*, 83, 1.

53. Being able to "buy out" of the ordeal is very unusual.

54. The sagibarons were judicial officers appointed by the king. This is one of the few laws that give any indication of their function. Since their value was the same as that of a count, one might expect them to be able to preside over a court, presumably a lesser court than the one presided over by the count. However, section 4 of this law below makes it seem as if the sagibarons were performing a function similar to that of the rachimburgi.

55. The manuscript tradition here is very confused but the intent of the law seems clear enough.

56. Sections 6 and 7 of this law (the sections involving basilicas) do not appear in that group of manuscripts regarded as the earliest redaction.

57. For an interpretation of this law, see the section on "Inheritance" in the Introduction. Cf. Cap. I, LXVI.

58. The Systematic Version of *Lex Salica Karolina* gives the father's sisters precedence over the mother's sisters (XXXIV, 3–4).

59. For a discussion of the parentela, see the Section on "Family and Kin Group" in the Introduction.

60. This item does not appear in the Systematic Version (XXXVI).

61. Note Cap. I, LXVIII below where the disposition does not exclude the wife: the children get one-half, the wife one-fourth, and the relatives the other fourth.

62. The penalty given here is for simple homicide—that seems to be a very light penalty since presumably a man cannot protect himself against a witch eating him.

63. Laws LXVa–e appear only in Herold or the Carolingian version of the *Pactus*.

64. Cf. XXIV, 5–6; XLI, 19–20.

65. Cf. XLI, 15.

66. Cf. XXIV, 8; XLI, 16.

67. Laws LXVf and g are found only in some of the B versions of the manuscript.

68. The amounts provided in this law would seem to be the fines due to the court, although the sums do seem to be low.

69. The capitularies were not part of the original "code" but were added during the reigns of Clovis's sons and grandson.

70. Cf. LIX.

71. Cf. LXII, 1.

72. The language of this law admits of an alternative reading that varies the meaning: "He who kills a freeman and it is proved against him that he killed him,

should make composition to the relatives according to law. His [the dead man's] children (*filius*) should get half the composition. Half of the rest should go to his mother, so that one-fourth of the wergeld comes to her. The other one-fourth should go to the near relatives, that is, to the three nearest on the father's side and three on his mother's side. If his mother is not living, the relatives should divide her half of the half-wergeld among themselves, that is the three closest from the father's side and three from the mother's side; whoever is the closest relative of the aforementioned three shall take [two parts] and leave a third part to be divided among the other two; then he of the remaining two who is the closer relative shall take two parts of that third and leave a third part to the other relative." This alternative translation would leave the wife in the same position as in the earlier law on this subject (LXII, 1) and considerably improve the position of the dead man's mother.

73. Ordinary homicide of a freeman, where the man was killed openly and could have protected himself, brought a composition of 200 solidi. But to kill a man and conceal the crime (to avoid paying composition) raised the composition to 600 solidi.

74. This penalty is the same as for death.

75. The two provisions of this law indicate that death by hanging was an ordinary penalty of the Frankish code. This may be true; but if so, the penalties must have been applied in cases not covered by the provisions of the laws. Death is a penalty provided only in the later capitularies; e.g., for procuring (Cap. III, LXLIX), for the offender who has run away to escape being summoned to court (Cap. IV, CXV), for marrying one's father's wife (Cap. VI, I, 2), for rape (Cap. VI, II, 2), and for killing a man without cause (Cap. VI, II, 3).

76. Cf. Cap. III, LXLV, and LXLVI.

77. This "Capitulary" is thought to have been issued in 524 by Kings Childebert I (511–558) and Chlotar (511–561).

78. Two forms of ordeal are found in *Lex Salica*, the ordeal of boiling water and the casting of lots. Ordeal by lot seems to have been used only in the case of slaves. See the discussion in the Introduction on "The Frankish Judicial System" and Wendy Davies and Paul Fouracre, eds., *The Settlement of Disputes in Early Medieval Europe* (Cambridge, 1986), pp. 11–19 and 221–222.

79. This seems to be an extremely high penalty for an unstated theft; presumably the fact that the stolen goods had been locked away is what makes it so serious.

80. This law provides that a guilty person might seek sanctuary in a church and that no one might drag him forth. However, Cap. VI, II, 2 below provides that the man who forcefully seizes a woman and ravishes her and seeks sanctuary shall be removed and sent into exile. If the woman consented to him and sought sanctuary with him, both could be removed and sent into exile.

81. The arpennis was a measure of 120 feet.

82. This seems to mean that these hundredmen were placed "in the king's trust" and therefore enjoyed the status of his followers.

83. Clovis I (481–511).

84. Childebert I (511–558).

85. Chlotar I (511–560/1).

86. Theuderic III (687–690/1).

87. Clovis IV (690/1–694/5).

88. Childebert III (694/5–711).

89. Dagobert III (711–715).

90. Chilperic II (715–721).

91. Theuderic IV (721–737).

92. Interregnum (737–743).

93. Childeric III (743–751). The dates in Notes 83–93 are taken from Patrick Geary, *Before France and Germany* (Oxford, 1988), pp. 323–333. The significance of this king list is not clear nor how the sum of 78 years was arrived at.

94. Cf. footnote 75 above and LXXV, 2.

95. Cf. LXXV, 1.

96. Cf. XXIV, 2.

97. Cf. XXIV, 3 and S.V. XXXIII, 3, where the sums are 100 solidi and 62 1/2 solidi respectively.

98. Cf. XLIV where the provisions are quite different.

99. The amounts provided in this and the following sections do not agree with the amounts provided in XXIV, XLI, and XLVe above.

100. Chilperic I (561–584).

101. The laws of this capitulary are very obscure. Perhaps this law means that beyond the Garonne another form of inheritance (i.e., Roman) might hold, but on this side the same form of inheritance will hold as held in Thérouanne.

102. Cf. Alexander C. Murray, *Germanic Kinship Structure*, pp. 79–87.

103. Cf. note 78 above.

104. See the interesting discussion of the procedures outlined in this law in Paul Fouracre, " 'Placita' and the Settlement of Disputes in Later Merovingian Francia," in Wendy Davies and Paul Fouracre, *Disputes in Early Medieval Europe*, pp. 39–41.

105. Capitulary II (LXXIX and LXXX).

106. Cf. XLI, 10 where the wergeld for a Roman who pays tribute is 62 1/2 solidi.

107. Cf. XXXIII, 2–3.

108. Cf. XXVII, 4 where the amount is 3 solidi for a stolen hobble and XXVII, 28 where the amount is 15 solidi for a stolen fishing net.

109. Cf. XXXIII, 1 and 4–5.

110. Cf. II, 1 and 2 where the sum varies from 3 solidi to 15 solidi depending upon which of several enclosures is involved.

111. Cf. XXVII, 23–25.

112. Cf. XXI, 1–3.

113. Cf. X, 5 and XXVII, 33.

114. Cf. XXXII, 1–4 where the penalty varies between 15 solidi and 45 solidi depending upon who does the tieing up and who is tied.

115. Cf. XXII, 31–32 where the penalty varies from 15 solidi to 45 solidi depending on whether the plowed land is sowed or not.

116. Cf. XXVII, 7 and 12 where the penalty is only 3 solidi if nothing was taken but 15 solidi plus the value of the objects taken plus a payment for the time their use was lost if something was taken.

117. Cf. XLVIII, 1–4.

118. Cf. XV, 1.

119. Thought to be Childebert II, king of Austrasia 575–595 and of Burgundy 592–595.

120. I take this to mean that grandchildren step into the succession in place of their father or mother—i.e., they share their parent's portion of the inheritance.

121. In general, the penalties or punishments provided in this series of laws are much more severe than those of the main code.

122. Cf. LXL, 1 where sanctuary seems inviolable and also XV, 2 where the penalty is only 62 1/2 solidi.

123. The kind of homicide spoken of here seems to be the kind done in stealth or ambush, where the victim had no chance to defend himself. Before this time, such homicide was compensatable. Cf. The Seven Types of Cases, VIII, 1–7.

124. This law may refer to some kind of inquest procedure.

125. Cf. the decree of King Chlotar (LXXXIV).

126. Ibid.

127. This is the only place where a royal notary has indicated his official participation in issuance of the laws.

128. I, 1.

129. I, 2.

130. II, 12 and 13. Evidently the compiler of the later law mistakenly combined the two earlier laws.

131. VII, 2.

132. XXXI, 1.

133. XXIX, 9.

134. Ibid.

135. IX, 3.

136. XXI, 3.

137. XXIX, 6.

138. III, 7.

139. Cf. XXIX, 14 where the penalty is 15 solidi for cutting off another man's ear.

140. Cf. XXXIII, 2 where the penalty is 45 solidi.

141. XXIV, 2.

142. VII, 3.

143. XXI, 4.

144. XXVII, 17.

145. XXIX, 4 where the penalty is 50 solidi.

146. XXIX, 13.

147. XVII, 2.

148. Cf. LV, 1 (where the same penalty is provided) and XIV, 9 where the penalty is 100 solidi).

149. Cf. XIV, 6 where the penalty is 62 1/2 solidi for each of a band of men.

150. XXIX, 2.

151. XXVIII, 2.

152. XIV, 10.

153. XIV, 11.

154. XXIV, 6.

155. XXVI, 1.
156. XXIX, 1, 15 and 17.
157. XLI, 11.
158. XLI, 13.
159. XIV, 4.
160. XIX, 1.
161. XXXIX, 4.
162. Cf. XLI, 15 where the qualification "before she can bear children" is added.
163. LV, 7.
164. LI, 1.
165. XIII, 14.
166. XXIV, 4 and XLI, 18.
167. XXIV, 8; XLI, 16; and LXVe, 3.
168. LIV, 1.
169. LIV, 3.
170. XLI, 21.
171. One would expect the penalty to be 200 solidi.
172. The penalties in these laws are three times those for normal homicide, the term "murder" denoting that the homicide was done in stealth or ambush—at any rate, the victim had no time to defend himself/herself. Cf. LXIII, 1.
173. Cf. LIV, 1 and The Seven Types of Cases, VII, 4.
174. Cf. XXIV, 8 and The Seven Types of Cases, VII, 3.
175. Cf. XXIV, 4 and The Seven Types of Cases, VII, 1.
176. This is the only reference to the value of a bishop; the amount is equivalent to that of an antrustion. No other members of the clergy are given a value in the *Pactus*, although the *Lex Salica Karolina* (Title VI in the Systematic Version) gives 300 or 600 solidi for a deacon and 600 solidi for a presbyter.
177. Cf. XLI, 5 where the term antrustion does not appear but instead the phrase *"in truste dominica"* is used.
178. This capitulary does not appear in the *Monumenta Germaniae Historica* version. It is taken from Karl August Eckhardt, *Pactus Legis Salicae, II, 2, Kapitularien und 70 Titel-Text* (Göttingen, 1956), pp. 450–456.
179. Title X in this translation.
180. Title XIII, 9 in this translation.
181. Title XV in this translation.
182. Title XXIV, 7 in this translation.
183. Title XXXV, 8 in this translation.
184. Title XLIV in this translation.
185. Title XLV in this translation.
186. Title XLVI in this translation.

Lex Salica Karolina Systematic Version

1. This translation is of the Systematic Version of *Lex Salica Karolina*, a revision prepared in 802–803 during the reign of Charlemagne. This is the most radical revision of the code: it omits the Malberg glosses, simplifies the context, and improves the Latin. The Systematic Version of this revision (a private compilation

probably made in northern Italy [Friuli] in the early ninth century) attempted to reorganize the material in such a way that all the provisions dealing with a similar subject were brought together; thus all the material on procedure is brought together at the beginning of the code, all the material on theft is together, all that on animals, etc. The *Lex Salica Karolina* contains only the laws from the original 65-title version; it does not contain the capitularies added by Clovis's sons and grandson and the other miscellaneous material.

2. The prologue here is known as the "long prologue" and was added to the laws some time during the eighth century. Note the emphasis here on the Catholicism of the Franks which did not appear in the earlier version.

3. The numbers given in brackets refer to the numbers in the standard version of the *Lex Salica Karolina*.

4. The *Pactus* version does not distinguish between "lesser" and more serious offenses; all unjust accusations bear a composition of 62 1/2 solidi.

5. Cf. *Pactus* LV, 7 for this item and *Pactus* LXVb for item 2. In the *Pactus* version, neither of these provisions is necessarily Christian. The *Pactus* version does not have anything corresponding to items 3 and 4 about deacons and presbyters.

6. *Pactus* LIV, 2 refers to a sagibaron or count who is a servile dependent of the king.

7. *Pactus* XVI, 2 and 5 do not appear in this version; also *Pactus* XVI, 15–21.

8. *Pactus* XLI, 10 provides a composition of 62 1/2 solidi for the Roman; the 45 solidi composition seems more reasonable since it would mean that a barbarian of comparable status would be worth twice as much, i.e., 90 solidi.

9. Items 13 and 14 in this title do not appear in the *Pactus* version.

10. *Pactus* XLI, 14–21 are omitted from this version.

11. The *Pactus* version includes slaves with Romans and half-free men (*lidi*). *Pactus* XLII, 5 does not appear in this version.

12. This provision combines *Pactus* XVII, 4 and 5.

13. Items 10 and 11 here correct *Pactus* XVII, 11 and 12.

14. This provision corrects *Pactus* XXIX, 2 where the amount is 62 1/2 solidi.

15. *Pactus* XXIX, 4 has 50 solidi.

16. *Pactus* XXIX, 8 has 35 solidi.

17. *Pactus* XXIX, 9 has 9 solidi.

18. *Pactus* XXIX, 18 provides for a payment for the doctor also.

19. *Pactus* XXXII, 3 provides 30 solidi (which is the sum one would expect).

20. *Pactus* LV, 1 provides 62 1/2 solidi here; the following title (S.V. XXI, 1) also provides 62 1/2 solidi for the same offense.

21. *Pactus* LV, 5 provides 45 solidi instead of 62 1/2 solidi.

22. *Pactus* LV, 6 provides 30 solidi instead of 15 solidi.

23. S.V. XX and XXI are basically repetitive.

24. *Pactus* LV, 2 and 6 provide 15 solidi for destroying a tomb and 30 solidi for destroying a basilica. This provision combines the two.

25. This item does not appear in the *Pactus* version.

26. This item corrects *Pactus* XLVIII, 3 where the amount given is 15 solidi.

27. *Pactus* LIII, 3 has six solidi instead of nine solidi.

28. The 30 solidi have been added from *Pactus* LIII, 7.

29. Both this item and *Pactus* XIX provide a composition of 200 solidi where one would expect death by an herbal potion (a secret form of homicide) to be three times the normal composition.

30. *Pactus* LIX, 3–4 gives the mother's sisters precedence over the father's sisters.

31. This payment should be 7500 denarii or 187 1/2 solidi (cf. *Pactus* LXIV, 2)—but this is a very high payment for simply calling someone a witch, whereas in the following item one pays only 200 solidi when a witch eats a man.

32. This should be 240 denarii (see *Pactus* XII, 2).

33. *Pactus* LXV, 2 gives 35 solidi here.

34. *Pactus* XXXIII, 1 cites the "bird or fish hunt" instead of "various hunts."

35. *Pactus* XXXIII, 3 provides 30 solidi instead of 35.

36. No number is given in the text. *Pactus* IV, 1 gives one-half triens.

37. Does not appear in *Pactus* VIII.

38. This sum would seem to be too low. It does not appear in *Pactus* VIII.

39. "Beyond the Loire" indicates that the original code was issued some time after the defeat of the Visigoths by the Franks at Vouillé in 507. The location of the Carbonaria Forest is thought to be some place in the Low Countries between the Moselle and the North Sea, the traditional home of the Salian Franks at the time Clovis became king in 481.

Bibliography

Primary Materials

EDITIONS OF *LEX SALICA*

There is no single critical edition of *Lex Salica*. The most recent editions, and the most reliable, are by the German legal scholar Karl August Eckhardt. All have been used in preparing this translation.

Karl August Eckhardt, ed., *Lex Salica 100 Titel-Text, Germanenrechte Neue Folge* (Weimar, 1953). In this volume Eckhardt surveys the text tradition of the 100-title text (Pepin I's reform of the law), provides a text of this version and a translation in German.

Karl August Eckhardt, ed., *Pactus Legis Salicae, I, Einführung und 80 Titel-Text, Germanenrechte Neue Folge* (Göttingen, 1954). In this volume Eckhardt provides a long introduction to the problem of producing a critical text of the Salic law, surveys the surviving manuscripts, analyzes the various families of texts, and provides an offprint of Herold's text (B. J. Herold, *Originum ac Germanicarum antiquitatum libri*, Basel, 1557), which seems to have been based on one or more manuscripts that no longer survive.

Karl August Eckhardt, ed., *Pactus Legis Salicae, II, 1, 65 Titel-Text, Germanenrechte Neue Folge* (Göttingen, 1955). In this volume Eckhardt reviews the manuscript tradition of this version of the laws and offers an edition with German translation of the 65-title text.

Karl August Eckhardt, ed., *Die Gesetze des Merowingerreiches 481–714, I, Pactus Legis Salicae: Recensiones Merovingicae, Germanenrechte Texte und Übersetzungen*, 2nd ed. (Göttingen, 1955). Here Eckhardt provides a revised version of the 100-title text with German translation.

Karl August Eckhardt, ed., *Pactus Legis Salicae, II, 2, Kapitularien und 70 Titel-Text, Germanenrechte Neue Folge* (Göttingen, 1956). In this volume Eckhardt provides a text and German translation of the capitularies and the 70-title text (*Lex Salica Karolina*).

Karl August Eckhardt, ed., *Pactus Legis Salicae, I, 2, Systematischer Text, Germanenrechte Neue Folge* (Göttingen, 1957). This volume contains a text of the *Lex Salica Karolina*, Systematic version, with German translation.

Karl August Eckhardt, ed., *Pactus Legis Salicae. Monumenta Germaniae Historica, Legum Sectio I, Leges Nationum Germanicarum*, Vol. IV, Part I (Hanover, 1962). This volume contains an edition of the main 65- and 70-title versions of the

Pactus, plus the capitularies. Eckhardt offers a single version of the text with the major variants in eight parallel columns.

Karl August Eckhardt, ed., *Lex Salica. Monumenta Germaniae Historica, Legum Sectio I, Leges Nationum Germanicarum*, Vol. IV, Part II (Hanover, 1969). Here Eckhardt presents a text of the 100-title version, with the major variants in eight parallel columns, and then he offers an edition of that version of the 70-title *Lex Salica Karolina* known as the "Systematic Version" because it has been rearranged to bring together all the laws dealing with a single subject.

In addition to the above editions of *Lex Salica*, there are a number of older editions that are still useful. Only the most important or most accessible are noted here.

J. Fr. Behrend, 2nd ed. rev. by Richard Behrend, *Lex Salica* (Weimar, 1897).

Alfred Boretius, ed., *Capitularien zur Lex Salica* (Berlin, 1874).

Heinrich Geffcken, *Lex Salica zum Akademischen Gebrauche* (Leipzig, 1898).

Petrus Georgisch, *Leges Francorum Salicae, Corpus Iuris Germanici Antiqui* (Halae Magdeburgecae, 1738).

J. H. Hessels, *Lex Salica: the ten texts with the glosses and the lex emendata.* With notes on the Frankish words in the *Lex Salica* by H. Kern (London, 1880).

J. M. Pardessus, *Loi Salique, ou Recueil contenant les anciennes rédactions de cette loi et le texte connu sur le nom de lex emendata avec des notes et dissertations* (Paris, 1843).

Ferdinand Walter, *Lex Salica Heroldi et Lindenbrogii und Lex Salica Eccardi et Schilteri, Corpus Iuris Germanici Antiqui*, Bd. I (Berlin, 1824).

OTHER CONTEMPORARY PRIMARY MATERIAL

Although the commentaries on Frankish legal customs in this volume have been based almost exclusively on the *leges*, there are a number of other contemporary sources that might expand our information about Frankish life. Other than the laws, the most important legal sources are the formulae, collections of forms that legal students or notaries might use in the preparation of legal documents. The most important historical source is Gregory of Tours, full of information but also full of prejudice. The *Notitia Dignitatum* is a late Roman document outlining the various offices in the Roman army and administration; some of this information applied to Gaul—but how many of these offices were carried over by the Franks is a matter of controversy. The canons of the church councils are very interesting, but since there was no regular system of church courts to apply them, it is difficult to evaluate them.

W. Arndt and Br. Krusch, eds., *Gregorii Turonensis Opera, Monumenta Germaniae Historica, Scriptores Rerum Merovingicarum* (Hanover, 1885).

Stephanus Baluzius, ed., *Marculfus Formulae, Capitularia Regum Francorum*, Vol. 2 (Paris, 1677).

Edwardus Böcking, ed., *Notitia Dignitatum et administrationum omnium tam civilium quam militarium in partibus orientis et occidentis* (Bonn, 1829–1853), Bd. II: *in partibus occidentis*.

O. M. Dalton, *The History of the Franks by Gregory of Tours*, 2 vols. (Oxford, 1927).
Gregory of Tours, *History of the Franks* (selections translated with notes by Ernest Brehaut) (New York, 1969).
Caroli de Clercq, ed., *Concilia Galliae, a. 511–a. 695, Corpus Christianorum, Series Latina* (Turnholti, 1963), Vol. 148A.
Theodore John Rivers, *Laws of the Salian and Ripuarian Franks* (New York, 1986).
Alf Uddhom, ed., *Marculfi Formularum, Collectio Scriptorum Veterum Upsaliensis* (Uppsala, 1962).

LAW BOOKS THAT WERE CONTEMPORARY WITH OR INFLUENCED *LEX SALICA*

Franz Beyerle, ed. and trans., *Gesetze der Burgunden, Germanenrechte*, X (Weimar, 1936).
Eduardus Böcking, et al., eds., *Codex Theodosianus*, Vol. 2, Part 2 of *Corpus Juris Romani Anteiustiniani* (Bonn, 1842).
L. R. deSalis, ed., *Leges Burgundionum, Monumenta Germaniae Historica, Leges, Sectio I, Tomus II, Pars I* (Hanover, 1892). (Includes also *Lex Romana Burgundionum*.)
Katherine Fischer Drew, trans., *The Burgundian Code* (Philadelphia, 1949).
Gustavus Hänel, ed., *Breviarium Alarici, Lex Romana Visigothorum* (Leipzig, 1849).
C. H. Monro, *The Digest of Justinian* (Bks 1 to 15), 2 vols. (Cambridge, 1904–1909).
J. B. Moyle, *The Institutes of Justinian*, 5th ed. (Oxford, 1913).
Clyde Pharr, et al., trans., *The Theodosian Code* (Princeton, 1951).
S. P. Scott, *The Civil Law*, 7 vols. (Cincinnati, 1932).
S. P. Scott, trans., *The Visigothic Code*, 2 vols. (Boston, 1910).
Alan Watson, ed., *The Digest of Justinian*, 4 vols. (Philadelphia, 1985). Theodor Mommsen's 1868 edition, with English on facing pages.
K. Zeumer, ed., *Lex Visigothorum, Monumenta Germaniae Historica, Leges, Sectio I, Tomus I* (Hanover and Leipzig, 1902).

ESSENTIAL AIDS IN DEALING WITH THESE SOURCES

Adolf Berger, *Encyclopedic Dictionary of Roman Law*. Transactions of the American Philosophical Society, New Series, Vol. 43, part 2 (Philadelphia, 1953).
C. D. DuCange, *Glossarium Mediae et Infimae Latinitatis* (Paris, 1840–1850), 7 vols.
J. F. Niermeyer, *Mediae Latinitatis Lexicon Minus (A Medieval Latin-French/English Dictionary)* (Leiden, 1976).

Secondary Materials

ROMAN GAUL, GERMANIC MIGRATIONS, ESTABLISHMENT OF THE FRANKISH KINGDOM

Olwen Brogan, *Roman Gaul* (London, 1953). Rather superficial on Gaul in the Late Empire.
D. A. Bullough, "Early Medieval Social Groupings: The Terminology of Kinship," *Past and Present* no. 45 (November, 1969), pp. 3–18. Heavily legalistic in its in-

sistence on differences in meaning between classical and postclassical terms of family relationship.

Cambridge Medieval History, Vols. I and II (Cambridge, 1911–1913).

Felix L. S. Dahn, *Die Könige der Germanen, Bd. 7: Die Franken unter der Merovingen*, 3 vols. in 2 (Leipzig, 1894–95). An older work containing more detail than most recent ones; interpretations somewhat dated.

Margaret Deanesly, *A History of Early Medieval Europe, 476–911* (London, 1956). One of the few general surveys of this time period in English.

Emilienne Demougeot, *La Formation de l'Europe et les invasions barbares*, 2 vols. in 3 (Paris, 1969–79). A standard work.

Samuel Dill, *Roman Society in Gaul in the Merovingian Age* (London, 1926). An older work, never really completed by its author before his death, but still containing interesting information based primarily on literary sources.

Samuel Dill, *Roman Society in the Last Century of the Western Empire*, 2nd ed. rev. (London, 1925). An older work, but completed and revised by an able classical scholar; still useful.

K. F. Drew, "The Barbarian Kings as Lawgivers and Judges," in *Life and Thought in the Early Middle Ages*, ed. Robert S. Hoyt (Minneapolis, 1967). A brief overview supplemented by and partially replaced by Patrick Wormald listed in next section.

Numa Denis Fustel de Coulanges, *Histoire des institutions politiques de l'ancienne France*, 6 vols. (Paris, 1888–1892), especially Vols. 2–4. A very famous work, now dated, that did much to establish the argument for an unbroken link between Roman Gaul and Merovingian France.

Patrick J. Geary, *Before France and Germany* (Oxford, 1988). An uncomplicated account of Merovingian Gaul, pointing out the bias against the Merovingians introduced by Carolingian authors.

F. D. Gillard, "The Senators of Sixth-Century Gaul," *Speculum* LIV (1979), pp. 685–697. An attempt to reassess what Gregory of Tours meant when he used the title "senator."

Walter Goffart, *Barbarians and Romans A.D. 418–585: The Techniques of Accommodation* (Princeton, 1980). A reassessment of what the Roman practice of hospitality meant in connection with settlement of the Germanic barbarians in the Western Empire; not very useful for the Frankish settlement, however.

L. Halphen, *Les Barbares des grandes invasions aux conquêtes turques du XIe siècle* (Paris, 1926). Standard work.

Louis Halphen, "Germanic Society in the Early Sixth Century," in *The Barbarian Invasions*, ed. K. F. Drew (New York, 1970). A translation of that part of the above work dealing with the subject.

Jean Hubert, et al., *Europe in the Dark Ages* (translated from the French *L'Europe des invasions*) (London, 1969). A work of art history, very beautifully done; argues for the continuation of imperial artistic and technological influence in the barbarian kingdoms, even in Merovingian Gaul.

R. Koebner, "The Settlement and Colonization of Europe," *Cambridge Economic History*, Vol. I rev. (Cambridge, 1966). A rather dated treatment tracing the movement of the Germanic peoples into the Roman Empire—emphasizes the holdover of the villa organization of the Empire into the Germanic kingdoms.

Auguste Longnon, *Géographie de la Gaule au VIe siècle* (Paris, 1878).

Ferdinand Lot, *The End of the Ancient World and the Beginning of the Middle Ages* (New York, 1931).

Ferdinand Lot, *Les Invasions germaniques* (Paris, 1935).

Ferdinand Lot, Christian Pfister, and François L. Ganshof, *Histoire du moyen âge, Vol. I: Les Destinées de l'empire en occident de 395 à 768* (Paris, 1940). Good for the invasions and political history of Merovingian Gaul, but with little on institutions, etc.

John Matthews, *Western Aristocracies and the Imperial Court, A.D. 364–425* (Oxford, 1975). Contains a chapter on the southern Gallic nobles primarily associated with the new capital at Arles in the early fifth century.

Michael McCormick, *Eternal Victory: Triumphal Rulership in Late Antiquity: Byzantium and the Early Medieval West* (Cambridge, 1986). Arguing for the continuity of Roman political ideas.

Lucien Musset, *The Germanic Invasions: The Making of Europe A.D. 400–600* (London, 1975), trans. by Edward and Columba James of *Les Invasions: les vagues germaniques* (Paris, 1965). Probably the best survey in English of the Germanic movements and the Roman reaction.

Henry A. Myers and Herwig Wolfram, *Medieval Kingship* (Chicago, 1982). With some interesting material on Frankish kingship.

Henri Pirenne, *Mohammed and Charlemagne* (New York, 1957). Argues for the economic continuation of antiquity through the Merovingian period.

Henri Pirenne, "Le Trésor des rois mérovingiens," *Histoire économique de l'occident médiéval* (Paris, 1957), pp. 118–126. On the grave goods from Chilperic I's tomb.

Henri Pirenne, "De l'état de l'instruction des laiques a l'époque mérovingienne," *Histoire économique de l'occident médiéval* (Paris, 1957), pp. 137–150.

Maurice Prou, *La Gaule mérovingienne* (Graz, 1969—reprint of Paris, 1896). An old standard work but fairly elementary and ideas old fashioned.

Maurice Prou, *Les Monnaies mérovingiennes* (Graz, 1969—reprint of Paris, 1896). Contains an assessment of the problems associated with the denarius-to-solidus ratio used in the Salic code.

Charles M. Radding, *A World Made by Men: Cognition and Society, 400–1200* (Chapel Hill and London, 1985). With an interesting argument that the Romans and Germans had achieved essentially the same outlook on the world by the fifth-sixth centuries.

Katharine Scherman, *The Birth of France: Warriors, Bishops and Long-Haired Kings* (New York, 1987). An assessment based on a rather uncritical use of the literary sources.

Raymond Van Dam, *Leadership and Community in Late Antique Gaul* (Berkeley, 1985).

J. M. Wallace-Hadrill, *The Barbarian West 400–1000* (London, 1962). Important work by a master of the craft.

J. M. Wallace-Hadrill, *Early Germanic Kingship in England and on the Continent* (Oxford, 1971).

Dorothy Whitelock, *The Beginnings of English Society*, 2nd ed. rev. (Harmondsworth, 1972). Does not bear directly on the Franks or Gaul, but contains a number of interesting comments on the significance of the blood feud that might
apply to the Franks as well as to the Anglo-Saxons.

Erich Zöllner, *Geschichte der Franken bis zur Mitte des sechsten Jahrhunderts* (Munich, 1970). A new edition of the Frankish portion of Ludwig Schmidt's *Geschichte der Deutschen Stämme bis zum Ausgang der Völkerwanderung*, with archeological material added by Joachim Werner.

SECONDARY MATERIALS RELATING TO LATE ROMAN AND EARLY GERMANIC
(ESPECIALLY FRANKISH) LEGAL DEVELOPMENT

Karl von Amira, *Germanisches Recht, Bd. I: Rechtsdenkmäler* (Vol. 5.1 of *Grundriss
der Germanischen Philologie*), 4th ed. by Karl August Eckhardt (Berlin, 1960).
This revision of a standard work on early Germanic legal developments surveys
the problems about *Pactus Legis Salicae*, Eckhardt here offering essentially the
same analysis he gave in his volumes of the *Germanenrechte* and *Monumenta
Germaniae Historica*. He notes that von Amira had regarded the Malberg glosses
as the earliest remnants of a Germanic language—Eckhardt does not actually
deny this but certainly plays it down. Material on the Franks is pp. 39–56.

Robert Bartlett, *Trial by Fire and Water: The Medieval Judicial Ordeal* (Oxford,
1986).

Heinrich Brunner, *Deutsches Rechtsgeschichte*, 2 vols. (Leipzig, 1906), Vol. II, 2nd
ed. by Claudius Frh. von Schwerin (Munich and Leipzig, 1928). Another standard treatment of early Germanic legal history.

Knut Jungbohn Clement, *Forschungen über das Recht der Salischen Franken vor und
in der Königszeit* (Foreword and Register of Malberg and other Frankish words
by Heinrich Zoepfl) (Berlin, 1878). Clement gives Merkel's text, a German translation, and Zoepfl's explanations of Frankish terms.

Friedrich Christoph Dahlmann-Waitz, *Quellenkunde der deutschen Geschichte*, 10th
ed. by Hermann Heimpel and Herbert Geuss, Vol. 2, Sections 39–54 (Stuttgart,
1971). A standard bibliography of sources and literature of German history.

Wendy Davies and Paul Fouracre, eds., *The Settlement of Disputes in Early Medieval
Europe* (Cambridge, 1986).

Jean Gaudemet, "Le Bréviare d'Alaric et les épitomes," *Ius Romanum Medii Aevi*,
Pars I, 2 b aa β (Milan, 1965). (The series *Ius Romanum Medii Aevi* began pub-
lishing in 1961 under the auspices of the Collegio Antiqui Iuris Studiis Proveh-
endis in Milan. It has not been active in recent years.

S. L. Guterman, *From Personal to Territorial Law* (Metuchan, New Jersey, 1972).
Although this is a fairly recent work, it represents an earlier generation of scholarship.

H. F. Jolowitz, *Historical Introduction to the Study of Roman Law*, 2nd ed. (Cambridge, 1952). Standard text.

Wolfgang Kunkel, *An Introduction to Roman Legal and Constitutional History*, 2nd
ed. (Oxford, 1973). A brief but good treatment.

Ernst Levy, "Vulgarization of Roman Law in the Early Middle Ages," *Medievalia
et Humanistica* I (1943), pp. 14–50. Levy is the authority on this subject.

Ernst Levy, *West Roman Vulgar Law: The Law of Property* (Philadelphia, 1951).

Alexander C. Murray, *Germanic Kinship Structure: Studies in Law and Society in Antiquity and the Early Middle Ages* (Toronto, 1983).

Karin Nehlsen-von Stryk, *Die boni homines des frühen Mittelalters: unter besonderer Berücksichtigung der frankischen Quellen* (Berlin, 1981). A survey of the appearance of this term in medieval laws and collections of formulae—good for legal bibliography.

Barry Nicholas, *An Introduction to Roman Law* (Oxford, 1962). Good treatment—very brief.

Pierre Riché, "Enseignement du droit en Gaule du VIe au XIe siècle," *Ius Romanum Medii Aevi*, Pars I, 5b bb (Milan, 1965), 3–10.

Hans-Achim Roll, *Zur Geschichte der Lex-Salica-Forschung. Untersuchungen zur deutschen Staats- und Rechtsgeschichte. Neue Folge, Bd. 17* (Aalen, 1972). Lists major editions of *Lex Salica* to 1875.

P. H. Sawyer and I. N. Wood, eds., *Early Medieval Kingship* (Leeds, 1977).

Ruth Schmidt-Wiegand, "Die kritische Ausgabe der *Lex Salica*—noch immer ein Problem?" *Zeitschrift der Savigny-Stiftung für Rechtsgeschichte*, Germanistische Abteilung 76 (1959). An analysis of Eckhardt's editions in *Germanenrechte*. Concludes that Eckhardt has not produced a critical edition.

Rudolf Sohm, *Der Process der Lex Salica* (Leipzig, 1971—reprint of Weimar, 1867). Comments on various provisions of Salic law; outdated.

Rudolf Sohm, *La Procédure de la Lex Salica* (Paris, 1873). Not as dated as the previous volume but still not very helpful.

Simon Stein, "*Lex Salica* I," *Speculum* (April, 1947) and "*Lex Salica* II," *Speculum* (July, 1947). An attempt to demonstrate that *Lex Salica* was a ninth-century Frankish forgery. Does not prove this point, but does give a clear picture of the difficulties faced by the various editors of *Lex Salica*.

Paul Vinogradoff, *Roman Law in Medieval Europe*, 2nd ed. (Oxford, 1929). Remains the only general treatment in English of the decline of classical Roman law in the early Middle Ages and the revival of Roman law beginning in the eleventh and twelfth centuries.

Giulio Vismara, "Edictum Theodorici," *Ius Romanum Medii Aevi*, Pars I, 2 b aa α (Milan, 1967). Demonstrates that the Edict was of Visigothic origin rather than Ostrogothic as thought previously.

Alan Watson, *The Evolution of Law* (Baltimore, 1985). Places the Germanic kingdoms in a long line of legal development.

Wilhelm Wattenbach–E. Levison, *Deutschlands Geschichtsquellen im Mittelalter*, Vol. I, Part I: *Die Rechtsquellen* by Rudolf Buchner (Weimar, 1953). Standard reference work—gives a brief survey of the editions and families of manuscripts of *Lex Salica*.

H. J. Wolff, *Roman Law: An Historical Introduction* (Norman, Okla., 1951).

Ian Wood, "Kings, Kingdoms and Consent," in *Early Medieval Kingship*, ed. P. H. Sawyer and I. N. Wood (Leeds, 1977), 6–29.

Patrick Wormald, "*Lex Scripta* and *Verbum Regis*: Legislation and Germanic Kingship, from Euric to Cnut," in *Early Medieval Kingship*, ed. P. H. Sawyer and I. N. Wood (Leeds, 1977).

SECONDARY MATERIALS ON FRANKISH INSTITUTIONS

W. Marjolijn J. de Boer Avé Lallement, *Early Frankish Society as Reflected in Contemporary Sources, Sixth and Seventh Centuries*. Unpublished Ph.D. dissertation, Rice University, April, 1982.

Bernard S. Bachrach, *Merovingian Military Organization 481–751* (Minneapolis, 1972).

Joseph Balon, *Études franques, I: Aux origines de la noblesse* (Namur, 1963).

Joseph Balon, *Ius Medii Aevi*, Vol. 3: *Traité de droit salique—Études d'exégèse et de sociologie juridique* (Namur, 1965). An important study of the content and meaning of the Frankish laws.

K. Bosl, *Frühformen der Gesellschaft im Mittelalterlichen Europa: Ausgewälte Beiträge der Mittelalterlichen Welt* (Munich, 1964). An important study, but material is based primarily on information from Gregory of Tours rather than from the laws.

Carlrichard Bruhl, *Fodrum, gistum, servitium regis: Studien zu den wirtschaftlichen Grundlagen des Königtums im Frankenreich und in den frankischen Nachfolgestaaten Deutschland, Frankreich und Italia bis zur Mitte des 14. Jahrhundert*, 2 vols. (Köln, 1968). Tries to chart the kings' journeys through their domains in order to collect food and lodging as part of their economic income. Not much here before the Carolingians, however.

Julius Goebel, Jr., *Felony and Misdemeanor* (New York, 1937, repr. Philadelphia 1976). Contains a considerable amount of information on the Frankish legal system.

Heike Grahn-Hoek, *Die fränkische Oberschichte im 6. Jahrhundert* (Sigmaringen, 1977).

Roger Grand, *Recherches sur l'origine des Francs; Ouvrage posthume complète, augmenté et publié par les soins de Suzanne Duparc* (Paris, 1965). A strange combination of an old romantic view of the Franks and a detailed collection of information from Tacitus, Lives of the Caesars, Gregory, and the Salic law—with a fairly lengthy discussion of the archaic features of those laws. He concludes that the Franks were pirates in origin, from Scandinavia.

Alfred von Halban, *Das Römische Recht in den germanischen Volksstaaten*, 3 vols. (Breslau, 1899–1907), Vol. 2 (1901) for Franks. Plays down the role of Roman law in the barbarian laws except for influence exerted through the church.

F. Iresigler, "On the Aristocratic Character of Early Frankish Society," in *The Medieval Nobility*, ed. T. Reuter (Amsterdam, 1979), pp. 105–136.

Edward James, *The Origins of France: From Clovis to the Capetians 500–1000* (New York, 1982). A good brief topical treatment with an excellent bibliography.

Hansjörg Krug, "Untersuchungen zum Amt des 'centenarius'-Schultheiz," Pt. I, *Zeitschrift der Savigny-Stiftung für Rechtsgeschichte*, Germanistische Abteilung, Vol. 87 (Weimar, 1970), 1–31. Krug traces this term from the Roman military usage, to the *Theodosian Code*, to the Franks and Lombards. He also notes the Germanic aspects of the office.

Peter Lasko, *The Kingdom of the Franks* (New York, 1971).

T. Reuter, ed., *The Medieval Nobility: Studies on the Ruling Classes of France and*

Germany from the 6th to the 12th Century (Amsterdam, 1979). An important work, especially the chapter by Iresigler cited above.

Pierre Riché, *Education and Culture in the Barbarian West Sixth through Eighth Centuries*, trans. from 3rd French edition by John J. Contreni (Columbia, SC, 1976). Has a section on legal education in Gaul in the fifth and sixth centuries.

R. Sprandel, "Struktur und Geschichte des merovingischen Adels," *Historische Zeitschrift* 193 (1961), 33–71.

C. Verlinden, "Frankish Colonisation: A New Approach," *Transactions of the Royal Historical Society*, 5th series, Vol. 4 (1954), 1–17. Denies that the present linguistic frontier was the result of Salian settlement in the area in the fourth and fifth centuries—the frontier is rather the result of a much longer process that began long before the fourth century and continued long past the fifth.

J. M. Wallace-Hadrill, *The Long-Haired Kings* (New York, 1962, repr. Toronto, 1982). A very important work on various aspects of Frankish political and social history.

Suzanne Fonay Wemple, *Women in Frankish Society: Marriage and the Cloister 500 to 900* (Philadelphia, 1981).

Karl Ferdinand Werner, *Histoire de France*, Vol. I: *Les Origines* (Fayard, 1984).

SECONDARY MATERIALS BASED ON ARCHEOLOGICAL AND/OR OTHER
ANTHROPOLOGICAL RESEARCH

Nils Åberg, *Die Franken und Westgoten in der Völkerwanderungszeit* (Uppsala, Leipzig, Paris, 1922).

R. V. Colman, "Reason and Unreason in Early Medieval Law," *Journal of Interdisciplinary History* IV, 4 (Spring, 1974), 571–591.

Barry Cunliffe, *Greeks, Romans and Barbarians: Spheres of Interaction* (New York, 1988).

Arthur S. Diamond, *Primitive Law, Past and Present* (London, 1971).

Arthur S. Diamond, *Comparative Study of Primitive Law* (London, 1968).

Max Gluckman, *Custom and Conflict in Africa* (Oxford, 1955).

Margaret Hasluck, *The Unwritten Law in Albania* (Cambridge, 1954).

Bruno Krüger, et al., *Die Germanen: Geschichte und Kultur der germanischen Stämme im Mitteleuropa, Bd. II: Die Stämme and Stammesverbände in der Zeit vom 3. Jahrhundert bis zur Herausbildung der politischen Vorherrschaft der Franken* (Berlin, 1983). Traces movement of the Franks by archeological remains. Note map of settlements of *laeti* with Germanic Reihengräber.

Edouard Salin, *La Civilisation mérovingienne*, 4 vols. (Paris, 1949–59).

Malcolm Todd, *Everyday Life of the Barbarians, Goths, Franks and Vandals* (London and New York, 1972). Relies heavily on archeological evidence mostly from outside the boundaries of the Roman Empire.

J. M. Wallace-Hadrill, "The Graves of Kings: An Historical Note on Some Archaeological Evidence," in *Early Medieval History* (New York, 1976).

Index

University of Pennsylvania Press
MIDDLE AGES SERIES
Edward Peters, General Editor

F. R. P. Akehurst, trans. *The* Coutumes de Beauvaisis *of Philippe de Beaumanoir.*
1992
Peter L. Allen, *The Art of Love: Amatory Fiction from Ovid to the* Romance of the
Rose. 1992
David Anderson. *Before the Knight's Tale: Imitation of Classical Epic in Boccaccio's*
Teseida. 1988
Benjamin Arnold. *Count and Bishop in Medieval Germany: A Study of Regional
Power, 1100–1350.* 1991
Mark C. Bartusis. *The Late Byzantine Army: Arms and Society, 1204–1453.* 1992
J. M. W. Bean. *From Lord to Patron: Lordship in Late Medieval England.* 1990
Uta-Renate Blumenthal. *The Investiture Controversy: Church and Monarchy from the
Ninth to the Twelfth Century.* 1988
Daniel Bornstein, trans. *Dino Compagni's Chronicle of Florence.* 1986
Betsy Bowden. *Chaucer Aloud: The Varieties of Textual Interpretation.* 1987
James William Brodman. *Ransoming Captives in Crusader Spain: The Order of Mer-
ced on the Christian-Islamic Frontier.* 1986
Kevin Brownlee and Sylvia Huot, eds. *Rethinking the* Romance of the Rose: *Text,
Image, Reception.* 1992
Matilda Tomaryn Bruckner. *Shaping Romance: Interpretation, Truth, and Closure in
Twelfth-Century French Fictions.* 1993
Otto Brunner (Howard Kaminsky and James Van Horn Melton, eds. and trans.).
Land and Lordship: Structures of Governance in Medieval Austria. 1992
Robert I. Burns, S.J., ed. *Emperor of Culture: Alfonso X the Learned of Castile and
His Thirteenth-Century Renaissance.* 1990
Davis Burr. *Olivi and Franciscan Poverty: The Origins of the* Usus Pauper *Contro-
versy.* 1989
Davis Burr. *Peaceable Kingdom: A Reading of Olivi's Apocalypse Commentary.* 1993
Thomas Cable. *The English Alliterative Tradition.* 1991
Anthony K. Cassell and Victoria Kirkham, eds. and trans. *Diana's Hunt/Caccia di
Diana: Boccaccio's First Fiction.* 1991
John C. Cavadini. *The Last Christology of the West: Adoptionism in Spain and Gaul,
785–820.* 1993

Brigitte Cazelles. *The Lady as Saint: A Collection of French Hagiographic Romances of the Thirteenth Century.* 1991

Karen Cherewatuk and Ulrike Wiethaus, eds. *Dear Sister: Medieval Women and the Epistolary Genre.* 1993

Anne L. Clark. *Elisabeth of Schönau: A Twelfth-Century Visionary.* 1992

Willene B. Clark and Meradith T. McMunn, eds. *Beasts and Birds of the Middle Ages: The Bestiary and Its Legacy.* 1989

Richard C. Dales. *The Scientific Achievement of the Middle Ages.* 1973

Charles T. Davis. *Dante's Italy and Other Essays.* 1984

Katherine Fischer Drew, trans. *The Burgundian Code.* 1972

Katherine Fischer Drew, trans. *The Laws of the Salian Franks.* 1991

Katherine Fischer Drew, trans. *The Lombard Laws.* 1973

Nancy Edwards. *The Archaeology of Early Medieval Ireland.* 1990

Margaret J. Ehrhart. *The Judgment of the Trojan Prince Paris in Medieval Literature.* 1987

Richard K. Emmerson and Ronald B. Herzman. *The Apocalyptic Imagination in Medieval Literature.* 1992

Theodore Evergates. *Feudal Society in Medieval France: Documents from the County of Champagne.* 1993

Felipe Fernández-Armesto. *Before Columbus: Exploration and Colonization from the Mediterranean to the Atlantic, 1229–1492.* 1987

Robert D. Fulk. *A History of Old English Meter.* 1992

Patrick J. Geary. *Aristocracy in Provence: The Rhône Basin at the Dawn of the Carolingian Age.* 1985

Peter Heath. *Allegory and Philosophy in Avicenna (Ibn Sînâ), with a Translation of the Book of the Prophet Muḥammad's Ascent to Heaven.* 1992

J. N. Hillgarth, ed. *Christianity and Paganism, 350–750: The Conversion of Western Europe.* 1986

Richard C. Hoffmann. *Land, Liberties, and Lordship in a Late Medieval Countryside: Agrarian Structures and Change in the Duchy of Wrocław.* 1990

Robert Hollander. *Boccaccio's Last Fiction: Il Corbaccio.* 1988

Edward B. Irving, Jr. *Rereading* Beowulf. 1989

C. Stephen Jaeger. *The Origins of Courtliness: Civilizing Trends and the Formation of Courtly Ideals, 939–1210.* 1985

William Chester Jordan. *The French Monarchy and the Jews: From Philip Augustus to the Last Capetians.* 1989

William Chester Jordan. *From Servitude to Freedom: Manumission in the Sénonais in the Thirteenth Century.* 1986

Ellen E. Kittell. *From Ad Hoc to Routine: A Case Study in Medieval Bureaucracy.* 1991

Alan C. Kors and Edward Peters, eds. *Witchcraft in Europe, 1100–1700: A Documentary History.* 1972

Barbara M. Kreutz. *Before the Normans: Southern Italy in the Ninth and Tenth Centuries.* 1992

E. Ann Matter. *The Voice of My Beloved: The Song of Songs in Western Medieval Christianity.* 1990

María Rosa Menocal. *The Arabic Role in Medieval Literary History.* 1987

A. J. Minnis. *Medieval Theory of Authorship.* 1988

Lawrence Nees. *A Tainted Mantle: Hercules and the Classical Tradition at the Carolingian Court.* 1991

Lynn H. Nelson, trans. *The Chronicle of San Juan de la Peña: A Fourteenth-Century Official History of the Crown of Aragon.* 1991

Charlotte A. Newman. *The Anglo-Norman Nobility in the Reign of Henry I: The Second Generation.* 1988

Joseph F. O'Callaghan. *The Cortes of Castile-León, 1188–1350.* 1989

Joseph F. O'Callaghan. *The Learned King: The Reign of Alfonso X of Castile.* 1993

David M. Olster. *Roman Defeat, Christian Response, and the Literary Construction of the Jew.* 1993

William D. Paden, ed. *The Voice of the Trobairitz: Perspectives on the Women Troubadours.* 1989

Edward Peters. *The Magician, the Witch, and the Law.* 1982

Edward Peters, ed. *Christian Society and the Crusades, 1198–1229: Sources in Translation, including* The Capture of Damietta *by Oliver of Paderborn.* 1971

Edward Peters, ed. *The First Crusade: The* Chronicle of Fulcher of Chartres *and Other Source Materials.* 1971

Edward Peters, ed. *Heresy and Authority in Medieval Europe.* 1980

James M. Powell. *Albertanus of Brescia: The Pursuit of Happiness in the Early Thirteenth Century.* 1992

James M. Powell. *Anatomy of a Crusade, 1213–1221.* 1986

Jean Renart (Patricia Terry and Nancy Vine Durling, trans.). *The Romance of the Rose or Guillaume de Dole.* 1993

Michael Resler, trans. Erec *by Hartmann von Aue.* 1987

Pierre Riché (Michael Idomir Allen, trans.). *The Carolingians: A Family Who Forged Europe.* 1993

Pierre Riché (Jo Ann McNamara, trans.). *Daily Life in the World of Charlemagne.* 1978

Jonathan Riley-Smith. *The First Crusade and the Idea of Crusading.* 1986

Joel T. Rosenthal. *Patriarchy and Families of Privilege in Fifteenth-Century England.* 1991

Teofilo F. Ruiz. *Crisis and Continuity: The Urban and Rural Structures of Late Medieval Castile.* 1993

Steven D. Sargent, ed. and trans. *On the Threshold of Exact Science: Selected Writings of Anneliese Maier on Late Medieval Natural Philosophy.* 1982

Sarah Stanbury. *Seeing the* Gawain-*Poet: Description and the Act of Perception.* 1992

Thomas C. Stillinger. *The Song of Troilus: Lyric Authority in the Medieval Book.* 1992

Susan Mosher Stuard. *A State of Deference: Ragusa/Dubrovnik in the Medieval Centuries.* 1992

Susan Mosher Stuard, ed. *Women in Medieval History and Historiography.* 1987

Susan Mosher Stuard, ed. *Women in Medieval Society.* 1976

Jonathan Sumption. *The Hundred Years War: Trial by Battle.* 1992

Ronald E. Surtz. *The Guitar of God: Gender, Power, and Authority in the Visionary World of Mother Juana de la Cruz (1481–1534).* 1990

William H. TeBrake. *A Plague of Insurrection: Popular Politics and Peasant Revolt in Flanders, 1323–1328.* 1993.

Patricia Terry, trans. *Poems of the Elder Edda.* 1990

Hugh M. Thomas. *Vassals, Heiresses, Crusaders, and Thugs: The Gentry of Angevin Yorkshire, 1154–1216.* 1993

Frank Tobin. *Meister Eckhart: Thought and Language.* 1986

Ralph V. Turner. *Men Raised from the Dust: Administrative Service and Upward Mobility in Angevin England.* 1988

Harry Turtledove, trans. *The* Chronicle *of Theophanes: An English Translation of* Anni Mundi *6095–6305 (A.D. 602–813).* 1982

Mary F. Wack. *Lovesickness in the Middle Ages: The* Viaticum *and Its Commentaries.* 1990

Benedicta Ward. *Miracles and the Medieval Mind: Theory, Record, and Event, 1000– 1215.* 1982

Suzanne Fonay Wemple. *Women in Frankish Society: Marriage and the Cloister, 500– 900.* 1981

Jan M. Ziolkowski. *Talking Animals: Medieval Latin Beast Poetry, 750–1150.* 1993

This book has been set in Linotron Galliard. Galliard was designed for Merganthaler in 1978 by Matthew Carter. Galliard retains many of the features of a sixteenth century typeface cut by Robert Granjon but has some modifications which give it a more contemporary look.

Printed on acid-free paper.